AF600256

BY THE GRACE OF GOD

Francoist Spain and the Sacred Roots of Political Imagination

By the Grace of God

Francoist Spain and the Sacred Roots of Political Imagination

WILLIAM VIESTENZ

UNIVERSITY OF TORONTO PRESS
Toronto Buffalo London

Toronto Buffalo London
www.utppublishing.com

ISBN 978-1-4426-4757-2

Library and Archives Canada Cataloguing in Publication

Viestenz, William, author
By the grace of God : Francoist Spain and the sacred roots of political imagination / William Viestenz.

(Toronto Iberic studies)
Includes bibliographical references and index.
ISBN 978-1-4426-4757-2 (bound)

1. Spanish literature – 20th century – History and criticism. 2. Religion and politics – Spain – History – 20th century. 3. Spain – Politics and government – 1939–1975. 4. Religion and literature – Spain – History – 20th century. 5. Religion in literature. 6. Politics in literature. 7. National characteristics in literature. I. Title. II. Series: Toronto Iberic

PQ6073.P6V53 2014 860.9'382 C2014-901985-8

University of Toronto Press acknowledges the financial assistance to its publishing program of the Canada Council for the Arts and the Ontario Arts Council, an agency of the Government of Ontario.

University of Toronto Press acknowledges the financial support of the Government of Canada through the Canada Book Fund for its publishing activities.

For Kristi and Audrey

Contents

Acknowledgments

I owe the existence of this book to the input and generosity of many people spanning several institutions and time periods. I especially owe a debt of gratitude to my intellectual mentors at Stanford University, particularly Hans Ulrich Gumbrecht, Vincent Barletta, Hayden White, and Marilia Librandi Rocha. I likely would have never attended graduate school without the guidance and encouragement of Jorge Brioso at Carleton College. I also thank Xavier Pla for his hospitality in Girona and for providing supporting materials on Joan Sales. Mario Santana very generously shared his bibliography on Luis Martín-Santos. My good friend Robert Kirsch served as a sounding board for many of the ideas that became central to the work and suggested many fruitful theoretical avenues to explore. A number of the ideas that grew into chapters of the book began as discussions with colleagues in graduate courses at Cornell and Stanford, and for that I especially thank Henry Berlin and Todd Mack.

I would be remiss if I did not recognize the support and intellectual guidance of my colleagues at the University of Minnesota. Material assistance for *By the Grace of God* has come from research funds provided by the College of Liberal Arts and the Department of Spanish and Portuguese. In terms of intellectual support, Ofelia Ferrán's critical eye improved to a great extent the introduction and conclusion to this book, and Ana Paula Ferreira has helped me think through the contribution of Iberian studies to my methodological approach. The mentoring I have received and the respectful support of my work in the Department of Spanish and Portuguese and Institute for Global Studies has been fundamental in my ongoing maturation as a scholar, and for that I am grateful.

My wife, Kristina, has never wavered in her encouragement of my work and has patiently and graciously supported me as I finished the book. I have learned a lot from her sharp attention to detail and refusal to compromise on things that truly matter. My parents, Anne Lambert and Ray Viestenz, have always been staunch backers of my decision to study Iberian literature and culture, even if it did not seem like a sound economic decision. I struggle to match their loyalty, generosity, and inextinguishable work ethic.

To Joan Ramon Resina, to whom I dedicate this book, I owe my identity as a scholar. Joan Ramon's guidance has taught me that every disciplinary paradigm carries ethical implications that have tangible consequences beyond the ivory tower, something that reminds me daily of the value of the work that we do. I will consider my career successful if I can acquire even a fraction of Joan Ramon's intellectual fearlessness, dedication to his students, and *bon seny*.

BY THE GRACE OF GOD

Francoist Spain and the Sacred Roots of Political Imagination

1 Introduction: *La España Sagrada* as a Political Category

But by the grace of God I am what I am

1 Corinthians 15:10

Lo sacro es una categoría que se basta a sí misma

María Zambrano

Francoist Spain, Post-Secularism, and a Sacred Politics

"Francisco Franco, Caudillo de España, por la gracia de Dios." This inscription appeared on Spanish coins throughout the Francoist dictatorship, which officially lasted from 1939 until the *Generalísimo*'s death in 1975. Neither king nor priest, Franco nevertheless conceptualized his right to sovereignty around a political theology. As the Caudillo articulated in a 1942 speech to the Frente de Juventudes, greatness and decadence always coincide with the union or divorce of the spiritual and national (Díaz-Plaja 116). A modern-day manifestation of a monarchical divine right, Franco's mission to frame Spain as the last bastion of Catholic ideals appeared to replicate a model of sovereignty that the rest of Europe jettisoned in the eighteenth and nineteenth centuries. Nearly forty years after his dictatorship ended, the Francoist alliance of the political and theological has gone from seeming anachronistic to topical with the emergence of post-secularism.[1] Post-secularism, and a general belief in the residual, often problematic presence of theological concepts within post-Enlightenment Western liberalism, leads one to question the extent to which contemporary political thought still makes use of a sacred-profane Manichaeism, and moreover the problem of defining national truth in sacred terms. Liberalism may have succeeded in nominally separating the church and the state, but such a superficial dualism neglects the fact that secular political imagining still covertly makes use of a discourse that relies on the sacred.

Thinking of a return of the sacred to political thought calls to mind the words of the German political theorist Carl Schmitt, who believed that "all significant concepts of the modern theory of the state are secularized theological concepts" (*Political Theology* 5, 36). Schmitt's thought may be susceptible to hyperbole, but the modern secular nation certainly continues to organize itself around myths, symbols, and hallowed spaces that are consecrated and set apart from profanation by both internal and external enemies of the state. Propagating and consecrating these narratives and holy national spaces hinges on ritually celebrating traditions, in addition to annually commemorating historical moments that collapse linear time into a circular repetition.

One of the secular state's adapted theological concepts that relies on the sacred is sovereignty, which can become manifest in different ways. Sovereignty, whether bestowed onto a single individual, as it was for Franco, divided among various organs of government, or subsumed by the normative constitutionality of law, carries the illocutionary force to dictate the moral and ethical contents of the nation's structures of identification. With the sovereign force of popular will, for example, the 1978 Spanish Constitution's Título preliminar anoints Castilian as the language of the state, describes the form and colouration of the national flag, and consecrates several universal ideals as inherent to the collective image of the body politic, such as liberty, justice, and political pluralism and equality. As a sacred document, a constitution endorses a particular image of collective identity and attaches various ideals to the state. When a nation's sacred precepts are thought to be endangered, modern liberal democracies tend to revert to a hierarchical, top-down form of governance that resembles a divine mandate. In fact, many modern liberal democracies like Spain permit the law to be suspended during a crisis, consolidating power in the hands of the military and select politicians and effectively disregarding the sovereignty of popular will.[2] As regards Spain, the fifty-fifth article of the Constitución allows for the suspension of rights "cuando se acuerde la declaración de un estado de excepción o de sitio." Western democracy, in other words, folds into its founding documents loopholes that at once allow for a sacred imagining of national identity and mechanisms to defend the inviolable precepts of the state when laws that surge from the collective will of the public are proven insufficient or undesirable.

By demonstrating the pratfalls inherent to a sacred imagining of national identity, Francoist Spain and the literature this environment produced can help to expand and modify conversations on post-secularism and the role of religion and theology in political thought. In addition, a retrospective analysis of the Caudillo's political ideology and its attendant oppression helps to pinpoint those areas of Spain's transition to democracy that insidiously embody Francoist principles. In *By the Grace of God*, I first propose that Francoist Spain is an ideal representation of how consolidating sovereignty and projecting national identity through sacred imagining is liable to purifying, exclusionary violence. The Spanish Civil War transformed, during the dictatorship, into an ongoing "cruzada nacional" as a result of the ever-present spectre of the enemy's re-emergence, justifying violent reprisals in the name of purity and unity. By framing the Nationalist movement as a crusade, Franco created a political environment structured around crisis, emphasizing to a high degree the decisionistic, exceptional nature of his sovereign power. In lieu of referring to his political program as an ideology, Franco frequently promulgated a *doctrina* that drew upon a deep sacred well of national spirituality. Impinging upon national unity in any way was not just a crime – it was a "pecado contra la Patria," as Franco explained to the Consejo Nacional del Movimiento in 1941. From this perspective, the divine conferral of grace onto Spain's line of sovereign rulers, from the Catholic kings to Franco himself, was the impetus driving the nation's historical destiny. To use a turn of phrase by Manuel Vázquez Montalbán (2003) about "la aznaridad," this was not so much "por el imperio hacia Dios" as "por Dios hacia el imperio." *La gracia de Dios*, as adopted by Franco, thus resembled Aristotle's unmoved mover: an eternal vital force that imparts motion onto finite objects and beings without ever being moved itself.[3]

Franco based his metaphysical cosmology on Roman Catholicism, but his conception of Spanish identity transferred the concept of the sacred onto secular territory.[4] By treating certain leaders of Spain's past, such as the Catholic King Ferdinand and Queen Isabelle, as apostolic models for the violent purification of unwanted elements, and promoting symbols of Castilian culture as emblematic of the entire nation-state, Franco demonstrated the symbolic exclusion that stems from consecrating one nationalism at the expense of others within the same sovereign space.[5] In 1959, while inaugurating the Valle de los Caídos – itself a veritable temple that commemorated dead Nationalist soldiers but excluded *los vencidos* – Franco demanded a "pureza de intenciones" stemming from the "mandato sagrado" of the dead (Díaz-Plaja 305–6). For nearly forty years, this sacred mandate was in constant danger as a result of the latent spectre of the Anti-España, which was often tied to anarchists, atheists, communists, Freemasons, and Catalan and Basque separatists. Franco's 1959 homily at the Valle de los Caídos adopted a semantics originating in the theological and spilled it over into the secular realm. Like a religious cult, civic duty in Francoist Spain demanded unflagging commitment from its members, and a stress on national unity led to an obsession with purification. In addition to the *Reyes Católicos*, St Teresa of Ávila was another historical protagonist favoured by the regime. As Richards notes,

Ávila "was pure because she was believed to be of 'a noble family', an 'old Christian family … clean of any strain [*raza*] or blemish [*mácula*] of Moors or of Jews'" (50). The case of St Teresa of Ávila demonstrates the ease with which Franco uprooted a theological discourse that linked sacrality to purity and transferred it to areas of secular governance. Ávila's purely Catholic *raza* could be applied to a secular *raza castiza* in order to construct an ideal image of Spanish identity inconsistent with leftist political ideologies and the cultural and linguistic identities of peripheral nationalities. Spanish national identity, in other words, came to resemble an exceptional sacred cult.

However, a ritual celebration of collective origin, a belief in the latent presence of the profaning enemy, and a constant commemoration of sacrifices for the nation are also present to varying degrees in modern democracies. As Émile Durkheim wrote in reference to the underpinnings of religious imagination, "No society can exist that does not feel the need at regular intervals to sustain and reaffirm the collective feelings and ideas that constitute its unity and its personality" (322). If a government accesses national truth by way of the sacred, as I argue it was throughout the Francoist regime, does this tend to favour hierarchical forms of governance? Post-secularism questions whether a nation can symbolize its collective feelings and ideals through a democratic consensus or if a single hegemonic power must render decisions that are collectively binding when a consensus between multiple parties is unreachable. Much of this debate stems from the hefty criticism of John Rawls's theory that a modern democratic society is ordered by an overlapping of consensus regulated by a commonly understood conception of justice and fairness. In his introduction to *Political Liberalism*, Rawls himself accepts, however, that when people, even in democratic societies, think of their good as "a transcendent element," compromise is rarely admitted (xxviii). In my own thought, one of the most important contributions of the sacred to political imagination is its ability to consecrate transcendental "goods," which are then used to bind a collectivity together. The sacred, in short, makes an element transcendental. The best way to reconcile two competing claims to sacred, transcendental truth within a single polity is a problem that democratic liberalism continues to work out. On a philosophical level, this quandary also interrogates the extent to which nuance is permitted when two or more partisan factions reach a stalemate over sacred, and therefore "unquestionable," truths. Is pluralistic compromise a myth, or does a continued reliance on the sacred compromise the liberalist public sphere by making transcendental truths fall beyond the possibility of discussion? Many authors in Francoist Spain pondered these same questions in an effort to make sense of the Spanish Civil War, to theorize the structure of Francoist ideology, and, more importantly, to consider alternative organizations of the state in a post-dictatorial epoch. In a twenty-first-century moment of post-secularity, it is important to take heed of these writers' discoveries.

As an extreme case where the sacred's link to national imagination and political authority was hyper-evident, Francoist Spain, which has traditionally been viewed as an outlier in twentieth-century Western political thought, thus becomes a counterpoint to the dissonant and nonlinear development of secularity. As with most movements that begin with the prefix *post*, post-secularism is not merely a return to the religious after a period of secularity; rather, democratic liberalism never adequately assimilated pre-modern, pre-Enlightenment strategies of social organization that consolidated power around a monarchical divine right, or even more primitively, with totemic identification. Schmitt believed that his theory of sovereignty – he who decides on the exception – was surpassed by the Enlightenment conferral of power onto the organic unity of the people's will (*Political Theology* 5, 48–9). Jürgen Habermas counters Schmitt's position, asserting that an inclusive, bourgeois public sphere evolved in the eighteenth century that redefined the "political" as "the symbolic representation and collective self-understanding of a community" (18). The problem is that the public sphere of the modern secular nation is not inclusive, ineffective in giving the body politic direct access to its legislators, and susceptible to lobbying and the unilateral exertion of sovereign power. As Talal Asad notes, "The public sphere is a space *necessarily* (not just contingently) articulated by power" (184).

If post-Enlightenment secularity has failed to do away totally with viewing national identity as a sacred absolute, Franco's Spain is a convincing example of the violence inherent to theorizing a pluralistic, multicultural state through exception and monism. An "overlapping of consensus" is easy to achieve if the parameters of the public sphere are purposefully designed to admit only those of a similar belief structure. A study of the role of the sacred in Nationalist Spain thus serves as a cautionary tale for those post-secular scholars arguing for the return of a religious sensibility to modern Western liberalism. By studying the nefarious consequences of taking a rhetoric of sacred purification and exceptionalism to an extreme, as Franco did, it is easier to link the failures of secularity, such as the residual presence of hierarchical power within the public sphere, to a continued dependence on sacred national imagining. The ease with which Franco was able to slip sacred discourse into the secular realm also helps to expand the post-secular debate by revealing why liberalism has failed to achieve a clear separation from its theological roots.

The political theorist Anthony Smith recently proposed a vertical theory of nationalism in which deeply rooted communions of sacred belief serve as the pillars of collective identity. In opposition to the idea that the nation is a relatively recent construct, Smith argues, "We must go beneath the official positions, and even the popular practices, of modern nationalisms to discover the deeper cultural resources and sacred foundations of national identities; and that in turn means grasping the significance of the nation as a form of communion that binds its members through ritual and symbolic practices" (18). This take on nationalism helps to explain Franco's maintenance of power after the Spanish Civil War, which relied heavily on acquiring symbolic capital from a heavily Catholic base that had never embraced liberalism and the rabid anti-clericalism that became synonymous with social conflict in Spain during the nineteenth and twentieth centuries. Spanish post-war history, however, reveals that founding a national identity is often the work of consecrating the historical validity of one sacred communion at the expense of others. This exclusionary logic is linked to such things as scapegoating, which is meant to quell discord, and calls to sacrifice in order to validate national purification and symbolize unceasing loyalty to the regime. Where Anthony Smith's thought most resonates is the belief that an endorsing of rituals and symbols deeply rooted in a collective's cultural history goes with the foundation of national identity.[6] My own study, which views Francoist Spain as a limit case, maintains that political imagination nevertheless counts on the vertical, exceptional character of sovereignty for its coherence and legitimization, with the modern nation-state becoming a battleground for acquiring the symbolic capital used to validate the diffuse presence of sacred sources of cultural identity. Once a nation consecrates a particular modality of political identity, rituals and symbols are projected from the centre of the nation, binding the body politic together, and excluding those whose presence would profane the state's preferred image.

The Sacred's Slippage into the Profane

In this book, when I argue for the presence of a theological core at the heart of Franco's vision of Spain, I am proposing that a division between the sacred and the secular is far from being a fixed caesura, which is my second main tenet.[7] In strict etymological terms, the sacred simply means "set apart," "cut and left out," and is related to the Castilian verb *sacar*. Despite its putative isolation, the sacred tends to spill over, both semantically and conceptually, into secular discourse. Giorgio Agamben refers to this slippage as the "signature" of secularization: "Signatures move and displace concepts and signs from one field to another (in this case, from sacred to profane, and vice versa) without redefining them semantically" (*Kingdom* 4). Indeed, this is the reasoning behind setting apart the sacred in the first place: the secularized profane, like a magnet, is attracted to what is protected. The sacred maintains a magnetic charge only by constructing a public myth of the profane's existence, and Franco attempted to derive his charisma from this very dialectic. In 1942, while celebrating the anniversary of the Nationalist uprising, the Caudillo homed in on one of his favourite targets, the Freemasons: "El medio más poderoso que encuentra el extranjero para intentar minar su unidad y destruir su libertad y fortaleza" (Díaz-Plaja 113). In the previously cited inauguration speech at the Valle de los Caídos, Franco warns of the anti-España's imminent return, noting that "la anti-España fue vencida y derrotada, pero no está muerta" (306). The positive qualities of a sacred object function only by simultaneously excluding what does not belong, meaning that the profane always lurks as a negative, contradictory element whose dialectical tension constitutes a polarity. This is Hegel's classic definition of a dialectics, where every thesis embodies its own antithesis.

Spanish literature produced throughout the dictatorship frequently references, and productively converts into a poetic sign, Franco's use of *la España Sagrada*, revealing on a more general basis the slippage between the sacred and the profane. In chapter 3, I show how fascism and anarchism, conceived as political cults, rely on the same modes of symbolic consecration as Catholicism in Joan Sales's novel *Incerta glòria*. Sales novelizes the need for set-apart identifying symbols in the collective imagining of a group. A social collective, whether on a small scale or an entire body politic, affirms its identity and moral paradigms by consecrating certain images and attaching to those symbols metaphysical belief structures. Setting apart, however, also means cutting and leaving out, and this aspect of the sacred comes to fruition in chapter 4 in an analysis of Juan Goytisolo's *Conde Julián*. In the novel, Julián wins back sovereignty after being exiled from the Iberian Peninsula, yet his substitution of *la España sagrada*'s sacred symbols of belonging comes at the expense of horrific displays of violence.

In light of Goytisolo's assault on Spain's sacred forms, the third tenet of this book is thus the need for a constant negotiation between the positive, indeed inextricable, contributions of the sacred to the political and the nefarious consequences of taking to an extreme a logic of purity and negation of the enemy. Franco usurped a model of power consistent with Carl Schmitt's supposedly antiquated theory of the sovereign exception, yet other writers whom I study, such as Joan Sales in chapter 3 and Salvador Espriu in chapter 7, still advocate for the use of the sacred as a political tool without putting forth doctrines of exclusion and violence. Habermas's public sphere, like Schmitt's sovereign exception, finds a strong connection between social cohesion and the consecration of symbolic representations. Habermas, however, stresses that post-Enlightenment self-understanding remains conscious of plurality and difference in the secularization of state power. The sacred, rather than being a hidden underpinning of national imagining, is made explicit as a positive tool for political organization, but with an acceptance of plurality and self-imposed limitations on unilateral power.

In many of this book's chapters, placing blame on a sacrificial victim is central to the political rituals of reconciliation that ultimately define the parameters of national citizenship. I argue that Joan Sales and Salvador Espriu particularly promote political visions of the sacred that eliminate the sacrificial rituals that bring about "peace" and "unity" after a period of civil discord. Espriu proposes a transcendence of Spain's sacred/profane dialectic, redeeming Iberia with both a new proper name – Sepharad – and a more equitable moral compass that distributes leadership among *diversos homes* and *diverses parles*. In Espriu's collection of poetry entitled *Setmana santa*, a particular verse puts forth that "harsh punishments are stored in old symbols."[8] While Goytisolo's Julián reaffirms the centralizing, violent exclusion embedded within the regime's marks of identity, Espriu erects an entirely new poetic sign that structurally alters Iberia's institutional arrangement, dividing sovereignty among the myriad cultural centres of the Peninsula. Using Smith's terminology, Espriu poetically constructs a temple in *La pell de brau* where multiple sacred sources of national identity are called to congregate. A new Iberian project of political partnership requires not leaving the past behind but rather subsuming a communal responsibility for history's travails into the newly consecrated symbol of Sepharadian collective identity: the blood-stained, ragged bull's skin hoisted into the air in the first poem of *La pell de brau*: "The bull, in the sands of Sepharad / attacks the stretched out hide / and transforms it, hoisting it into the air, into a flag."[9] In contrast to the line of Spanish political thought sketched in chapter 2, which investigates the nineteenth- and early-twentieth-century roots of Franco's political theology, a counter-current of federalist sovereignty proposed by writers such as Valentí Almirall, Francesc Pi i Maragall, and Enric Prat de la Riba influence Espriu's Iberianist proposal. Emphasizing the construction of a temple through dialogue and negotiation also channels Habermas's democratic public sphere.

The Sacred and Metaphysics

Francoist Spain, like a wolf that never bothered donning sheep's clothing, refused to cloud the distinction between, in Carl Schmitt's words, the omnipotent God and omnipotent lawgiver (*Political Theology* 36).[10] By virtue of being Caudillo *through* God's grace, Franco possessed a papal infallibility wrought from conviction. It is useful to think of Franco – a mortal manifestation of Spain's eternal *bienes espirituales* – through Ernst Kantorowicz's theory of the king's two bodies. Kantorowicz argues that during the Middle Ages sovereignty began to be thought of as divided between two entities: the *corpus naturale* of the king as a mortal, finite human being and the *corpus mysticum*, or the essential placeholder of power that could not be destroyed. The immutability of the king's mystical body protected the institution of sovereignty against the instability of the mortal beings to which it corresponded.

Throughout *By the Grace of God*, I will frequently refer to the metaphysical nature of the sacred, and in doing so I am thinking of the sacred as a symbolic shell that is imbued with essential qualities and meanings linked to national identity. Like a tabernacle, a nation's sacred core is purposefully mysterious – always open to interpretation and speculation. The projection of national sacred truth is not unlike a *corpus mysticum*, with content and symbolism determined by the *corpus naturale*'s sovereign power. Sovereignty, in other words, can function as a sort of symbolic capital, which in Franco's lexicon is to be equated with the possession of God's grace. In chapter 4, Julián's redemption in Goytisolo's novel maintains the sovereign order founded on violence that originally expelled the protagonist from the Peninsula. The *corpus mysticum* remains, but its symbolic content – through the conquest of sovereign power – is rearticulated, but without transcending a destructive oscillation of constitutive and constituting violence. In chapter 5, Juan Benet's woolly guardian of Región, Numa, repeats the dialectic of *corpus naturale* and *corpus mysticum* and perhaps best fictionalizes the Francoist conflation of the omnipotent God and the omnipotent lawgiver. In *Volverás a región*, Benet imbues the metaphysical shell of sacred sovereignty with a morality referred to as *rencor*, which I link to Nietzsche's *ressentiment*. Sovereignty always extends outward from a moral imperative, and for Benet *rencor* constitutes a modality of Being that is productive only in its constant negation of outsiders, whose murders are given a sacrificial dimension by being blamed for social discord. In both Benet's and Goytisolo's work, exerting sovereign power hinges on introducing a sacred time into the linear thrust of profane history. Periodically inserting sacred time returns a society back to its origins and reaffirms ideological divisions. This assures that a culture's sacred-profane dialectic never reaches a moment of transcendence that would reconfigure the structure of the state.

The sacred tends to conceptually meld itself with Aristotelian metaphysics, creating a perception that consecrated objects are beyond the reach of negotiation and reconfiguration. As is indicated by Zambrano at the beginning of this introduction, the sacred is a category that justifies itself without external support. In this sense, Aristotle would argue that the sacred possesses a metaphysical nature. Aristotle's philosophy of first causes, later simply known as the *Metaphysics*, investigates the variety of ways that objects are derived from essences, how objects are moved with a purpose, or telos, in mind, and the negative forces that bring movement to a standstill. In short, all things "that are produced are produced by means of something, and from something, and become something" (*Metaphysics* 141). In certain cases, matter originates from matter: a bowl proceeds from bronze, and a coin proceeds from gold or silver. In other cases, a thing will originate from a beyond-the-physical "form" that imbues essences into objects: "Is there, then, in existence such a thing as the essence of the very nature of entities or not? For whatsoever is the very nature of a thing is the essence of that thing" (136). For the chain of causes to not reach back into infinity, Aristotle theorizes the presence of an original first cause, which justifies itself and requires no external support. Essences, or first causes, are immutable and do not change, a concept that becomes quite powerful when conceptualizing political identity as if it were an "unmoved mover" – from whence the state's sacred precepts proceed. Indeed, Franco's definition of the nature of God's grace is a veritable discourse on what the Caudillo determines to be the first causes of Spanishness.

The grave error in this line of thought is that national identity is not truly a metaphysical substance; rather, it is a modality – a proposition open to affirmation, negation, or debate. When a particular modality of national Being is consecrated, metaphysics becomes synonymous with the sacred, thus discouraging any effort to view the state as merely one proposition among many possibilities. Claude Lefort posits that any collective that frames its origin in non-theological terms simply tends to replace, *mutatis mutandis*, the sacred with metaphysics: "Any society which forgets its religious basis is laboring under the illusion of pure self-immanence" (224). Pure self-immanence, in the words of Zambrano, is a category that, like the sacred, "se basta a sí misma." The shift from thinking of "Spanishness" through religious terms to a category of self-immanence takes place at the end of the nineteenth century, with the emergence of regenerationist discourse. As I explore in the next chapter, this is a key moment where the sacred slips into secular rhetoric in order to reaffirm the metaphysical truth of the nation, a transition that later proved very useful to Francoist ideology.

If a state's reason for being is perceived as an essential given rather than a normative "overlapping of consensus," disagreements revolving around national identity tend to escalate quickly into irrational exhibitions of violence. Whenever a profaning force challenges the sacred, rational dialogue tends to be entirely absent. Durkheim maintains a similar thesis, arguing that in sacred rituals where taboos are suspended, primitive peoples "shriek and become carried away, feeling the need to tear and destroy" (303). In chapter 5, I analyze Mercè Rodoreda's novel *La mort i la primavera*, which precisely details the disarray introduced into a village by the sacrilege of its annual traditions. Joan Sales's analysis of war in chapter 3 also reflects this proposition, emphasizing that the original impetus of a conflict soon dissolves into an unconscious drive to destruction the more that the enemy adulterates the sacred objects of its antagonist. The sacred, in short, tends to have the effect of arresting cognition, encouraging partisan tension, and fuelling mindless violence. This is all due to the always-already nature that a sacred object pretends to project, as though it were an objective and immobile given that is ineluctably tied to national identity. A nation's *bienes espirituales*, in other words, become a metonymic extension of the state once they assume a sacred mood.

But how does an arbitrary, negotiable modality appear to be a sacred truth within human consciousness? In chapter 6, I explore Luis Martín-Santos's assimilation of Heideggerian time, which is a propulsion originating in the past that sweeps up an individual. In his novels *Tiempo de silencio* and *Tiempo de destrucción*, sacred models of national self-imagining, as well as the traditions that a state exploits in order to project identity, limit an individual's horizon of existential possibility and trick one into adopting particular poses and attitudes. Thinking of metaphysical sacred truth as unquestionable is a false consciousness made possible by a subject not having experienced his or her community's origins. When an individual is born or comes of age, he or she is entering mid-conversation into a terrain with an already-sophisticated system of symbolic reference points. Spain's most celebrated symbols of identity, such as bullfighting, and its starkly demarcated layers of privilege and gender are thus never questioned, because an individual mindlessly accepts the sacred thrust of tradition without reasoned thought, a hallmark of how human consciousness experiences the relationship between time and being. Martín-Santos's solution is to think of Spain as an ill patient, which draws on his experience as a psychotherapist. For Martín-Santos, the infirm nation can progress only by transcending its sacred-profane dialectic, which begins with a "de-sacralization" and ends with "sacrogenesis." Through sacrogenesis, a new modality of behaviour represented by a different set of symbols is endorsed, rerouting history's propulsion towards the future.

Spain's "Time of the Sacred": Literature as a Political Matter

By the Grace of God is the first sustained analysis within cultural studies of *la España sagrada* as a political category and tool for national imagination, especially from an Iberianist optic.[11] I explore the issue primarily through literary close readings, but from a multidisciplinary angle that gathers primary documents from the Francoist dictatorship, philosophies that exerted a strong influence on Spanish literature, such as works by Ortega y Gasset, Unamuno, Sartre, and Nietzsche, sociological interpretations of religion and post-secularism, and political theory. Close readings tend to become confined, abstracted realities, which I tried to avoid by locating the individual chapters within a broader political and philosophical conversation related to the hidden signature of the sacred embedded within secular political imagination.

Chronologically, my study focuses on a twenty-year span that covers the crux of the dictatorship, beginning in 1948, the year in which Sales commenced *Incerta glòria*, and concluding in 1970, the publication date of Goytisolo's *Reivindicación del conde don Julián*.[12] The chronological span corresponds, not coincidentally, to a post–Second World War retrenchment within Francoist rhetoric of a sacred mandate to promote Spain's Catholic first causes. Of the three main pillars of Francoism – the church, the military, and the Falange – Catholicism took on an increasing importance within the regime's propaganda in this time span. In a Bakhtinian sense, the literary works that I examine assimilate this maturation of Francoist ideology, as though it were a chronotope reflecting an idiosyncratic interrelation of time and space.

I found these particular authors especially compelling for two primary reasons. First, each text contributes a distinct component to the theory of the sacred that I argue is predominant in the conceptualization and praxis of Francoist political ideology. Sales, for example, perceives the existential thirst for consecrated cultural symbols in the mobilization of political will and the presence of a scapegoating mechanism at the heart of the post-war consolidation of the Spanish state. Goytisolo, for his part, unfurls the nefarious consequences of resorting to exclusionary violence whenever the state's sacred principles are in extremis. Benet and Rodoreda each explicate the view that ritual violence is a precondition for the maintenance of sacred time and that metaphysical essences are mistakenly projected outside the self, despite the fact that their true reality lies within discourse. Martín-Santos and Espriu, meanwhile, endeavour to step outside the thrust of sacred time in order to recalibrate the terms of social identity and political inclusion. In a manner similar to how the philosopher Vico perceives each individual nation as an outgrowth that participates in a universal history, the theoretical coincidence of these literary texts along the same longitudinal line – the sacred underpinnings of political imagination – germinates, without substantial redundancy, a macro-image of the Francoist conceptualization of the Spanish state.

Admittedly, *By the Grace of God* includes a relatively small selection of texts; however, my intention was to cover a wide swathe of experience within and in relation to the Spanish state during Francoism – the second reason behind my selection of these particular works. I culled the set of close readings from externally and internally exiled writers.[13] Sales and Espriu, for example, were internally exiled writers living in Catalonia; Rodoreda, herself a Catalan novelist, was externally exiled in first Paris and later Geneva; Goytisolo, also from Barcelona but with a familial heritage from the south of Spain, observed Francoism from his perches in Paris and Morocco; Martín-Santos, of Basque origin, belongs to a select class of novelists that best capture the quotidian experience of post-war Madrid; and, finally, Benet, a close friend of Martín-Santos, travelled through the same literary haunts in the capital city but also worked as an engineer in rural Castile and León and lived in the provincial city of Oviedo.

In a broader sense, I contend that the texts in *By the Grace of God* contribute significantly to an understanding of a political problematic. A vestigial inheritance of Hegel's theory of symbolic art, in which aesthetic reality cannot be a genuine expression of the true Idea it purports to replicate, is the notion that the cognition of political and social truth somehow exceeds the horizon of discourses rooted in the imagination. Highly influenced by Hegel, Lukács's *Theory of the Novel*, one of the more influential and widely read interpretations of the genre, views the novelistic world as autonomous and organic; a realty produced by the imagination in which "all that becomes visible is the distance separating the systematisation from concrete life; a systematisation which emphasises the conventionality of the objective world and the interiority of the subjective one" (70).

The rounded interiority of the novelistic world, far from participating in objectivity, reflects the introversion of the subjective – and therefore humanistic – realm. Lukács postulated that the historico-philosophical realities of each age condition the emergence of aesthetic form, and in the case of the novel the growth of a bourgeois Weltanschauung produced "the epic of an age in which the extensive totality of life is no longer directly given, in which the immanence of meaning in life has become a problem, yet which still thinks in terms of totality" (56). The novel's bracketed subjectivity produces a sterility caused by the absence of immanent meaning. Lukács thus mutes to a great extent the political potential of the novelistic form; in theory, the novel can be an imaginative projection of only an interiorized world turned away from the totality of the community. The introversion of the novelistic milieu would thus be apolitical and never a disclosure of something in common. Returning to the Hegelian roots of Lukàcs's theory, one could argue, as does Theodor Adorno, that all attempts to restore aesthetic art – not just the novel – to a social function are "doomed," because "artworks detach themselves from the empirical world and bring forth another world, one opposed to the empirical world as if the other world too were an autonomous entity" (1). It is this elision of aesthetics from the empirical world in favour of a detached, alternative reality that gives force to modernist discourse, especially in the "high" period between the two world wars.[14]

Against both the insuperable dyad of imagination and truth-perception and the radical autonomy of the aesthetic form, the literary texts studied in *By the Grace of God* challenge the notion that political truth exists prior, and external, to discourse. The works propose that the aesthetic regime of art, far from being an island unto itself, plays a crucial role in the disruptive subversion of official, essentializing proclamations of a nation's sacred character. In particular, the texts together produce a distinct vocabulary meant to, at once, relativize the truth content of Francoist ideology and problematize Spain's cultural symbolic distribution, which is the cauldron within which political imagination takes shape and is refashioned. In that sense, literary discourse, like all aesthetic work, is an inherently political act that argues against the possibility of first philosophies, such as Franco's expropriation of *la España sagrada*, by showing any given perception of national identity to be one of many possible manners of granting a metaphysical truth-value to the horizontal comradeship of a polity. As *Conde Julián* reveals, the Francoist interpretation of Spanish first causes is the result of possessing symbolic capital and not successfully connecting to a primordial truth "out there" waiting to be uncovered. The locus of national truth, in other words, exists solely within the symbolic field and is itself a form of imagination, an assertion that disallows any application of the correspondence theory of truth to political identity. The aesthetic regime of art, thus, serves as an ideal instrument for both the desacralization of essentialized national identity and the production of new forms of culture, consciousness, and political imagination.

Any essentialist assertion that the innate character of the nation is self-evident must be reaffirmed by the representations of aesthetic works within the cultural field, lest that systematic demarcation of the sensible – to use a term created by Jacques Rancière – seem arbitrary and without universal foundations. For this reason, as Rancière puts it, "politics is an aesthetic matter, a reconfiguration of the way we share out or divide places and times, speech and silence, the visible and the invisible" (*Politics* 203). Inverting the formula, aesthetics, including the literature studied in this book, is also a political matter because of its subversive potential to reapportion space and time and offer visibility to those areas of cultural life previously silenced. This attitude is neatly summed up by Juan Goytisolo, who argues that the political role fulfilled by the writer is aided by the discovery of "un lenguaje nuevo" that possesses a breadth of symbolic reach that exceeds the parameters of traditional discourse. Without discounting the uniquely aesthetic value of the literature I study, a text such as *La pell de brau* also possesses an important political dimension by virtue of its imaginative potential to rearticulate the Francoist distribution of cultural and political life. Imagination is intricately bound to the act of cognition, which ultimately affects the way in which a reader of Espriu, for example, might *perceive* and adjudicate reality. The aesthetic regime of art, far from simply deepening an understanding of political problematics that putatively exceeds its scope, may actually be the ground zero from which the disruption of ideology, lived experience, and collective understanding emerges. Rancière's political approach to aesthetics, at this point in the book, is merely speculative. In the conclusion, I test the validity of the theory by using as a praxis the knowledge gained from my close readings of the novels and poetry in the forthcoming chapters.

Though the sacred core of Franco's political philosophy has not been approached from the vantage point of cultural studies, authors working in political theory, historiography, and nineteenth-century literary studies have broached the issue. These include historical accounts of Franco's life, such as Paul Preston's *Franco*, and interpretations of the Caudillo's political program, such as Michael Richards's *A Time of Silence*, which studies Franco's purification of Spain and his political structure of autarky. Also of historical importance is Julián Casanova's *La iglesia de Franco*, an in-depth study of the Roman Catholic Church's complicity with the Franco regime, and Francisco Sevillano's *Franco: Caudillo por la gracia de Dios*. On the level of political essay, Vázquez Montalbán's *Los demonios familiares de Franco* investigates the inseparability of Franco's absolute power and his demonizing of separatist movements, leftist political ideology, and Freemasonry. Carl Schmitt's philosophy plays a key role in my theorization of sovereignty and was greatly informed by nineteenth-century Spanish thinkers such as Donoso Cortés. Schmitt's influence in Spain is thus the object of a body of scholarship, most recently in José Luis Villacañas's *Poder y conflicto: ensayos sobre Carl Schmitt.*

In terms of literary studies, Noël Valis's innovative 2011 exploration of religious imagining in nineteenth- and early-twentieth-century literature entitled *Sacred Realism* finishes chronologically where this book leaves off, with the Spanish Civil War, and therefore provides an excellent historical backdrop to Francoist ideology and the conversion of *la España sagrada* into a literary sign. From a different angle but with a similar methodology, Jo Labanyi's foundational text *Myth and History in the Contemporary Spanish Novel* investigates many of the same texts as my own study, contextualizing the structural tendencies of Francoist ideology through close readings. Labanyi's analysis goes part and parcel with my own belief that Franco's *gracia de Dios* consecrated a set of symbols meant to define the parameters of national belonging and codify the state's social structure, movements that are inextricably tied to mythic imagining. Both of these studies, I would add, tend to pay scant attention to non-Castilian cultural production, a complication that I will next discuss.

Iberian Studies: A Parallax View

This study represents a contribution to the burgeoning field of Iberian studies, a methodological shift to the traditional approaches of Hispanism. My selection of texts places novels and poetry from the Catalan literary tradition up against stalwarts of the Castilian canon, which redeems a sorely underrepresented text such as Sales's *Incerta glòria* and better contextualizes a well-studied novel such as *Tiempo de silencio*. Joan Ramon Resina's *Del hispanismo a los estudios ibéricos*, which compiles essays that appeared in publications throughout the 2000s, and edited volume, *Iberian Modalities*, frame the parameters of the shift to Iberian studies, which he deems a "propuesta federativa para el ámbito cultural." A federalist approach to disciplinary pedagogy mirrors the counter-symbolic partition of the Iberian peninsula developed in the thought of Joan Sales and Salvador Espriu, who both advocated decentralization and an inclusion of the periphery in resolving the state's problematics. Resina trenchantly argues that the evolution of scholarly discipline is always bound to the political, especially in Hispanism, which materialized as a post-imperial nationalism that amputated "amplios segmentos de la imagen cultural de la Península" (29). Hispanism, as Resina postulates, succeeds because of its categorical abstraction of all Iberian cultures into two monolithic geopolitical blocs: Spain and Portugal. This binary taxonomy of Iberia's myriad nationalities on a political level bleeds into the field of cultural production, converting the Peninsula's array of diverse aesthetic objects into standardized, consumable forms that slot unproblematically into the monolithic national culture promoted by each individual state. To that end, a novel like Mercè Rodoreda's *La plaça del diamant*, a harsh depiction of the Civil War and post-war period in Barcelona that resonates with Joan Sales's *Incerta glòria*, fares better as *La plaza del diamante*, a social-realist novel to be indexed between Ferlosio and Cela. From an Iberian studies optic, one would argue not that the latter statement is untrue; rather, it is only half of the story.

My own study considers the sacred as a poetic sign that infiltrated all parts of Spain implicated by Francoism, meaning, on a very basic level, that a cultural analysis of peninsular literature would be grossly incomplete if limited only to Castilian language and culture. Resina's argument that a shift to Iberian studies be made on both ethical *and* epistemic grounds is thus quite convincing, as "la perspectiva tradicional del hispanismo ha conformado y limitado su objeto de estudio ... los estudios ibéricos buscan su legitimación en un *argumentum ad verecundiam*" (159). A part of the process of legitimizing Iberian studies is the appearance of books such as my own that derive a real, tangible epistemological value from rethinking traditional methods of researching peninsular literature. This goes beyond a simple recuperation of works written in a minority tongue; examining the cultures that bore the regime's greatest blunt force strengthens an examination of how Franco's political theology reverberated in the aesthetic regime of art.

What separates Iberian studies from the more tested, schematic approaches of comparative literature? Comparative literature tends to approach separate literary traditions systematically, as if they were apples and oranges – two distinct kinds of fruit that happen to share thematic similarities. The recent formulation of Iberian studies to which I subscribe thinks of the Catalan, Galician, Basque, Portuguese, and Castilian canons as conditioned by similar structural processes and are, therefore, highly interrelated in a foundational sense. In scholarly terms, I believe that adopting a pluralistic approach that thinks of Iberia's multiple cultural nations as competing, yet in many ways complementary, entities is more intellectually fruitful vis-à-vis the modus operandi of traditional Hispanism.

Once the critic places Iberia's literary nations into a dialectical matrix, the objects observed – such as the literary texts in *By the Grace of God* – become unstable and open to reinterpretation. For this reason, I would suggest that thinking of Iberian studies as simply a paradigm shift has the potential, depending on how one interprets the meaning of *paradigmatic*, to underestimate the movement's epistemic potential. In corporatese, a paradigm shift implies a change of perspective, but the movement does not necessarily alter the quality of what is observed.

Returning to my previous comparison, the happenstance sharing of thematic qualities does not fundamentally alter the composition of the apple and banana, regardless of the perspective from which one views the fruit. A paradigm shift, essentially, presupposes that some "undiscovered" element of what is observed comes to light as the result of a perspectival deviation. One could also think of a paradigmatic shift, as does Ferdinand de Saussure, who originally used the term *associative relations* in his *Course in General Linguistics*. There, a paradigmatic or associative relation entails the substitution of one predicate term for another that bears a strong mnemonic similarity (122–31). A paradigmatic shift in this sense would think of the move from Hispanism to Iberian studies as the arbitrary substitution of a like term and not a significant linear progression. The danger here is the possibility of misinterpreting Iberian studies as simply Hispanism by another name – putting lipstick on a pig, essentially.

As an alternative to paradigmatic substitution, I propose to approach Iberian studies following Slavoj Žižek's articulation of a parallax shift in which the object of study undergoes a fundamental displacement alongside the change in position of the observer. Under the terms of a parallax effect, there occurs a distinct mediation between subject and object "so that an 'epistemological' shift in the subject's point of view always reflects an 'ontological' shift in the object itself" (*Parallax View* 17). An epistemological shift in the scholar's line of sight thus signals an ontological shift in the object of study – through an Iberian studies perspective, in other words, what constitutes the sign "Catalan literature" or "Castilian literature" changes in fundamental ways, opening up both new avenues of study and reformatting the previous dispositions that mediated "known" objects of scholarship.

In *España invertebrada*, Ortega y Gasset surmises that if the Catalans and Basques had been given the responsibility of developing the Iberian Peninsula instead of the Castilians, "lejos de arribar a la España una, habrían dejado la Península convertida en una pululación de mil cantones" (41). Leaving aside the political implications of such a phrase, which I discuss elsewhere, it is worth considering that viewing both Hispanism's cultural canon and the political reality of the Iberian Peninsula as a series of limbs, each of which offers a different perspective of a seemingly inviolable – indeed, sacred – main trunk is a superior epistemological approach, especially from a parallax view in which that trunk becomes increasingly ductile, on an ontological level, with each added observation. On an ethical level, Resina's proposal mirrors, to a certain extent, this book's conclusion: that viewing Iberia as a matrix of several sacred communions of national identity, as "una pululación de mil cantones," positively reveals the highly repressive nature of the decisionistic brand of sovereignty wielded by Franco. The sacred ought to be used, on a supra-national level of governance, as a determinant structure of national identity while imposing a self-limit on apocalyptic violent exclusion.

2 "He aquí una plenitud española": Catholicism, Cultural Regeneration, and Spanish Essentialism

De entre los escombros tradicionales,
nos urge salvar la primaria sustancia
de la raza

José Ortega y Gasset

Por dios hacia el imperio: Spanish First Causes

Francisco Franco consolidated his sovereign power around what Anthony Smith would call a national communion of Catholicism, with the Spanish Civil War being interpreted not as a rebellion but, rather, the start of a crusade. "La gloriosa cruzada nacional" was meant to maintain Spain as the last bastion of the Catholic faith, plotted against the rabid atheism of the Soviet Union, Moorish Islam, and the religious pluralism of the West. I have framed Franco's advocating of political theology as a corollary to democratic liberalism's uneven development, which is only now, with the emergence of post-secularism, becoming an object of study. Francoism in Spain, however, was not an ex nihilo ideology birthed out of thin air. This chapter investigates the multifarious underpinnings of *la España sagrada*'s twentieth-century articulation by Franco, which adopted facets from a heterogeneous set of political and intellectual movements that preceded the regime. This involved political thinkers who strictly linked Catholicism to Spanish identity, such as Jaime Balmes's philosophy of history; theorists who justified violent, decisionistic displays of power in order to appropriate national being, such as Juan Donoso Cortés's 1849 meditation on authoritarian dictatorship in times of crisis; as well as philosophical movements, such as Krausism and the Generación del '98's regenerationist discourse, which argued for the rational existence of a sacred *raza castiza.*

The capacity of literary authors during Francoism to engage in a dialogue with *la España sagrada* also depended on the inheritance of a particular cultural discourse from the previous century. The efforts of authors influenced by Krausism, like Clarín, in the late 1800s and the use of culture as a basis for political structure by the Generación del '98 aestheticized the sacred, creating a precedent for challenging the State's political theology through such mediums as the novel and poetry. The Generación del '98, particularly through the meditations of Ortega y Gasset, shifted the paradigm of Spanish sacred identity from the theologico-religious realm to the cultural field of production, obviating a focus on political theology in the endorsing of a politics modelled on literary figures like *el Quijote.* Franco's facile displacement of the sacred onto secular discourse, promoting both Catholicism and the sacrosanct Castilian countryside as the heart of *la raza castiza,* was thus an already well-established literary trope. Franco, in a sense, translated the Generación del '98's historical project into a political praxis.

Francoist ideology originally drew together the Nationalist cause around three pillars: the church, the military, and the Falange. At first glance, it appears that the Caudillo's shift to a strict political theology based on Catholicism, and away from Fascism, was a later development influenced by the events of the Second World War. Indeed, Franco's reliance on the Falange in the 1930s and early 1940s was eventually substituted with a turning to Opus Dei, a Catholic lay organization, whose members were made governmental ministers in the 1950s. Opus Dei's emergence is traditionally attributed to the stigma attached to the Falange's fascist loyalties after the Second World War and the need for economic stabilization of the 1950s, which introduced technocrats into government ministries. However, the infiltration of the ultra-conservative religious organization began in the realm of intellectual thought and scientific inquiry. Throughout the 1940s, Opus Dei slowly acquired control over the Consejo Superior de Investigaciones Científicas, whose mission was precisely to reconstruct traditional culture through the sphere of education and research.

The disjuncture between the Falange and Franco was reflected in each party's respective slogan. Every peseta came inscribed with "caudillo por la gracia de Dios" underneath the Generalísimo's visage. Franco's self-given title contrasted with the epigraph that appeared at the beginning of each issue of *Jerarquia,* the "revista negra de la Falange," which read "Para Dios y el Cesar." This efficiently communicates the philosophical breach between that organization and Franco's earnest belief that he possessed a divine right tied to the messianic redemption of a defamed spiritual community, a manoeuvre that Juan Goytisolo mimics in his *Reivindicación del Conde Julián*. In asserting that sovereign power is "para el Cesar *por* Dios," Franco drew upon a mythological past that predated the nineteenth century's long series of conflicts between the state, the church, and Spain's various incarnations of liberalism, and reached back to the divine mandate the Catholic kings exploited in their fifteenth-century *reconquista* of the Iberian Peninsula. The 1492 edict expelling the Jews from the Iberian Peninsula, in fact, began with "Los Reyes Fernando e Isabel, por la gracia de Dios." The ideological shape of *Nacionalcatolicismo*, which carried the slogan of "por el imperio hacia Dios," actually reverses the conceptual underpinnings of Francoism, which rearranges the preposition *por* and uses the spiritual fount of God's grace as the metaphysical first mover that pushes Spain towards its dreams of empire and gives the country its reason for being.

Though Franco's loyalties shifted to Opus Dei after the Second World War, the regime originally framed the Nationalist victory in 1939 as a re-established connection with the eternal spiritual fount of the nation. On 2 April 1939, Radio Española declared for the first time that "España, con el favor de Dios, sigue en marcha" (Díaz-Plaja 11). The imposition of God's grace, or favour, allows for the re-engaging of Spain's march towards empire, but this should not be confused with a progressive theory of history. Hegel, the famed proponent of a Protestant vision of historical development, views the movement towards spirit's absolute attainment as a series of steps: "The world spirit has an infinite urge and an irresistible impulse to realize these stages of its development; for this sequence and its realization are its true concept" (*Hegel Reader* 404). To Franco the country's dalliances with liberal, non-Catholic forms of governance are the anti-Spain and thus totally excised from history. Under this rubric, the truth of Spanish political identity is an a priori concept absolutely present, in full plenitude, at the moment the nation came into being. The historical rise of political liberalism is thus construed as a lengthy profanation, a series of steps taken without *la gracia de Dios* that secularizes the purity of the state. From the same Radio Española transmission: "El amor y la espada mantendrán, con la unidad de mando victoriosa, la eterna unidad de España" (Díaz-Plaja 11). The regime thus conceptualizes *la eterna unidad de España* as an Aristotelian first mover, and whoever has a finger on the pulse of this immemorial origin possesses *la gracia de Dios* and the permission to make state decisions without fear of profanation.

Re-establishing a link to Spain's eternal fount of unity in fact participates in the same Generación del '98 discourse of regeneration that gripped the country at the end of the nineteenth century. Like an electrical plug that had been disconnected from its outlet, the antediluvian vital force of Spanishness simply needed revivification after a lifeless period. This concept, incidentally, mirrors Ortega y Gasset's disavowal of Alfonsan Restoration politics, which the philosopher viewed as yet another layer of historical detritus heaped atop Spain's hidden primary substances. To Ortega, Spanish traditionalism was an inert structure out of touch with "la primaria sustancia de la raza, el módulo hispánico" (*Meditaciones* 172). Ortega believed that there existed a latent and authentic Spanish race buried deep within the recesses of a profane agglomeration of historical sediment. If the traditional apparatus of Spanishness were to be burned, one would find "como una gema iridiscente, la España que pudo ser" (172). A progressive and innovative vision of history is thus eschewed in favour of a turning back to Spain's *circunstancias* in order to re-establish a connection with the sacred, and therefore indestructible, origins of the nation. The Spain that could have been is thus also a Spain that is always already there, waiting to be dusted off, re-appropriated, and brought to the surface. Combining a rediscovery of Spain's authentic form with a repressive, authoritarian form of governance based on crisis, however, led Franco even earlier, to the 1840s.

Nineteenth-Century Spain: *Cuando la legalidad no basta*

In the hundred years leading up to the Spanish Civil War, the country was threatened with foreign invasion, fought wars over monarchical succession, experienced declining imperialistic and economic fortunes, and turned back revolts against absolutist leadership. Amid this chaos, a series of political thinkers appeared in the 1840s whose views on political theology, history, and dictatorship echo Franco's self-imagining. For example, a Catholic, anti-Hegelian philosophy of history that locates the origin of public power in a divine first cause was heavily promoted by anti-liberal thinkers such as Jaime Balmes. Balmes, a Catholic priest from Vic, melded Spanish tradition with that of the church and reacted against Enlightenment social contract theories of political order promoted by European philosophers such as Rousseau.[1] Against Rousseau and the natural goodness of humankind, Balmes presented a metaphysics of morality whose origin is sacred and dictated by "la ley eterna" and "los principios eternos" (*Lógica y ética* 166). Public power, by the same token, stems from a natural right emanating from God, which for Balmes is the surest antidote to anarchy. Balmes, who died at the age of thirty-eight in 1848, feared the implications of the French Revolution and was also troubled by the historical questions revolving around Spain's monarchical split upon Ferdinand VII's death in 1833.[2]

Balmes's Catholic philosophy of history places the absolute character of both morality and power in the origins of civilization, meaning that truth is not progressively attained through the advancement of spirit, à la Hegel. Rather, God's natural law, which prefigures the structure of social hierarchies and relationships, is already fully formed *in illo tempore* – like Ortega's *gema iridiscente* – but becomes corrupted over time by the profaning touch of human beings. As Balmes notes, the moral value of public power "se funda en la ley natural," but it suffers "la variedad e inestabilidad de las cosas humanas" (*Lógica y ética* 202–3). In line with this philosophy of history, Franco's re-establishment of Spain's eternal unity, which is accessed through the apostolic intercession of the Catholic kings, articlulates the liberal Second Republic as a profaning movement that, without a hold on *la gracia de Dios*, is also out of line with *los principios eternos* of the nation. Balmes's simplistic summation of his political thought seems quite in line with both Francoism and Ortega's *España que pudo ser*: "nosotros nos fundamos en lo que *es*; nuestros adversarios se fundan en lo que *puede* ser" (*Obras completas* 711). An *España que pudo ser* is, of course, a Spain that is already *there* but hidden from view.

Balmes, like Franco in the 1930s and beyond, integrates Catholicism into an understanding of Spain's essential character and excoriates liberalism for its ignorance of the nation's hallowed origins. In 1845, not long after General Narváez's *pronunciamiento* and the passage of a moderate constitution influenced by French models, Balmes cautioned against ruling without knowledge of "la España antigua, de la España religiosa y monárquica, de la España de las tradiciones" (*Obras completas* 209). Balmes yokes this with a belief that Spain was in spiritual peril caused by foreign models of thought. Balmes certainly promoted a political theology that looked to religion as the metaphysical anchor that dictated a state's morality and decision calculus, but unlike Franco and his own contemporary Juan Donoso Cortés, he feared repressive absolute power. Balmes was of the view that "es preciso no contar demasiado con los medios represivos" (977), and believed that anarchy is less fearsome than an absolute monarchy (979).

The notion of restoring order by the sword, as promoted by Radio Española in 1939, harkens back to Hobbes but also resonates strongly with the Spanish nineteenth-century political theorist Juan Donoso Cortés. In his famous 1849 discourse on dictatorship, Cortés, in a harangue against revolution, justified dictatorial action during moments of crisis, basing his theory on a comparison with God's tendency to change the course of natural events by breaking dictums that he himself established. Cortés, an ardent monarchist who supported Isabella II's claim to the throne, aimed to justify General Narváez's use of expanded authoritarian power in order to put down a series of revolutions during the late 1840s, and in so doing, abandon the moderate constitution of 1845. Cortés distilled dictatorship down to two forms: a movement from above, emanating from established government, and an impulse from below, brought on by popular revolution. He metaphorically links both variants to knife-like instruments: "Se trata de escoger, por último, entre la dictadura del puñal y la dictadura del sable: yo escojo la dictadura del sable, porque es más noble" (*Ensayo* 261). Cortés prefers "dictatorship from above," or the dictatorship of the sabre, because it replicates God's propensity to break with natural law and is carried out through the actions of an already installed sovereign power, rather than an ad hoc plebeian mob. In short, a dictatorship of the sabre is a form of absolute power emanating from a sole, sovereign individual who decides on exceptions to constitutional law: "Cuando la legalidad basta para salvar la sociedad, la legalidad; cuando no basta, la dictadura" (243).[3] Spanish dictatorship, as theorized by Cortés, depends on the existence of crisis and adopts a model of sovereignty rooted in theology, an inheritance that Franco used to great benefit. This is why, in both the regime's initial Radio Española transmission and in speeches throughout the dictatorship, it was necessary to emphasize that the Civil War was never completely finished: "España sigue en pie de guerra contra todo enemigo del interior o del exterior" (Díaz-Plaja 11).

Like Balmes, Cortés trenchantly promoted a non-Hegelian philosophy of history that was worked into a justification for political theology. The *Ensayo sobre el catolicismo, el liberalismo y el socialismo*, written in 1850 and simultaneously published in Paris and Madrid, considers politics the final link of a chain that begins with religion and morality. Through Catholicism "entró el orden en el hombre, y por el hombre en las sociedades humanas" (65). Every political question is therefore also a theological question, and a Catholic metaphysics is the filter through which one arrives at the truth of Spanish governance. For Cortés, Catholicism is God's unique Spanish manifestation, but at the same time "Dios era *unidad* en la India, *dualismo* en Persia, *variedad* en Grecia, *muchedumbre* en Roma" (65). In all situations, God initiates historical movement while representing the absolute fulfilment of the plenitude of truth. God is thus "eterno reposo y autor de todo movimiento; es inteligencia suprema, voluntad soberana" (65). Being "author of every movement" mirrors, *mutatis mutandis*, Aristotle. Both Cortesian and Francoist thought reveal, however, another uncertain truth about a sacred vision of history. If God is an eternal prime mover, and the passage of time only adulterates and blasphemes a country's holy origins, then the supreme power wills its own distancing from the world. One could take this idea further. A solution to a culture's separation from is divine origins is to stridently admonish those who desire change and to institute ritual sacrifice in order to set history's clocks back to zero when the nation's sacred image is in peril, in order to touch base with eternal origins. A scapegoating of internal discord onto victims who are framed as "outsiders" or "foreigners" thus becomes a favoured practice of the Franco regime, disqualifying liberal movements and ideologies from even belonging to Spanish history. Liberalism, and its various incarnations, was a sickness infecting the degenerate national body, a condition remedied via military and dictatorial surgery, with the sword *que mantiene la unidad espiritual* functioning as a scalpel that excises cancerous, profaning tumours – a dictatorship of the sabre.

Nineteenth-century Spain, which produced writers like Balmes and Cortés, is best understood as a series of short-lived and mostly futile attempts by moderates, liberals, and progressives to lessen the sphere of influence of the church and catch up to the standards of religious and political tolerance set by other parts of Europe and the United States. Indeed, the second president of the First Republic, Francesc Pi i Maragall, interpreted the period beginning with Fernando VII's death in 1833 and ending with the Alfonsan Restoration as a dialectic of reaction and revolution. Valis, in her investigation of the role of the sacred in Spain's nineteenth- and early-twentieth-century literary imagination, argues that the church–state tension that deepened after Ferdinand VII's death, and more or less continued into the twentieth century, was a "struggle over competing authorities [that] was played out repeatedly in Catholic Spain, with no side really winning the big prize until, perhaps, Franco" (32). Valis is right in that the breach between Spanish liberalism and traditionalism transcended a theoretical disagreement concerning the role of religion within a secular state. In nineteenth-century Spain, the question revolved around first the division of sovereign power and the slow displacement of the old regime's absolutism to the purely symbolic constitutional monarchy of the Alfonsan Restoration and its *turno pacífico*, which of course ended up being anything but peaceful. Simply branding the pre-history of the Spanish Civil War as a conflict pitting Spanish liberals against its reactionary responses, however, seriously oversimplifies the geographic, class, and national complexities of a state comprising multiple cultural and linguistic centres. As is very well detailed in Sales's novel *Incerta glòria*, this lack of a liberal consensus continued to exert a damning influence on the Republican side's lack of a cohesive war effort in the late 1930s.

Spanish Regenerationism: Displacing the Sacred onto the Secular

In the last quarter of the nineteenth century, philosophies such as Krausism attempted to reconcile, on an intellectual scale, the same breaches between liberal thought and theology that were prevalent on Spain's political stage and led to the reactionary writings of Balmes and Cortés. As Valis persuasively demonstrates, this is the moment when Catholicism began to be seen "as a problem for the individual and for society" (2) and the juncture where the polemics surrounding the sacred character of Spanish identity and thought shifted prominently into the literary realm, a tradition that I argue remained prevalent throughout Francoism.[4] The Krausist movement, for example, aimed to reconcile positivistic rational inquiry with religious faith and establish an environment of free inquiry. This was the philosophy's central attraction to Clarín, as Kronik notes: "What bonded Alas to the Krausist movement ... was a series of abstract positions: its reconciliation of rational philosophy with Christian religion, its creed of tolerance, its thirst for knowledge coupled with an ethical bias" (5). Approaching the sacred through rational inquiry, however, tends to have the effect of profaning the emblematic images and personages of a collective's identity. Joaquín Costa's famous dictum that Spain slam shut El Cid's "sepulcro a doble llave" perhaps best exemplifies this phenomenon. Costa, an emblematic figure of *regeneracionismo*, a movement that used Krausism as a point of departure, exhorted the country to leave behind the historical thrust of its imperial past and look to different horizons. This same methodology is worked out at great length in Luis Martín-Santos's fiction, which I explore in chapter 6, yet Martín-Santos understands better than Costa the intense seductive hold that sacred cultural symbols possess.

Critics of Costa's brand of regeneration tended to fall back onto sacred figures like El Cid in a retrenched essentialization of Spanish being. Ramón Menéndez Pidal, for example, saw in the Cid an aesthetic prime mover that defined the essentially realist and "close to reality" nature of Spanish prose. For Miguel de Unamuno, in turn, *lo castizo* was defined as a combination of idealism and realism typified in the complementary relationship between Sancho Panza and Don Quijote, respectively. To some members of the Generación del '98, like Unamuno, Krausism's most obvious fault was its foreign origin, yet the notion of appropriating spiritual truths through rational inquiry remained patent. Much of the rhetoric that emerged from turn-of-the-century *regeneracionismo*, especially in Ortega's work, co-opted the same notion of recovering an internal, essential Spanishness forged by the community's collective living together that one finds in Francoist thought. Regenerationism, despite de-emphasizing Balmes's and Cortés's insistence on Catholic theology, maintained the political structure of *la España sagrada* by interpreting the essential metaphysical truth of the nation through secular figures culled from, for example, the literary realm. Members of the Generación del '98 thus attached the sacred, non-questionable aspects of Spanishness to classic cultural figures such as Don Quijote, Don Juan, and la Celestina, to use three protagonists from a famed work by Ramiro de Maeztu. When Franco finally arrived onto the scene in the 1930s, therefore, he inherited two critical discourses: one from the nineteenth century linking Spanish metaphysics to Catholicism and dictatorship, and the second, a regenerationist philosophical tradition that had argued for the rational, objective presence of, in Ortega's words, *una plenitud española* that could be recuperated from its imperilled state.

One of the principal tenets of Ortega's 1914 essay, *Meditaciones del Quijote*, is the value of cultural study and philosophical reason in the production of the primary truths that ought to serve as the foundation for policies cultivated by political authorities. Ortega contrasts the nineteenth century with the twentieth, and particularly lambastes figures such as Cánovas for "desatender todo lo inmediato y momentáneo de la vida" (67) through an abstract obsession with political and social ills. According to Ortega, Spanish culture consists in a series of *circunstancias* embodied by sacred figures like el Quijote that serve as a window opened up to universal, objective truths: "La cultura nos proporciona objetos ya purificados, que alguna vez fueron vida espontánea e inmediata, y hoy, gracias a la labor reflexiva, parecen libres del espacio y del tiempo, de la corrupción y del capricho" (68). Culture produces, in other words, monadic, deistic protagonists of history whose solidification shields the profane corruption of spontaneous, chaotic time. At this point, Ortega had not yet theorized his *razón vital* but nevertheless saw in the work of philosophical reflection the tool by which the consecration of cultural objects occurs. Ortega, better said, saw in *his* work the ideal mechanisms for deciding upon and maintaining *la España sagrada*. Free from the effects of time and space, purified cultural objects become a bridge between the momentary, spontaneous flow of everyday life and the deeper, immobile eternal truths of the environment from which a culture historically develops.

The salient point to take away from Ortega is that his discourse imports a sacred–profane dialectics into secular subject matter rooted within cultural and literary studies. Encapsulated within the figure of Don Quijote, for example, Ortega sees "la indicación de una posible plenitud" (*Meditaciones* 46) that is accessible through redemptive reflection. Reaching the plenitude of sacred objects is equivalent to a meeting with the divine: "No hay cosa en el orbe por donde no pase algún nervio divino: la dificultad estriba en llegar hasta él y hacer que se contraiga" (78). In his famous metaphor of phenomenologically interpreting an orange, so well satirized as an apple by Martín-Santos in *Tiempo de silencio*, Ortega calls this hidden idea, or essence, of the thing a third dimension, which becomes patent only through an active *ver intelectivo*. Though funnelling Plato's notion of the Idea, Ortega is also fundamentally Aristotelian in his naming God as the origin of an object's third dimension: "Pues bien, la tercera dimensión de la naranja no es más que una idea y Dios es la última dimensión de la campiña" (116). Discovering a latent Spanish essence through a reflective analysis of *quijotismo*, and framing such an endeavour as a redemptive mission of salvation, creates an ontological philosophy that bears striking resemblances to the ideological framework of Francoism described above. In both cases, much of the nineteenth century and its political struggles are glossed over in favour of acquiring deeper truths that stretch back to time immemorial. A ritual return to national essences is, moreover, the pathway to social regeneration, a gesture that both reaffirms the essentialist understanding of the nation proffered by idolizing sacred personages such as Teresa de Ávila and Don Quijote and precludes thinking through the nation in alternative terms, with alternative cultural figures.

Ortega's quest to place his finger on the pulse of Spain's "unmoved mover" was matched by other members of his generation, especially Miguel de Unamuno. Unamuno, demonstrating a level of xenophobia that differed from Ortega's Germanophilia, qualified Krausism as a "barbarismo" whose minor impact could be compared to a "vacuna" that "evita la viruela" (39).[5] As a response, Unamuno converted the term *casticismo* into a philosophical category, arguing for the pure presence of a secularized caste of "Spanishness" hidden, vertically, deep in the state's layered sediment. By discovering a *casticismo* "puro y sin mezcla de elemento extraño," Unamuno believed that he had arrived at "lo eterno" of Castilian consciousness. Unamuno arrived at this lofty understanding of Castile's eternal truth by harmonizing the province's "idealismo quijotesco con su realismo sanchopancino, esfuerzos que se revelan en el fruto más granado del espíritu castellano, en su castiza y clásica mística" (27, 76). That a national spirit could be scientifically unveiled through thought merely replicated Hegel's enslavement of spirit within the confines of the sensible world. Unamuno, in other words, de-emphasized Spain's essential Catholicity but maintained a political theology predicated on a rationalized sacred essence rooted in the everyday – *lo castizo*. In turn-of-the-century Spain, therefore, intellectuals considered the final two steps of August Comte's three stages of social progress – theology, metaphysics, and positivism – to be mutually dependent. An individual could still pursue the primary causes of Spanish character and search for absolute national truths, through positivistic rational inquiry and "intellective seeing." For Comte, of course, this proposal would appear completely absurd.

This tactic, in any event, was enormously useful to Francoism, making it unsurprising that the Generación del '98 played a role in his historical project, as Manuel Vázquez Montalbán has asserted. Montalbán, thinking in particular of Maeztu's writings, sees in *el '98* a "reaccionarismo regeneracionista que atribuye parte de los males finales de España al abandono de las peculiaridades que la hicieron grande, catolicidad, unidad, etcétera" (*Los demonios* 48). Ortega, Unamuno, and Maeztu, in fact, represent how an explicitly theological political ideology can be divested of its religious overtones yet maintain the sacred as a tool that defines what belongs and what ought to be excluded from the nation. Returning to Comte, the first two stages of social progress – the theological and metaphysical – are functionally the same, with abstract notions merely replacing supernatural deities. It is no surprise then that Franco could take the metaphysical apparatus provided by the Generación del '98 and easily revert to a fundamentally theological understanding of Spain's essential character. In summation, the nineteenth century, particularly Cortés's theory of dictatorship, provided a manual for exploiting crisis in order to violently repress liberal resistance to authoritarian power; the early twentieth century, in turn, created the ideological foundation for using metaphysics to structure society around its first causes, i.e., objective truths that are accessible via rational reflection.

Catholicism as a Social Force: 1936

The adoption of influential philosophical and theological discourses from the past certainly contributed to Franco's charisma. Catholicism remained, throughout the

Second Republic, a powerful social force with great organizational valence. This reliance on Catholicism as a metaphysical foundation for national identity particularly profited from a groundswell of popular dissatisfaction with the Second Republic's efforts to deem the religion socially irrelevant. Manuel Azaña not only disqualified Catholicism as an objective truth from whence to derive sovereignty, but also cast aside religion as a potent social force, even going so far as to assert that "Spain has ceased to be Catholic" (cited in Valis 49).[6]

The fractured nature of Spanish liberalism was never able to create a stable and enduring structure of national belonging able to funnel the effervescent social forces of an anxious body politic into a cohesive sacred communion where the purely secular state would be worshipped. Catholicism, for all intents and purposes, remained a very deep-seated part of the public sphere throughout the nineteenth and twentieth centuries, meaning that Franco's framing of the Nationalist revolt as a glorious Catholic crusade benefited greatly by adopting rhetoric, imagery, and rituals already steeped in a long history of sacralization. During the Spanish Civil War, the rabid anti-clericalism of certain components of the Republican side only fuelled the ire of a disenchanted Catholic national communion as a result of the very visceral, passionate responses that sacrilege provokes. The irrational nature of sacrilege is present in Joan Sales's work, but also reappears, in an allegorical realm, in Rodoreda's *La mort i la primavera*, which I investigate in chapter 5.

At the conclusion of the Spanish Civil War, at which point an already incoherent Republican effort was even further fragmented by exile and imprisonment, a Catholic source of national identity remained unchallenged. The British historian Michael Richards convincingly argues this point, proposing that "the Francoist side ... had a more coherent and durable nationalist vision than the Republicans" (3). The Nationalists, in other words, were better able to consolidate multiple factions – monarchists, Carlists, fascists, the clergy, and others – into a single sacred communion. By eventually opting to hitch his horse to Opus Dei, rather than to the brand of Fascism linked to the Falange that was roundly defeated by Allied forces in the Second World War, Franco strengthened his hold on the nation and his connection to *la gracia de Dios*. This occurred despite widespread famine and poverty throughout the 1940s and 1950s, an existential hardship that the regime attempted to assuage by promoting self-sacrifice as an enduring ideal, a tactic whose failure forced the Caudillo to open up the country to foreign tourism and investment in the late 1950s. In a sense, Franco was indeed *caudillo por la gracia de Dios*, with God's metaphysical reality not understood as a mysterious, objective given but rather derived from Catholicism as an effervescent social force.[7]

Richards's argument is persuasive in pinning Franco's symbolic prowess on the coherence of his vision, which was alluring to a citizenry that could identify the

Caudillo as a *corpus naturale* that resembled previous Spanish sovereigns. The symbolic power central to the exercise of sovereign authority requires uptake from significant sectors of the body politic. As Habermas writes, "Only by establishing a convincing connection between law and political power with religious beliefs and practices could rulers be assured that the people followed their orders" ("The Political" 17).[8] Once a new leader sways a populace's imagination, he or she then acquires the power to define the sources of national identity and the parameters of citizenship. The sacred functions essentially as a structure of power. In Francoist Spain, *la gracia de Dios* is central to this exercise of might and involves mimicking a previously legitimated model of practice and authority.

In the next chapter, I will discuss how the use of a metaphysical "given" in order to organize national unity is successful at the level of individual consciousness. Joan Sales's political thought, in addition to his largely unknown literary masterpiece *Incerta glòria*, emphasizes the need for human beings to ascribe themselves to consecrated images and moral doctrines in order to escape the existential dread of nothingness. The sacred, as a tool for political congregation, survives its theological beginnings through its implicit absorption into the formation of political parties and social movements. Affixing a metaphysical belief structure to icons, like national flags and literary figures, and thereafter protecting those consecrated objects from profanation, forges and protects collective identity. On a second level, Sales also explores Francoism's founding violence and the scapegoating necessary for the regime to quell discord after the Civil War and establish a "time of peace." This leads Sales to consider a form of sovereignty that is not based exclusively on an all-or-nothing structure of exclusion and inclusion, demonstrating a level of nuance absent from Franco's Manichaeism. Against thinkers like Cortés and Ortega y Gasset, Sales reaches back to Pi i Maragall and Prat de la Riba in a search for a federalist form of governance in which a sacred national communion can be founded while simultaneously recognizing the right of other groups to exist and participate in nation building.

3 Politics by Other Means: The Sacred Core of Collective Imagining

Ya que el cielo te desengaña de que has errado
en el modo de vencerle, humilde aguarda
mi cuello a que tú te vengues

Calderón de la Barca

Post-War *Stimmung*

Joan Sales's *Incerta glòria* stands alone by virtue of being a post-1939 interpretation of the Spanish Civil War from the defeated side published in Catalan. In addition, the concluding chapters of the novel, which are set years after the conflict, ruminate on the violent scapegoating inherent within Franco's self-coined post-war "peace." *Incerta glòria* is not only a superior representation of the war and its aftermath within the Catalan tradition but is concomitantly one of the most ideologically balanced works of literature published in Francoist Spain. On a Continental level, the novel captures a general mood within post-war Europe questioning the legitimacy of religious and philosophical paradigms in light of nearly incomprehensible displays of violence.

The novel is in turns told, in epistolary form, by three characters. A fourth character, Juli Soleràs, is deprived of official narration but dialogically appears in relation to the aforementioned narrators throughout the text.[1] Lluís de Brocà, a soldier on the Aragonese front with Soleràs, narrates the first part while on the front. The letters of his common-law wife, Trini, to Soleràs during the conflict compose the second. These two sections take place primarily in 1938 and 1939. The novel's final two chapters, narrated by an aged Cruells years after the conflict, ruminate on the conciliatory political processes that drive out violence with further violence and the productive potential of embracing victimhood. The final chapter, entitled "El vent de la nit," concludes in the mid-1960s, nearly thirty years after the novel's initial point of departure. The three interlocutors share an anarchist background prior to the war, but the narration ventures into the heart of what drives human projects and the fallacies that dictate ideological adhesion and faith-driven devotions in the search of an uncertain glory that "no sabríem definir" (*Incerta glòria* 21). I will suggest that Cruells's narrations, by virtue of their recollective tone and emplotment years into the evolution of Francoism, comment obliquely on the violent exceptionalism inherent to the regime's establishment of a sacred cult of national belonging.

Sales, upon returning to Europe after a period of exile in France, the Caribbean, and Mexico, began the novel in 1948, and it first appeared in December 1956, only after receiving a *nihil obstat* from the archbishop of Barcelona, which allowed publication despite protests by the regime's censors. The work was extensively amplified for the Gallimard French translation in 1962.[2] For the French translation, Sales restored the second and third parts of the novel, which the Spanish censors had mutilated, and also added a new fourth section entitled "Últimes notícies." Over the course of three decades, Sales continued to retouch and add to the novel, taking advantage of increasingly liberal censorship policies and adapting the work's thematics to his own evolving political and religious views. The novel's fifth Catalan edition, published in 1981 by Sales's editorial house Club dels Novel·listes, is the last version directed by the author himself, with the final section adopting the title "El vent de la nit," appearing as though it were a standalone text, but still counted as a fourth volume within the novel. In subsequent Catalan editions, the most noteworthy variances were considering "El vent de la nit" a standalone text and the inclusion of an introductory "Confessió de l'autor."[3] The opening "Confessió" is important both philologically and thematically. On one hand, it connects Sales's novel to the Catholic novel tradition popular in post-war Europe, which structured narration as a first-person testimonial reminiscent of St Augustine's *Confessions*. The "Confessió" is also essential in its foregrounding of the author's interpretation of the concept of glory, whose importance is evident in the very title of the work and derives from Shakespeare's *The Two Gentlemen of Verona*. Sales perceives that an agonizing "set de glòria" pushes humankind towards both love and war, with the latter being the case of his generation. The uncertain glory of an April day, besides being taken from *The Two Gentlemen of Verona*, undoubtedly also refers to the events of April 1931, with the proclamation of the Second Spanish Republic on the fourteenth and Francesc Macià's declaration of a Catalan Republic, resulting in the establishment of the first Generalitat in modern times, on the seventeenth.[4] One would be remiss not to note that the development that makes these glories uncertain also came to pass in April, eight years later, as Franco officially declares a definitive defeat of the Republic on the first of that month in 1939.

The unique evolution of *Incerta glòria* distinguishes the novel from and establishes commonalities with the other texts that I include in this study. The beginning sections of the work, set during and shortly after the war and written in the late 1940s, capture the welter of existential chaos indicative of warfare. However, because Sales expanded and retouched the novel over the span of three decades, especially in the late 1950s and 1960s, *Incerta glòria* also by and large reflects the zeitgeist of the time in which Goytisolo, Benet, Rodoreda, Martín-Santos, and Espriu crafted their literary works. Cruells's contributions to the narrative, set after the war, especially capture the intellectual and material poverty of the first decades of Francoism. This chapter follows a chronological path, with the next two sections focusing primarily on the wartime narrative and the final piece centred on the political dimension one can extract from both Cruells's post-war reflections and Sales's personal letters on the reiterative cycle of violence embedded in scapegoating.

(Prot)agonizing Existence

Perhaps the unique trait of Sales's novel is the manner in which the author contemplates the metaphysical dimension of being and consequently works through the question of who or what is the protagonist of existence. In reference to the novel's title, the notion of glory being uncertain denotes a latency inherent in moments of triumph. The docility of a clear April sky can rapidly become tempestuous and strewn with lightning, a mirror image of the sudden change of fortunes for Republican Spain in the decade of the 1930s. In one of the more complex moments of the novel's first section, Lluís explores a burnt and abandoned monastery where anarchist marauders dis-entombed the mummified remains of several monks and arranged the corpses in an obscene series of poses depicting a marriage. A sudden thunderclap shatters the immense silence of the situation, leading to a metamorphic shift in the atmospheric mood: "Alço els ulls a la finestra: el cel s'enfosquia en gradacions sobtades com si un tramoista anés apagant els llums d'aquell decorat de núvols" (66). Moments of uncertain glory, like the sound of thunder or the flash of lightning, are all explosions that initially strike the senses and the imagination in a significant way only to then disappear, as the result of the absence of force, just as rapidly as they first appeared. The frustration akin to never being able to capture lightning in a bottle is the same that fuels the fruitless attempts of Sales's protagonists to apprehend a concentrated and, most importantly, eternal sense of the glorious. In many ways, the pursuit of an indefinable yet meaning-saturated moment of glory correlates to an unconcealment of Being in Heidegger's late philosophy. Although glory, unfolding at incomprehensible and unpredictable intersections of history, and Being claim humankind and let themselves be established, one's nostalgia and will to administer both is never satiated. It might be said, furthermore, that pursuing glory through events such as war is akin to never becoming sustained in the lightness of Being because one views behaviour as wilfully instrumental. The moment in which one perceives glory *qua* glory a negation of the situation, centred on decadence and peril, is already present. Sales unerringly reiterates that without faith in a metaphysical transcendence beyond the repetition of time, humankind is destined to represent itself and the universe as absolute negation.

Incerta glòria, with the important exception of its third part and the concluding "El vent de la nit," is by all accounts a civil war novel. Unlike in most war narratives, however, the plot spends relatively little time detailing the battles themselves, which in temporal terms were short lived. What Sales, who fought with the Durruti and Macià-Companys columns on the Madrid and Aragonese fronts, best captures is the infinite waiting and forced indolence that filled the gaps between the exchanges of artillery fire and bomb detonations. In the case of Trini, who remains in Barcelona with her and Lluís's child while the men are on the front, Sales also communicates the interminable sense of longing that surrounds the infrequent correspondence from Soleràs and Lluís within a city whose inhabitants rarely venture into the outside world unless an air bombardment requires movement to a bomb shelter. Through all of these characters, Sales stresses the disjointedness and solitude of wartime and the manner in which the event either brought to a standstill or completely derailed the projects and pursuits that previously had distracted and motivated everyone. In such moments of discontinuity, soldiers like Lluís are able to step outside the circuitry of existence and ponder the philosophical ramifications of the situation to which they are subject. Trini, in particular, reflects that her previous belief in anarchism and her life's work as a geologist cannot wrest metaphysical meaning that would confer a sense of permanence onto existence. In a letter to Soleràs she notes, "A tu t'agrada passejar-te arran dels precipicis; ¡a mi em fan rodar el cap! Tot em va semblar inútil des d'aleshores, estudiar els mol·luscos del Carbonífer o posar fills al món, des del moment que el món no tenia ni podia tenir cap solta. No era més que un immens suburbi – però suburbi ¿de quina ciutat? – , un espai caòtic travessat de vies mortes i eriçat de pals sostenint teranyines de cables, tot sense cap objecte; un suburbi espantosament gris i incoherent, limitat per dos murs interminables: l'obscè d'una banda, el macabre de l'altra. ¿Quin sentit podia tenir res, si tot es reduïa a això?" (223).

Wartime, as the disentombing of mummies mentioned earlier shows, unveils the mystery of what Soleràs and others in the novel frequently refer to as the obscene and the macabre, which essentially represent the reproduction of the species and death. These two terms, like other apparent dualisms in the novel such as anarchism and Fascism, are not shown to be polar opposites but rather two meeting points along a circle. Within a Catholic context where ritual is intact, the notion of the sacred transfigures the vulgar, animalistic reality of the obscene and the macabre. The sacraments of baptism and last rites, for example, mask the fact that social renewal, or birth, often comes at the price of a founding violence. Failure to subscribe to the transcendental benefits of the sacraments, which absolve the recipient of both original sin and subsequent transgressions, unveils the futile, endless repetition of human endeavours, which are accompanied frequently by violence and conflict.

In a letter to Soleràs, Trini compares the change of seasons and a linden tree in her yard to her growing indifference towards geology because of the futility evident in the cyclical nature of history: "I el til·ler em semblava estúpid, com tot; cada any la mateixa comèdia, perdre les fulles, treure'n de noves, i tot plegat ¿per què? … És aleshores que vaig avorrir la geologia, que ens descobreix cínicament, potser més que cap altra cosa, aquesta interminable i inútil successió de fets idèntics, l'atroç monotonia de tantes i tantes capes de sediments, cada una d'elles representant desenes o centenars de milers d'anys, deposades l'una damunt l'altra fins a formar un gruix de diversos quilòmetres; l'abisme incomprensible del temps, que dóna nàusea" (227).

Before resorting to religious faith, Trini becomes obsessed with the obscene and the macabre, which in her words, are able to open "un pou als peus … un pou sense fons" (223) within one's consciousness. The obscene and the macabre, as mentioned earlier, form a wall at a meeting point that also represents the passage from one generation to the next. This liminal point becomes especially known during times of crises when antagonistic forces unveil and profane the sacred, discrediting the ambitions of a particular generation. Soleràs marks the beginning stages of the novel's narratological time as one such critical point, using the disentombed friars as an example: "La nostra època, que és imbècil i extraordinària, ha volgut esquinçar els vels que cobrien la mort i la naixença, l'obscè i el macabre" (54). In the modern period, this kind of crisis often entails war, which acts as an interstitial period between periods of peace and in Catalonia served as a period where the vast majority of churches were burned to the ground alongside other profaning acts, such as the opening of tombs that normally shield the dead from the living. This practice, as evidence of the repetition of history, is nearly synonymous with social upheaval in Spain. One notes, to cite a few examples, a similar level of anti-clericalism that accompanies the breakdown of social cohesion during the *setmana tràgica* in 1909, the nineteenth-century Cantonalist movement in which armed militias took possession of churches, and the 1835 worker revolts in Barcelona where convents were burned on *les Rambles*. In 1936, amid another interstitial moment of social dislocation, Trini and others reflect on everyday life outside of conflict, and it appears fraught with meaningless distraction and embalmed in grey. This is sacrilegious knowledge, as it deprives sacred rites, which transfigure the obscene and the macabre, of their structural power over society by disarming a belief in linear transcendence above and beyond the profane. The meeting point where the beginning and the end of existence intertwine, through the magical power of the sacred, tends to be cloaked in mystery. Soleràs, recalling a period of his youth, notes, "Ens fan i ens desfan, ens inflen i ens desinflen, i no hi ha res que apassioni tant el nen com aquest doble misteri: com ens fan, com ens desfan" (79–80). The scene Lluís encounters in the Olivel monastery perfectly captures the way an alpha and omega moment meet, as not only is the post-mortem fate of the body revealed but an Easter candle is phallically placed between a monk's legs, referencing the socially repressed vulgar reality inherent in the obscene. The anarchist marauders' arrangement of the monks in a marriage scene also emphasizes that in such a moment of social upheaval taboos are suspended and the consecrating power of ritual is diffused.

Trini senses that her newfound understanding of "l'abisme incomprensible del temps" nearly exceeds her ability to reason, and this has terrifying consequences for existence that result in nausea, which itself is a repudiation of inner content and an acknowledgment of the body as an objective container without essential, immutable contents. The body becomes "un pou sense fons," in other words. Trini demonstrates, in a fashion similar to Camus in *The Myth of Sisyphus*, that an absurdist understanding of life rests on the conflict of the limits of reason with what exceeds thought: the irrational. Camus writes, "This world in itself is not reasonable, that is all that can be said. But what is absurd is the confrontation of this irrational and the wild longing for clarity whose call echoes in the human heart" (21). Trini, a natural-born positivist seeking clarity in geological pursuit, realizes that reason reaches a limit that then requires either a leap of faith or a contentment with being restricted within the walls of the obscene and the macabre. Lluís, earlier in the novel, reaches a similar fork in the path. While comparing himself to the mummies at the Olivel monastery, he agonizingly notes, "Aquells objectes eren simplement incomprensibles. Una mòmia ens excedeix. Impossible imaginar que nosaltres serem algun dia això: un objecte. Un objecte que es pot dur d'aquí d'allà, rígid i buit; ¿buit de què? D'ànima, diràs tu; però i això ¿què és? … ¿Què tinc jo de comú amb una mòmia? Materialment tot, i no obstant res" (61).

Lluís appears to be near the same point Trini eventually reaches: doubtful of a permanent essence within the self and on the brink of a complete objectification of existence. A correspondence between the organicity of a living human body and a decomposing corpse is materially possible. Lluís's concluding words, however, are a residual no to nothingness – a reiteration of the possibility of the body possessing, whether naturally or through the pursuit of glory, a portion of the absolute. Both characters understand that in wartime, where profanation unveils the obscene and the macabre for what they truly are, the unabashed presence of death in the aftermath of a discharge of youthful ambition towards glorious ends shows the two limit points of existence to be co-extensive, creating existential doubt by diffusing the explanatory power of transcendental religious mythology, which Camus will call an irrational leap of faith beyond the confrontation that gives birth to the absurd.[5]

The bottomless pit of nothingness opened within Trini places her close to Jean-Paul Sartre's Antoine Roquentin in *Nausea*, not only because of her somatic reaction to the absurd, but also in the sense that viewing existence as meaningless is aporetic to external action. Without faith in an absolute, life takes on the guise of the absurd, and the only possible existential authenticity then becomes, following Camus, a recognition of life's limits and an extinguishing of eternal hope – two conditions that certainly characterize Trini. The point at which life is known as meaningless erects, concomitantly, a sense of freedom in the construction of the ego, if one embraces the absurd. This is demonstrated well by Sales in his portrayal of Soleràs. In *Being and Nothingness*, Sartre perceives the ego as a reflected nihilation of nothingness, an aporia if there ever was one, in order to assimilate a world of being through intentioned projects, meaning that every time one attempts transcendence towards a being-in-itself, it comes from a position of privation: "We rediscover non-being as a condition of the transcendence toward being" (*Being and Nothingness* 84). Sartre's consciousness is heavily latent with possibility; by being pure nothingness, humankind is the entity by which nothingness enters the world. This requires a pre-reflective *cogito* to produce an ego that is not at all programmed to adopt any particular mode of being. The future course of the reflected ego, defined by Sartre as metastable, is sustained by an infinite array of determinations that consciousness may take in assimilating Being. As an object reflected off the purely interior consciousness, the ego, as a unity of past and present experience, is not defined by Sartre in essentialist terms, and may at any time veer off course, or step away from its projects altogether. At this point, anxiety and nausea ensues, as consciousness becomes aware of its own freedom. This freedom of the being-for-itself, possible only as the result of its inherent nothingness, is the self's precondition for existence: "Let us understand indeed that this original necessity of being its own nothingness does not belong to consciousness intermittently and on the occasion of particular negations … consciousness continually experiences itself as the nihilation of its past being" (64).

In *Incerta glòria*, Soleràs best portrays the freedom of the being-for-itself upon betraying his column and passing to the fascist side soon after declaring his affection for Trini. Soleràs, when explaining his treachery while living with his aunt as a child, infers onto the duplicity that would later mark his fascist betrayal a permanence rooted in his childhood, comparing his mode of being to that of a phantasm that uneasily straddles the line between being and non-being: "¡Si et pogués fer comprendre els plaers subtilíssims de la fantasmagoria! Ser i no ser al mateix temps (pobre Shakespeare); ser un mateix i ser un altre: ¡Ser i no existir, existir i no ser, tot a la vegada! La personalitat desdoblada, l'evasió total, sensació vertiginosa que només pot donar la doble vida!" (203).

The "total evasion" that Soleràs places at the core of a double life pinpoints a negating of responsibility for the type of objectified ego one has historically constructed, certainly one of the principle tenets of Sartre's bad faith. In the novel, Soleràs often functions as a psychoanalyst, insinuating and untangling sentiments that the other characters only hint at digressively. Trini's grasp of the incomprehensible abyss of time and her endless inner well of nothingness are clear examples, as they come to fruition only after she and Soleràs spend an afternoon walking together, though her feelings of solitude and insignificance are present from the very onset of the second part of the novel. If Trini's newfound awareness of meaningless freedom equates her with Roquentin's nausea, Soleràs's always-already condition of embracing the absurd in full awareness of its implications brings him close to Camus's Don Juan, who "has chosen to be nothing" (*Myth of Sisyphus* 73) by accepting the limits of mortal existence, which entails an endless series of intensely passionate yet quite temporary actions. By loving everyone, Don Juan loves no one, just as Soleràs's phantasmagorical, shape-shifting nature allows him to be both everything and nothing at once.

Soleràs maintains a certain level of sincerity by maintaining cognizance of the synchronicity of being one thing in order to simultaneously make the negation that then allows being what one is not. Unlike many characters in the novel, Soleràs manages to avoid betraying his youth by embracing his condition of duplicity to the very end of his existence. Soleràs's example also demonstrates that bad faith, as Sartre argues, is a prerequisite for the very constitution of an existence outside of a primordial consciousness: "The condition of the possibility for bad faith is that human reality, in its most immediate being, in the intra-structure of the pre-reflective *cogito*, must be what it isn't and not be what it is" (*Being and Nothingness* 112). For there to be *a* reality outside of the nothingness at the origin of humankind, there must be a self-denial in the objectification of the ego; one *must* enter the world as a "no" to nothingness. Soleràs is, at least partially, the essence of Sartre's philosophy by being conscientiously aware that he exists in bad faith and that *that* is his precise mode of being. If consciousness acts sincerely, in Sartre's terms, and stops sustaining its being, all that is left to perceive is the only authentic material of existence – the pools of nothingness that would render all other substance transparent and anxiety-inducing, as Trini discovers.

Sartrean philosophy is totally lacking in a metaphysical dimension beyond the phenomenologically encountered object that would permit a subject to negate nothingness by aspiring to possession of absolute glory, which in Sales's terms would be the only authentic being-in-itself with a plenitude of meaning autonomous of other determinants. Campillo and Castellanos, in fact, convincingly argue that Sales's protagonists reflect that "l'heroisme i la voluntat de permanència que porten els homes a cercar «la incerta glòria d'un matí d'abril» … és producte de la recerca de la plenitud del sentit" (79). The plenitude of being, of which the main characters in the novel have only experienced a taste, fuels the insatiable drive that is sustained by faith. Trini's decision to convert to Catholicism from an atheistic perspective is initially a reaction to the inadequacy of the rational positivism that marked her pre-war life. She notes that religion once held little interest because "havia respirat en família un gran respecte per les ciències positives i una total indiferència per allò que en diuen «metafísica». Per a nosaltres era indiscutible que les ciències positives portarien, tard o d'hora, a la racionalització de la societat" (*Incerta glòria* 216). As stated before, this knowledge not only failed to rectify her feelings of emptiness but also fed a belief in the meaninglessness of the cycle of history. Trini, in short, seeks out a faith that is rooted in an idealism that Camus would disdainfully call a "rationalization of the irrational" in order to inauthentically overcome the absurd. Camus critiques existentialist writer Leon Chestov, for example, for rejecting a total acceptance of the absurd upon reaching the limits of rational categories. Chestov, despite discovering "the absurdity of all existence," responds that "this is God: we must rely on him even if he does not correspond to any of our rational categories" (Camus, *Myth of Sisyphus* 34). Neither can Trini accept this absurdity. She credits Soleràs's gift of a Bible as a preliminary step towards her conversion, which opens her eyes "a una altra vida on no arriba ni pot arribar el ridícul espantós d'aquesta" (*Incerta glòria* 346).

In another passage, Trini notes the extent to which her conversion transfigures the linden tree, which she previously associated with existential meaninglessness. She writes that the linden tree, "el tronc pelat del til·ler que jo veia a contrallum sobre el cel de posta, em va semblar que a aquell pal obscè i macabre li naixia un altre pal transversal … ¡alguna cosa a què arrapar-se! «La Creu o l'Absurd»" (231). Trini's turn to faith is not dependent on any dogmatic belief linked to an encyclopedic knowledge of Catholic practice or any credence given to the historical reality of the Genesis story or the Gospels, a stark contrast with Cruell's portrayal of her later in the novel when she is middle-aged and fully assimilated into institutional Catholicism, ardently attending Mass and reciting the rosary daily.

That Trini has not been indoctrinated since birth into a religious belief structure allows Sales to communicate the primal need that drives a mature consciousness, fully in possession of reason, to seek an organized system of beliefs unsupported by empirical proofs. Indeed Trini's Catholicism arises purely as a reaction to the immediate need for a supranatural world of permanence outside of an everyday reality that is chaotic, incoherent, and makeshift.[6] Her existential crisis and subsequent conversion echoes Roquentin's recognition of the meaning of life through an encounter with a chestnut tree, and places in doubt Carme Arnau's assertion that the *til·ler*'s importance rests on it being "un símbol d'amor i de fidelitat … Trini roman fidel al seu company, malgrat la forta atracció que sent per Soleràs" (118). Not only does Trini believe her marriage to be over at this point in the narrative, but Sales's text gives no indication that the reader should view the symbol in connection to its role in the Baucis and Philemon myth, as Arnau does somewhat flippantly. Sales, very much like Chestov, argues that the very existence of a limit point that reason cannot overcome is precisely the proof that there exists a glorious absolute that embodies goodness incompatible with the finitude of mortals. As Soleràs notes to Cruells later in the novel, "De fet no hi hauria d'haver res més que mal, de la mateixa manera no hi hauria d'haver més que tenebra absoluta, fred absolut, no-res en definitiva. El no-res seria l'única cosa que no plantejaria cap enigma" (659). Echoing Heidegger's questioning as to why there is something rather than nothing, Soleràs elucidates that an idealistic, invisible reality exists beyond our own that confers a sense of mystery onto a reality otherwise entrenched within a definite historical temporality. Soleràs's statement places the roots of evil firmly within the realm of human affairs and reminds one that the semantic origin of the concepts of "God" and "good" are one and the same.

Trini reduces life to a choice between the Cross and the absurd, a move that credits Soleràs's power of suggestion. Trini exclaims in another letter to Soleràs that "en Lluís és incapaç de sospitar que sóc cristiana … Sí; tu et vas adonar ben aviat que jo no podia suportar la buidor, que necessitava creure" (250). In a world in which all categories of reason are shown to be insufficient to understanding realities that exceed the capacity of consciousness, faith is all that is left to provide a stable footing and a remedy for anxiety, proving that the underpinnings of religious thought are truly dependent on feeling. Soleràs, though deprived of a chapter of his own narration, is enormously important by serving as Sales's philosophical voice and therefore revealing the process that foregrounds adherence to faith and the construction of the ego. Above all, Sales uses Soleràs to construct consciousness as a being-for-itself instilled with absolute freedom that is inevitably led down paths that appear forced, in spite of existing in a world in which arbitrariness is the rule.

The anxiety resulting from the absurd leads to a suspension of belief in mythology, creating foundational narratives that appear fantastic. Trini herself seems to grasp this phenomenon when comparing the sacrament of baptism to reading the Christ narrative to her child Ramonet. On one hand, she comments,

"El baptisme ... què vols que t'hi digui. Que tirant-li una mica d'aigua al cap acompanyant-ho d'unes paraules màgiques obtenim que se salvi algú ... ¿és que realment queda encara ningú capaç de creure una tal ... bestiesa?" (226). By the conclusion of the novel's second part, however, Trini will come to view religious faith as the essence of life, despite the puerile belief structure that it demands of its adherents. Her change in tone is astounding: "Jo crec amb tota l'ànima que si necessitem tant la poesia i la fe per no sentir-nos molt més desventurats que si no fóssim ni haguéssim estat mai és perquè la poesia i la fe són l'existència i la vida, perquè sense elles tot aquest món es desfaria en no-res com una vana fantasmagoria sense cap consistència. Si veiessis el Ramonet amb quins ulls escola rondalles ... ¡I com li agrada de saber que l'àngel de la guarda, el Nin Jesús i la Mare de Déu vetllen per ell; com el reconforta de saber-ho! ¡Ens sentiríem tan desemparats en aquest món si no hi hagués un altre món invisible per sostenir-nos!" (337).

Once again, Trini pinpoints affect as the crucial component that drives one to grasp faith and create explanatory events that provide coherent evidence of an "invisible world" beyond the phenomenological reality of appearances. Cruells, similarly, will later recognize that such biblical myths, in particular Christ's Passion story, are "a penes creïbles als ulls de la raó crítica" (460). The invisible supporting reality of faith is an antidote to the endless well of nothingness that fed Trini's anxiety prior to her conversion and existentially provides a platform of stable footing. In a fashion similar to how Plato's realm of absolute ideas provides a reliable model for humankind to recognize and theorize form, Trini's invisible metaphysical world of faith imposes constancy onto her empirical reality and enables mythological comprehension of phenomena that are otherwise ungraspable. Her commentary, at the very least, pinpoints religious thought as a response to a primal human feeling that arises amid an incoherent and contingent realm of reality that appears cosmologically abandoned. The role of faith as an antidote to existential anguish proves to be such a formidable temptation that Trini eventually argues for an infantilized understanding of Divinity: "¿Què importa que les figuracions que ens fem d'aquest món invisible que ens sosté siguin tan puerils ... ¿És que hi ha gaire diferència entre l'enteniment que tenim als tres anys i el que arribem a tenir passats els vint? ¿Com podríem arribar a afigurar-nos mai la Divinitat si no d'una manera tota infantil?" (337).

With religion re-establishing a constancy and transcendent influence over the realm of human activity, Trini is able to return to her geological studies by the end of the second part. Though geology had bored her "quan aquest abisme del temps m'havia aparegut de sobte sense sentit; ara hi retrobo al contrari com una mena de consol, com un sedant" (348). Trini also comes to see her marriage as over by the second part, and the freedom this confers onto her life is now absolutely bereft of the anguish and sickness onto death that marked her prior conception of existence: "Sóc soltera, lliure del tot; no estic lligada amb ell [Lluís] per res. És la sort que m'ha tocat enmig de la desgràcia" (346). Unbeknownst to Trini, the dualism she constructs between anarchistic, scientific positivism, and religious faith is in fact a point of convergence, like so many other binaries in the novel.

The invisible existence of an absolute ideal that confers stable meaning and is capable of osmotically being appropriated by finite mortal bodies rooted in time fuels the projects that Sales's characters construct in the shaping of their metastable egos. Though Trini sees the anarchist movement of the early 1930s as an integral element in the creation of a society free of metaphysics, the thirst that drives her adherence to the ideology is the same thirst that Catholic faith satisfies during the war. Trini, without conscientiously making this connection, sees a similar kind of faith in her atheist father, who created an anarchist pamphlet entitled *Blast* that she, Lluís, and Soleràs hand out on the streets. Trini laments those who fail to perceive any kind of mystery to existence. She reiterates that this in no way describes her father: "Ell creu; potser no s'acabe d'entendre gaire en què, però creu" (275). Belief in a mysterious glory is critical, and Trini herself subscribed to this same fascinating *misterium tremendum* rooted in an anarchist vision of society as a teenager participating in the student revolts that preceded the establishment of the Second Republic and, more particularly, the proclamation of a federalist Catalan Republic by Macià in 1931. The motivation that drove this project was precisely "una glòria que no sabríem definir": "¡Era una època exaltant aquella primavera de 1931! ¿N'hi haurà mai més cap de tan primavera com aquella? En Lluís i jo i tu i tots nosaltres, els estudiants revolucionaris, ens havíem trobat al palau de la Generalitat el 14 d'abril aquella tarda inoblidable ... ¡com espetegava al vent de primavera, quina alegria a tots els ulls, com podia aquella bandera lluminosa fer-nos sentir tots fills de la mateixa gran família! ¡Quina glòria la d'aquell 14 d'abril!" (270).

Glory, whether found in the ascension of a political ideal or in religious dogma, is intricately linked to the sacred in its ability to bind together a community, often around consecrated objects, such as a flag, that are endowed with an ideal that might be considered the hypostatic image of a social grouping's identity.

This is precisely what Émile Durkheim perceives as an elementary form of religious life. Durkheim notes that in primitive cultures, people confer onto totemic animals or objects a consecrated spirit, a sacred element, which creates a symbol that is nothing other than "society hypostasized and transfigured" (257). The sacred exists only within human consciousness and provides a principle by which a collectivity can organize and thereafter self-identify. This type of society perceives existence as a circle, with essential periods set apart for the performance of sacrifices and consecration rituals meant to spiritually regenerate the next iteration of the cycle. Outside of these meeting points, the sacred is set apart, and a series of taboos and prohibitions prevent profanation. These prohibitions extend to linguistic discourse. Soleràs references this dynamic when discussing the Olivel monastery's disentombed monks with Lluís: "Tu no ets un cadàver, res d'això, però amb tu puc parlar de cadàvers; ets de les poques persones amb qui se'n pot parlar en confiança. El macabre està interdit de la conversa; com l'obscè" (*Incerta glòria* 152–3). The totality of this sacralizing process is Durkheim's precise definition of religion: "A religion is a unified system of beliefs and practices relative to sacred things, that is to say, things set apart and surrounded by prohibitions – beliefs and practices that unite its adherents in a single moral community called a church" (46).

A society places the essence of its regeneration and power in the sacred object, and ritual sacrifice functions as a tool that members of a cult can use to assimilate, often in a very literal sense through dietary consumption, a material endowed with transcendental power. Durkheim's definition of religious life contextualizes the cycle of the obscene and the macabre, along with the logic of assimilating glory, in Sales's novel. It moreover demonstrates that religious practice involves not only an organized demagogic entity like Catholicism, but may refer, secularly, to any cult that could be defined as a moral community because of its internal organization around the consecration of a hypostatized ideal of the cult's adherents. Or in Trini's own words, it may refer to a "lluminosa bandera" that unites "els fills de la mateixa gran família" (270).

Sales is well aware of the closeness between religious practice and incipient political regimentation. One is reminded of Clausewitz in the sense that religion, like war, is the continuation of politics by other means.[7] Trini's reflections on her youth, in any case, reveal anarchism to be a religious organization like any other. Gerald Brenan's history of anarchism and anarcho-syndicalism echoes this, noting that the two essential aspects of Spanish anarchism are its idealism and moral-religious character (188). Brenan notes in particular that the 1902 general strike in Barcelona enthused workers and anarcho-syndicalists throughout Spain, particularly in Andalucía, where "an extraordinary ferment, as sudden and apparently as causeless as a religious revival, swept over the country districts" (174). Without delving too deeply into the niceties of the movement, I reference Brenan in passing only to stress the ease with which a primitive, circular conception of the sacred shifts from religious into secular and political realms in modern times.

Trini's letters, over the course of the novel's second part, shift in focus from her present existential anguish to the ideals of her youth. In the "Confessió de l'autor," Sales pinpoints that "hi ha un moment de la vida que sembla com si ens despertéssim d'un somni. Hem deixat de ser joves" (21). All of Sales's narrators take up this issue in their respective sections. Trini merely exchanges the cult of her youth with another belief structure, which in essence is a kind of distraction that fends off the anxiety inflicted by the meaningless freedom of human activity between the walls of the obscene and the macabre. Trini's husband, Lluís, makes a similar exchange after the war, leaving behind his youthful ideals of both anarchism and the defence of the *pàtria* for the cult of the marketplace by moving to the Americas to spread his family's noodle-making business. Glory, synonymous with absolute meaning, is always the object that drives human projects, and Sales importantly points out that the process occurs outside the confines of organized religion.[8] Glory is what gives logic to the absurd, but its possession is merely instantaneous and fugacious, as it inevitably gives way to the monotony of everyday life. As Soleràs explains to Cruells, this is how the cyclical repetition of the obscene and the macabre functions:

> La glòria ¿què és? ¿Una paraula vana? ¿No hi ha altra glòria que la vanaglòria. Sí, molt sovint no hi ha més que això, res més que paraules i paraules, bruit i furor per res; però algun cop, algun raríssim moment, la sentim com el que és: la plenitud de sentit, l'antiabsurd. No és altra cosa, és això; i és per això que la busquem, ¡una cosa que tingui plenament sentit! ¡Que valgui per ella mateixa, que sigui absoluta! El nostre error és buscar-la en aquesta vida; no pas que no s'hi pugui trobar, però no podríem suportar-la més que un instant: ens aniquilaria. Si no ens aniquila és perquè es dissipa; o bé es transforma en monotonia i finalment torna l'absurd … Era la glòria a condició que només durés un instant i que no es repetís. (663)

What will differentiate Trini and Lluís from Cruells later in the novel is the former's inability to solve a conundrum essential for Sales's generation: how is it possible for one not to betray the ideals of youth once the glorious has been grasped and subsequently lost? When sacrifice for that glory has been rendered futile, how does one move past a sacrificial mechanism that replaces one set of metaphysics for another, thereby maintaining the dialectic of the obscene and the macabre? This dialectic, as Soleràs's previous quotation demonstrates, is entirely dependent on a theory of social collectivization within a sacrificial structure that founds order through violence. The sacred, as Durkheim convincingly notes, is lethal when approached and, when profaned, it tends to lose its consecrated power and dissipate. In the above quotation, Soleràs finds this same element of risk in the pursuit of a glorious absolute, which tends to both annihilate its possessor and disappear. Soleràs paints the moment of this possession as an atemporal instant, a very brief stepping outside of finite time that reconciles a mortal with eternity. As I explore in chapter 5, this is precisely what Mircea Eliade calls sacred time.

Once a particular glorious absolute dissolves, it cannot reappear, and society is left stymied as nothingness becomes more perceptible than being itself. In the final two sections of the novel, Cruells, with the omnipresent intervention of Soleràs, reveals that the aftermath of a sacrificial crisis, where the members of a tribe disregard taboos and prohibitions, requires a logic of sacrifice that reinstitutes a new glorious ideal whose pursuit is destined to repeat the process. This gives a great symbolic import to the quotation by Gracián with which Sales opens the first part of the novel: "Qué veys? Veo, dixo Andrenio, que las mismas guerras intestinas de agora doscientos años" (23).

The Scapegoat Mechanism and the Mimetic Reduction of Difference

Through the wartime experiences of Lluís and Trini, Sales begins his analysis of war and violence from a point of departure that could not be more elementary: the structure of consciousness and the logic that gives birth to the ego. A moment of crisis reveals the need for humanity to base action according to the dictum of an invisible supra-phenomenal reality, and this process is the basis for the formation of a community held together by common moral tenets. This type of social organization fuels the onslaught of war, when two or more sides enter into conflict defending contradictory belief structures. Margarida Casacuberta has argued that *Incerta glòria*'s central tenet is that "l'única veritable heretgia és no creure en res. En aquest sentit, tots els personatges són uns grans pecadors que troben, això no obstant, la redempció en el penediment i la conversió" (48). In a leap of logic not altogether coherent, Casacuberta then questions, "què sentit té, doncs, la història en el sentit progressista i materialista del terme?" (49). What is clear in an analysis of Trini and others in the novel is that conversion is not at all motivated by a deep-seated guilt instilled by a stereotypically Catholic feeling of being a concupiscent sinner in need of expiation. Conversion, in both Lluís and Trini's cases, is the result of an ontological aporia that requires a metaphysical truth in order for life to advance beyond a point of undecidability. Casacuberta faults Sales's historiography for finding all ideologies to be one and the same, with the conversion to Catholicism being the only valid course of action. This, for Casacuberta, constitutes the "fi de la història." One can only assume that this refers to Francis Fukuyama's controversial work *The End of History and the Last Man*, which views all war as a conflict among competing ideologies that can be superseded only by the universal spread of liberal democracy. Casacuberta's fatal error is a failure to perceive Sales's equation of the "scarlet and the black" as the foundation of a theory of violence. Sales structures the Spanish Civil War as a mutual desire for the same object – what he calls a thirst for glory. The confrontation of a mimetic desire shared by both sides demands that an initial differentiation of causes at the beginning of the conflict eventually devolves into an orgy of violent paroxysms. At this juncture, all combatants become mutually unintelligible, because a need to completely annihilate the rival replaces the original object of desire (glory). It goes without saying that our recognition of this process is the fruit of René Girard's thought.

Girard argues that in a normally functioning society the maintenance of hierarchies with a strong semblance of differentiation among its members preserves order. Conflict, however, implies a dissolution, a "removal of differences and hierarchies which constitute the community in its wholeness" (*Things Hidden* 142). Prior to this point of indifferentiation, however, Girard questions what it is that incites what he calls a sacrificial crisis, where social rituals that re-enact the scapegoating of a surrogate victim fail to check a breakout of reciprocal violence among members of a community. The answer is that humankind, despite having its most basic needs of survival met, cannot fail to perceive a greater plenitude of being in an object possessed by a model: "Once his basic needs are satisfied (indeed, sometimes even before), man is subject to intense desires, though he may not know precisely for what. The reason is that he desires *being*, something he himself lacks and which some other person seems to possess. The subject thus looks to that other person to inform him of what he should desire in order to acquire that being. If the model, who is apparently already endowed with superior being, desires some object, that object must surely be capable of conferring an even greater plenitude of being" (*Violence* 146).

In this passage, Girard is defining a theory of mimesis and placing it at the root of actions that lead to violence. One desires an object not because of its innate value but rather because it is desired by a model, who thereafter is converted into a rival for the desired thing. Though this process begins as a one-to-one relationship, desire is infectious and eventually incites all members to pursue the same object. Girard analyzes this dynamic in the beheading of John the Baptist, where the choir joins Salomé's entreaty to see the murder brought to fruition. This unfettered mimesis ends in conflict, as a chain of reciprocal aggression takes root and a spirit of vengeance incites reprisals. Is it far-fetched to perceive Sales's conception of the glorious absolute as one such common object of desire that, when coupled with mimesis, enacts a period of senseless butchery? Cruells, in a conversation with Trini, echoes Girard's thoughts: "¡La causa! – vaig exclamar –, la causa en tot cas seria diferent per a cada u … però ¿quina és la causa de cada u? No, no és per la causa; han vingut a crucificar-se. Els uns i els altres, els uns als altres. És la mateixa història a totes les guerres i és per això que de guerra n'hi haurà sempre, sempre, sempre. Perquè l'home, que va ser creat per asseure's a prop del foc en companyia d'una persona estimada, necessita no obstant crucificar-se … ¡vostè no pot afigurar-se el que són capaços de sofrir i de fer sofrir quan arriba l'hora!" (461).

The wars change, as do the causes brandished by the different sides, but what remains consistent is a kind of death drive that persists despite all other material needs being met. Such an unconscious drive towards annihilation certainly recalls Freud's thanatos instinct that drives humankind to return to an originary, inorganic state from which "the attributes of life were at sometime evoked" (*Beyond the Pleasure Principle* 46).

What intrigues Sales is how wars begin as a conflict of distinct causes but end up with the conflict's individual participants being completely unaware of why they were initially incited to commit violence. At moment near the end of the Civil War, Cruells asks: "¿Qui els empeny? No pas la causa, que no la sap ningú, sinó la glòria, que la sent tothom" (461). In Sales's *Cartes de la guerra*, he echoes this sentiment: "¿Saben *ells* per què es maten? Es maten, em deia, perquè sí, pel gust de matar-se; no cerquis ideals ni res que s'hi assembli en les accions dels homes" (164–5). Cruells, who is recalling a conversation that takes place in the middle of the conflict years after the fact, argues that at the root of idealistic causes there exists a common denominator that reduces all combatants to a common structure of desire predicated on the existence of "glory," a higher plenitude of being, which is to be obtained at all costs. Far from proclaiming the end of history, and the end of all ideology, Sales is perceiving a universal human mechanism of both social crisis and re-socialization that begins with conflicting ideals but gives way to a metonymic shift that places a yearning for the violent elimination of the rival into the position formerly held by the desired object.

Girard, analyzing such diverse sources as classic mythology, Christianity, and structuralist anthropology, explains that as a sacrificial crisis proceeds in stages, the original object of desire is replaced by a desire to completely obliterate the mimetic obstacle. At this point, what was originally desired fades from consciousness: "Desire clearly understands that, in desiring what another desires, it makes a rival and an obstacle of this model. It would be wise to give up, but if desire were wise it would not be desire. Finding only obstacles in its path, it incorporates them in its vision of the desirable and brings them into the foreground; it can no longer desire without them and cultivates them avidly. Thus it becomes full of hatred for the obstacle, and allows itself to be scandalized" (*Scapegoat* 133).

Sales's frequent reference throughout the novel to the scarlet and the black, beyond being a nod to Stendhal, is also a critique of the similar colour scheme employed in both the anarchist and falangist shields, a not too subtle reminder that many anarchists became falangists after the war and that many supposed anarchist agitators were actually undercover fascist agents. That Sales notes a closeness between seemingly polarized schools of thought such as anarchism and fascism demonstrates the functioning of the *skandalon* (obstacle) in any mimetic reduction of difference. Soldiers on both sides, and under all different banners, desire glory, "que la sent tothom," but at a certain point in the conflict the common pursuit of a particular ideal intertwines the different rivals. In Sales's view, the existence of a faction of soldiers, of which he is a part, interested only in defending their nation are an obstacle to both anarchists and fascists in their respective attempts to violently lay claim to Barcelona and Catalonia on the whole. Though the anarchist and fascist ideals differ on paper, consorting with one another in order to destroy a hated obstacle reduces the two factions to a single force. As Sales notes in his *Cartes*, "Vet aquí un home que si l'han afusellat els feixistes és perquè no ho havien pogut fer abans els anarquistes; tot un símbol de la Catalunya crucificada entre dos lladres" (218). A mimetic structure of desire gives way to a reduction of differences in which a distinction of ideals is lost as a mutual obstacle is brought to the foreground. Destroying Catalonia, and the Second Republic, reduces the anarchist and fascist sides to a singular symbol that equates the two – the scarlet and the black of each side's respective flag – a clear demonstration of scandalizing resulting from the existence of a common *skandalon*.

Sales interprets war as a paroxysm of violence that reaches a point where senseless butchery is the only perceptible interest that a conflict's combatants have. War is a time of epiphany because it opens up the possibility of possessing glory, which is no longer set apart within a complex system of sacral ritual and protected by prohibition. Roger Caillois and other sociologists have argued that in the pre-modern era the festival acted as a similar interstitial interlude that removed prohibitions and opened up to the general public contact with the sacred. The festival is notably an interruption of the everyday that entails a collective gathering, transforms social life, and is a "phenomenon of such duration, violence, and magnitude, that it can only be broadly compared to days of pleasure with no thought for the morrow in complex civilizations" (161). As modernity evolved, the function of the festival lost importance, and Caillois argues that war is now, in the modern period, the only time that "introduces man to an intoxicating world in which the presence of death makes him shiver and confers a superior value onto his actions. He believes he will acquire a psychic vigor … out of proportion to mundane experiences" (173). The omnipresence of death in Sales's novel leads to such a trembling, as evidenced by Lluís's initial contact with the mummies at the Olivel monastery, whose visual ambush incites his ruminations on the limits of existence and the questionable presence of the soul. The urge to move beyond the mundane register of everyday experience is precisely the "fosc afany [que] ens mou" that Sales perceives in his generation, which seeks glory in two things: "sobretot en l'amor – i en la guerra" (21).

As evidenced by the dis-entombed mummies, Sales frequently emphasizes the paroxysm of violence and unbridled consumption of resources that he personally witnesses on the front in his *Cartes* and novelizes in *Incerta glòria*. The author directs his critique at both sides of the conflict. Lluís narrates an episode where the Fascists falsely surrendered a few soldiers in order to make the other side cease their attack and lay down their arms. In discovering the ruse, Lluís's battalion responds with unbridled fury, unleashing an assault that results in "una matança a l'arma blanca. Enfonsen el matxet en el ventre de tots, fins dels que cauen de genollons demanant misericòrdia" (163). One of the fallen fascist soldiers is later discovered genitally mutilated, leading Lluís to a bitter observation: "La guerra té coses ben desagradables. ¡Si un hi matés algú a qui tingués tírria! … el mal no és, doncs, que ens matem els uns als altres, sinó l'odi" (164). War, at a certain juncture, loses all sense of a justified cause that would give weight to a grudge proclaimed against a specific enemy. Violence committed in pursuit of a cherished ideal is one thing, and violence for violence's sake is another. Towards the end of his *Cartes de la guerra*, Sales remarks, "La guerra és una cosa tan cafre que només pot ser lícita quan reuneix dues condicions: una causa justa i una esperança fundada de guanyar-la. En aquestes altures, temo que la nostra, la que encara estem sostenint a desgrat de tot, ja no té cap de les dues; la causa justa, que era la defensa de Catalunya … I pel que fa a esperances de guanyar-la … potser que riguem per no haver de plorar" (251).

These ruminations on the progression of violence prove to be double-sided in the sense that a blind desire to obliterate one's rival is combined with an absolute commitment to self-immolation. In the *Cartes*, Sales writes that "ens sentim disposats a fer la guerra per tota l'eternitat abans que rendir-nos" (214). This remark, alongside Cruells's commentary on the universal need to self-immolate through crucifixion, emphasizes that war, like the festival of old, demands all prevailing energies of consumption both of the self and of the enemy.

Sales makes this observation in April 1938, well into the Spanish Civil War and past the point where total annihilation would have replaced initial desired causes in the mimetic structure of engagement. Cruells, a personification of Sales himself reconsidering the war years later, has the advantage of hindsight and thus homes in on the mimetic reduction of difference in the pursuit of glory. That Sales would reach this perspective based on experience gained from participation in a civil war is potentially illuminating. Carl Schmitt relates civil war closely to his theory of the partisan, in the sense that both exist at or just beyond the margins of bracketed Eurocentric state conflict where international law and war conventions are respected. War combatants demand total annihilation of the enemy when groups within the same legal order each believe they possess a justified cause. The only possible qualification of victory is therefore the complete conquest of the state and not simply obtaining a particular aim. Schmitt writes, "Civil war has something gruesome about it. It is fraternal war, because it is pursued within a common political unity that includes also the opponent, and within the same legal order, and because both belligerent sides absolutely and simultaneously affirm and negate this common unity. Both consider their opponent to be absolutely and unconditionally wrong" (*Theory of the Partisan* xv).

The failure to perceive in the enemy any semblance of rights and the unconditional demand for its annihilation places civil war at the limit point where Schmitt believes European rule of law gives way to partisan warfare.[9] Sales outlines, on a scale that begins with an individual's psychological propensity to link desire to violence and ends with a macro-perspective on the Spanish Civil War, how the transformation of bracketed war into an extremely violent exercise of resistance at all costs is fluid and unstable. The disappearance of known justifiable causes in *Incerta glòria* marks the point at which the margin separating these two forms of conflict disappears. Absolute enmity substitutes for ideological rhetoric, leading to the interminable exchange of terror and counter-terror until one side is obliterated and there is total consumption of resources.

As I will soon show in an analysis of the re-entombing of the Olivel monastery monks, Sales relates the re-establishment of Franco's "time of peace" in the 1940s to the production of a list of scapegoats onto whom the regime projects Spain's ills. I will investigate this dynamic still further in the final section of the chapter in which Cruells deconstructs the scapegoating dynamic and proposes an alternative principle of political congregation based on love. For Girard, scapegoating begins with the choosing of a victim, often innocent of any crime, but universally found at fault by all sides and therefore ejected from the community, bearing the weight of all cultural transgressions. Girard stresses that a subject at war, clouded in mimeticism, not loses only a sense of cause but also a sense of self and the ability to make decisions. At this point, with the subject now an automaton, all conflict with the mutual obstacle ceases, yet the appetite for death remains: "Submerged in mimeticism the subject loses awareness of self and purpose. Instead of rivaling the model he is transformed into a harmless marionette; all opposition is abolished and the contradiction of desire dissolves. But where now is the obstacle that was barring the war and pinning him down? The monster must be lurking somewhere; for the experience to be complete the monster must be found and destroyed. At this moment there is always an appetite for sacrifice that requires appeasement, a scapegoat to destroy" (*Scapegoat* 144).

The notion of a "monster lurking somewhere" very accurately characterizes Franco's belief throughout his dictatorship in the imminent return of the "Anti-España." To Girard, a community opposes a rising tide of vengeance through the sacrifice of a scapegoat, a critical move, as unrestricted violence "is an interminable, infinitely repetitive process. Every time it turns up in some part of the community, it threatens to involve the whole social body" (*Violence and the Sacred* 14–15). In order to break this vicious cycle, sacrifice is required in order "to stem this rising tide of indiscriminate substitutions and redirect violence into 'proper' channels" (10). The victim of such a sacrifice is a scapegoat.

Despite the innocence of the scapegoated victim, the persecutor and the public are convinced of his guilt, and yet in the aftermath of sacrifice the scapegoat undergoes a curious and paradoxical reversal of esteem. The public will sacralize the memory of the scapegoat due to its appearing as the cause of the "end to the crisis by eliminating all the interpersonal repercussions in the concentration of evildoing in the person of one victim. The scapegoat is only effective when human relations have broken down in crisis, but he gives the impression of effecting external causes as well, such as plagues" (*Scapegoat* 43). The community both fears the scapegoat, as it is the alleged cause of the indifferentiated cycle of violence whose return to society could bring war, and converts the victim into a consecrated symbol of the re-establishment of peace. To Girard the sacred is thus profoundly ambivalent, and both fear and esteem require setting sacred objects apart through taboo and ritual. The choice of the scapegoat is also a delicate matter, as it tends to be a marginalized member of society or a relatively recent newcomer onto the scene. The victim, however, cannot be too different from those involved in the circle of vengeful reprisals or it will fail to be a suitable substitute for those who are actually the cause of discord. The sacralization of the scapegoat is the very birth of myth, as it creates a founding narrative around a spiritualized entity that casts a veil over the macabre nature of society's founding and originary, obscene violence.

The victimary mechanism is essential to understanding *Incerta glòria*'s theory of violence and its overall theological structure. The mechanism is hinted at in the quoting of a popular song at the beginning of the first part's third chapter: "Van sortir sis toros, / tots sis eren dolents; / i aquesta ha estat la causa / de cremar-se els convents" (99). This song takes place before the 1836 revolt in Barcelona that burned convents throughout the city. The bulls are a kind of scapegoat by being innocent substitutions for the agitators, but their immolation does not quell the social crisis, the first Carlist war. Elsewhere in the novel, Lluís details another sacrificial process in his account of the re-entombing of the Olivel monks. The major of Lluís battalion, though chiefly to irritate a superior officer, insists on "restaurar l'ordre al monestir" (104). The battalion cannot restore order, however, by simply reinserting the monks into their niches and cleaning up debris. The major continues, "Un dia reintegrarem les sagrades mòmies – textual – als seus nínxols, enmig d'una solemne cerimònia: no hi ha cultura que valgui sense pompes fúnebres" (104). In order to truly restore order, the process must be ritualized, contextualizing the event within a historical expectation of restoring the sacred after a period of profanation.

The re-establishment of culture, therefore, imports a logic derived from a theologico-religious field of behaviour, a fact that the battalion's major is loath to admit in his speech to the townspeople during the war: "Que no s'hi equivoqui ningú: nosaltres no som clericals, però sí liberals, radicals i federals ... som els puntals dels ideals socials" (121). Like Trini, the major fails to perceive the close connection between the elementary forms of religious life and political ideology. The major and the other commanding officers do realize that rectifying a sacrilegious offence can satisfy all offended parties only by punishing a scapegoat before the eyes of the public, whose presence and acquiescence to the proceedings implies unanimous agreement. The scapegoats are not in fact the members of the anarchist committee that had masterminded the monastery's ruination, but rather "els sis imbècils" who had aided the committee's efforts. As stated before, this choice is a delicate matter. The village idiots are a marginalized social group, and Lluís implies that they acted without completely understanding the implications of what was demanded of them. Yet, by their association with the committee, they are not so innocent that one cannot easily substitute them as a surrogate for the anarchist agitators who have long since abandoned the place. The accused are in fact completely unaware of their role in the scandal, viewing the spectacle "amb ulls de lluç que no acaba de comprendre com l'han tret de l'aigua" (121).

Restoring order to the monastery takes on a religious character such as defined earlier by Durkheim, even though an "anti-clerical" military regiment performs the ceremony. Sales describes the grounds where the ritual takes place as swarming with life: "Tanta vida al bat del sol en aquella esplanada i allà dins tant immobilitat" (120). On one hand, therefore, we have a single moral community akin to a church that is collectively assembled to witness the resacralization of "les sagrades mòmies": "el moment de tornar al misteri el que és del misteri, d'estendre de nou aquell vel amb què s'ha de cobrir el macabre com si fos obscè" (121). The battalion does not literally sacrifice the scapegoats, but they are punished nonetheless, being charged with returning the corpses to their tombs, an act of prostration before the eyes of the public. The ritual, in its returning mystery onto mystery, places a veil over the violence committed against the clergy. This violent act of profanation symbolizes social crisis and the dislocation of that particular community, as most townspeople supported the monks but remained quiet for fear of anarchist retribution. In the eyes of the anti-clerical military officers, the ceremony reasserts the monks' sacred authenticity. Lluís's commanding officer Rebull, in fact, states in a commemorative speech, "Des d'ara sobre aquests cadàvers flotarà sempre l'esperit, és a dir, la cultura" (121). Returning mystery onto mystery in ritual form restores the sacred, re-spiritualizes a defamed object, and is proof that the traditional birth of culture is framed around a repressed, mysterious core of violence directed at a community member whose punishment will incite no reprisals. It is irrelevant that the military did not actually assassinate the "sis imbècils," because the logic and result of the ritual would have been the same: the reintegration and rebirth of a social collectivity hides the macabre – violence resulting in death and profanation – and treats the act of sacrifice, which is also a form of violence, as if it were the regenerating obscene.

The scapegoat mechanism is firmly present in Franco's own restoration of the sacred after excising the Second Republic's profaning presence in 1939. In order to restore order in the wake of a chaotic conflict, Franco had to locate the root cause of society's ills in a variety of figures, including Freemasons, Communists, Jews, and regional separatists. A cursory glance at the failed course of liberalism in Spain, and the socio-economic conditions that created turbulence throughout the Second Republic, reveals that many of Franco's *bestias negras* had little to do with the nation's most serious economic and intellectual inadequacies. The punishment and potential return of these scapegoated groups did, however, provide the narrative force for Franco's mythology of national rebirth and his belief in the sacred, exclusive qualities of *la raza*. Shovelling blame onto sacrificial victims was central to the regime's political rituals of reconciliation, which ultimately established the parameters for inclusion in the Caudillo's national cult of belonging.

Like Girard, Sales finds that scapegoating is ultimately the end of a mimetic confrontation of desire, where both cause *and* a sense of self are abandoned to an automaton state. Cruells, in the novel's final section set decades after the Civil War, remarks near the end of the work, "¡Si n'hem vist d'aquests robots sobre aquest món al llarg d'aquest segle! ¡Si n'hem vist d'atrocitats d'un cap de món a l'altre! I els robots voldrien que els homes no fossin més que robots, tots idèntics, tots fent i dient el mateix; acabaríem que no podríem fer res que ja no hagués estat fet milions de milions de vegades per altres robots. Abandonats a l'automatisme ¿fins on podríem caure? La caiguda és sense fi ja que no hi ha fons" (749).

The cycle of the obscene and the macabre will continue as long as authority figures, like the military in *Incerta glòria* or Franco in real life, produce the sacred by driving out violence with violence. At the moment that social crisis hits and glory appears to be within reach, the indifferentiation of causes will also begin, as will the process by which the participants of a conflict lose a sense of agency and act according to a violent, automatic impulse. This reaction demands the production of an innocent victim that all conflicting sides mutually sacrifice. In the final section of the novel and in texts Sales published elsewhere, the innocent victim on which the two sides agree is Catalonia – a scapegoating that I will develop in the next section. Implicit in the novel is that a civil war within Catalonia ultimately decided an originally Spanish conflict, and indeed the fall of Barcelona on 21 January 1939 precipitated the Nationalist takeover of the remaining Republican strongholds. All in all, the novel's conclusion ends in an aporia, unable to explicate fully a political dimension that depicts Catalonia as a victim sacrificed doubly by the fascist regime and the anarchist betrayal of the second Spanish Republic during the Civil War.

Beyond the Victimary Principle

Sales's conception of the structure of human consciousness, which shares many similarities with Sartre's philosophy in *Being and Nothingness*, is immutable in the sense that an ego must always strive towards a plenitude of being because it is finite and needs intentioned projects to distract itself from nothingness. Striving towards a plenitude of being through war has destructive ends as it degenerates into a mimeticism of desire that results in reciprocal acts of vengeance. A society quells runaway violence only by removing the contradiction of a mutual obstacle and searching out a surrogate victim in the scapegoat. In Lluís's description of the re-entombing of the Olivel mummies, sarcasm indicates that the narrator grasps the illogical construction of a victim who is not in fact the root cause of social discord, demonstrating the irony in responding to an act of violence through a similarly punitive measure. In the novel's third part, Cruells, in his recollection of the war, explicitly spells out a criticism of scapegoating that is only implicit in Lluís's Olivel episode: "Mostreu amb el dit un dolent a l'odi de les multituds, elles seguiran; ¿què importa que el dolent no sigui més que una paraula? L'aristòcrata, el burgès, el capellà, el semita, el feixista, el roig, no importa. Ja que és el dolent, ell en té la culpa; ¿la culpa de què? ¡De tot! ¡Mori el burgès, el capellà, el jueu, el feixista, el roig! ¡Visca la mort! Cremeu, mateu, emborratxeu-vos de sang: *qu'un sang impur abreuve vos sillons*. Sempre el mateix. La carnisseria" (460–1).

Cruells's reference to *La Marseillaise* pinpoints the expected outcome of the victimary principle: spilling blood perceived to be impure might satisfy the demand for vengeance of all who inhabit a particular space. A nation resolves the conflict of desires manifested in war and re-establishes unity by making one group culpable. It is once again appropriate to question whether Sales is truly conceptualizing the end of history. Casacuberta argues that Sales is proposing that the only valid course of action is "la creença en un déu que és el Déu dels catòlics" (44). According to Casacuberta, Catholicism for Sales would be what liberal democracy is for Fukuyama. Perhaps a better way to approach Catholicism in *Incerta glòria* is to question what Sales finds in religion that offers an alternative to the endless butchery that is the fruit of conflict by veiling the sacrifice of a surrogate victim, by maintaining the obscene and the macabre in a cloak of mystery.

Critics of Sales's novel, such as Joan Triadú and Campillo and Castellanos, have noted emphatically that the work belongs to the tradition of the Catholic novel only in a very general sense. Sales's Catholicism has always been problematic, perhaps because the author, like many protagonists in his work, was a late convert to the faith and brought to it a decidedly non-dogmatic understanding. In a loose sense, Triadú argues that "el terme «cristiana» que empra Sales … gaudeix d'una amplitud d'aplicació que tant permet parlar de Camus com de Gide i tant de Henry James com de Kafka" (426). Triadú pinpoints the influence of Dostoievsky as a critical component of Sales's religious thought, as do Campillo and Castellanos. In an overview of the Catholic novel tradition, the latter argue that Dostoievsky was important as a "model de literatura que penetra en la paradoxal condició humana i tradueix el rerafons sobrenatural de l'home. És en aquest sentit que esdevé un autèntic model per a la novel·la preocupada per la dimensió metafísica de l'existència" (71). This statement, considering the rampant existentialism throughout Sales's novel, seems completely reasonable. Xavier Pla also argues that it is convenient to call Sales's novel "Catholic," even though the term imposes an "impoverishing reductionism. The catholic novel is not a coherent and uniform ideological, aesthetic or formal current, but it is true that it was a meeting point for the literary and religious interest of some authors who … called Christianity into question" (119).

At the same time, other critics have framed Sales's novel as quite orthodox. Fuster writes that *Incerta glòria* is a "«novela católica», y de converso: crispadamente católica" (332). Perhaps the confusion stemming from how "Catholic" Sales's novel is results from the author's conception of Christ's crucifixion, which is so literal that it seems heterodox. This conception, in short, views Christ as a figure that discards the scapegoating mechanism through the redemption of the victim. Girard argues that this is the core message of Christ's passion, which seems unconventional because it is lost even by the most ardent practitioners of the faith, as evidenced by the church's repeated participation in victimary practices throughout its history. In Spain, this practice is particularly acute if one considers the logic of expulsion that accompanied the *reconquista* and *la Inquisición* in the fifteenth and sixteenth centuries and beyond. According to Girard, the most orthodox way to approach Christ is to view him as proof that "the victim-scapegoat is at the point of no return … Instead of casting it out he is himself cast out, thereby revealing to men the mystery of expulsion, the secret on which rests the positive dimension of Satan's power, its organizing force of violence" (*Scapegoat* 190). Christ is a revelatory figure by which the world is made aware of its persecution mentality and unconscious tendency to cast out violence by violence. Girard argues further that Christ teaches humankind its true vocation, "which is to throw off the hold of the founding murder," and resort to a principle of love over violence that exchanges an infinite series of vengeful reprisals for a benevolent reciprocity (*Things Hidden* 214). Cruells, in the quotation at the opening of this section, similarly decries the scapegoat mechanism, which he attributes to Christ's example: "Si és covard refusar la crucifixió quan Déu ens hi crida, és criminal refusar la felicitat quan Déu ens vol feliços. En Soleràs la refusava amb orgull; en fugia. S'obstinava a mirar fixament l'Obscè i el Macabre com si el tinguessin fascinat … El cristianisme és estrany, el cristianisme és absurd – i estrany i absurd com és, és l'única resposta. Déu assumint la immensitat de la nostra misèria i per això despullant-se de la immensitat de la seva glòria, oferint-se crucificat en espectacle obscè i macabre per redimir l'Obscè i el Macabre" (464).

Cruells notes that there are different points where God calls humankind to both crucifixion and happiness. Cruells places God's call to crucifixion and sacrifice, however, within a framework that characterizes Old Testament belief, who redeems the process by "despullant-se de la immensitat de la seva glòria" (464).

An outdated sacrificial framework is evident in the Old Testament, with Abraham's call to immolate Isaac being a clear example. In an analysis of Kierkegaard's *Fear and Trembling*, Jacques Derrida argues that Abraham's decision reveals the impossibility of ethical responsibility by rejecting universality in the unsubstitutability of the self: "As soon as I enter into a relation with the other, with the gaze, look, request, love, command, or call of the other, I know that I can respond only by sacrificing ethics, that is, by sacrificing whatever obliges me to also respond, in the same way, in the same instant, to all the others" (68).

The confrontation with the eternal that demands sacrificing a normalized ethical code certainly describes those who pursue glory at all costs in Sales's novel. Like Abraham, these characters sacrifice all the others to the One who is the source of the glorious. Sales and Girard demonstrate how this version of Old Testament theology results in a conflict that is ironically quelled only when the One, the scapegoat, is immolated on behalf of all the others. Cruells stresses that the Christian model inaugurates a new era that upends this cycle by offering a different path to both the glorious and the creation of the sacred: through a gift of absolute love. Instead of resorting to war, Sales offers love as an avenue through which an individual can osmotically appropriate an eternal sense of the glorious. Glory, pursued correctly, can become a foundational element of a lasting political structure by limiting conflict at the point where unfettered mimeticism would shift awareness away from stated cause.

Returning to the "Confessió de l'autor," Sales offers two avenues through which it is possible to grasp the absolute: war and love.[10] To Sales, the latter is made possible only by Christ's redemption of the former. Girard, somewhat abstractly, also argues that Christ's death diffuses an enslavement to violence in order to enter into a different realm, a "Kingdom of love, which is also the domain of the true God" (*Things Hidden* 197). Sales argues that Christ's crucifixion redeems the obscene and the macabre by offering humankind an ideal of love around which a cult can form without resorting to new sacrificial murder. In addition to the "Confessió de l'autor," Cruells reiterates the absolute quality of love near the end of the novel in a reference to the mythical figure Don Juan: "Però l'amor és absolut, no hi ha sinó l'amor que ho sigui – i ho és fins quan és fugaç, fins quan és pecat, fins quan és crim … Per breu que hagi estat, per culpable, per criminal,

¡era un instant d'absolut! Don Juan ho sabia prou; i amb ell tots el que han estimat en bé o en mal" (459). In lieu of representing the epitome of the absurd, as in Camus's thought, Sales's Don Juan finds that the absolute is approachable outside of violence. Don Juan's fatal flaw, under Sales's rubric, would be a lack of faith in a single source of love, which leads to a perfunctory series of peccadillos. Cruells, however, shows that pursuing the absolute through love can be an effective mode of political organization when coupled with faith. Unlike Don Juan, Cruells outlines through his revolutionary activities in the 1960s in "El vent de la nit" that a loving dedication to a single absolute ideal creates a kind of faith that, like violence, has a mimetic structure that draws adherents into a cult-like association through reciprocal acts of benevolence. This process occurs only by embracing victimhood and refusing to remain scapegoated, unsettling a political structure built upon the shrouding of foundational violence.

Cruells's path to this realm of thought begins by embracing of victimhood decades after the Civil War in the novel's final chapter, set in the mid-1960s. At this very late juncture of the narrative, Cruells's tone becomes less recollective and more activist with respect to the time of the emplotment of "El vent de la nit." He notes, shortly before proclaiming his faith lost, that "un s'arrapa al consol amarg de ser un vençut, de no tenir res de comú amb els vencedors d'aquest món" (609). Cruells, like Sales himself, spends time in a concentration camp in France after fleeing Spain and also is sent to the Caribbean for a spell before returning to the peninsula. At this point, his faith is already in a perilous state. The fatal blow comes when the archbishop of his diocese forbids him to preach in Catalan: "Quan l'arquebisbe m'interdigué la predicació, vaig desobeir; aleshores em privà de les llicències; no podia dir missa fins a nova ordre, m'era interdit fins i tot portar sotana ... vaig reaccionar molt baixament. Vaig perdre la fe" (609–10). Though Cruells is here at his lowest point, his return to Spain, along with his embracing of victim status, is an implicit refusal to be relegated to the status of a scapegoat. Like Sales, Cruells refuses to remain exiled and bear the weight of the transgressions that Franco expiated from the country in order for a "time of peace" to take effect.

The scapegoat's continued presence, after all, is revelatory in disentombing the violence on top of which the regime founds a darkness of silence. "El vent" that arises within the shadows of "la nit" is a product of Cruells regaining his faith and the possibility of resurrecting the absolute ideals of his youth by pursuing love in lieu of war. This turn occurs when a group of seminarians in May 1966 come to visit his small industrial parish in response to accounts of Cruells being a *rojo* priest during the war and his renown for refusing to yield to his archbishop's demands. The seminarians wish to march on Barcelona to support student riots against the regime, a symbol of the increased role that a post–Vatican II church played in challenging Franco's authoritarianism.[11] Cruells, despite initial trepidation, eventually joins the group, compelled by a somewhat abstract belief in love, which he claims is "la claror que ens ve de dalt; aquest món no seria més que un mal somni sense aquesta claror" (720). With his hopes renewed, Cruells regains his faith.

The demonstration in Barcelona is notable, compared to the pre–Civil War anarchist demonstrations outlined earlier in the novel, for the absence of any violent intent. Cruells writes that "és un pecat molt greu insultar un germà, escopir-li a la cara, fer-li la cigonya o coses pitjors per arrencar-li declaracions" (722). Cruells thus rejects, prima facie, obtaining goals through violence. He will then declare that the priests' very duty is to lead by example through docile protest: "Farem ara el nostre deure; preguem per tots els nostres germans, policies, estudiants i obrers, i que la nostra mansuetud sigui per a tots ells una claror de pau en l'amor a Crist" (722). Faith in an ideal of love, following Christ's example, demonstrates Girard's theory of benevolent reciprocity. Cruells writes that "la fe ... ¡la fe se'ns comunica per contacte! Com una flama" (761). Faith is the light, in other words, that reveals what the night's darkness hides, and one cannot help but think of Nietzsche's Zarathustra and his proclamation that the night is also a sun. Benevolent reciprocity is a substitute for a mimetic reduction of difference, which leads to a mutual hatred for a declared obstacle. It is also an alternative path to the sacralization of an ideal. Love for an ideal, and a faith in its singularity, has the potential to congregate a moral community and to infectiously spread, "com una flama," through the same mimeticism of desire that results in scapegoating.[12]

Cruells's belief in the organizational potential of love requires a concept of the political that allows for the transcendence of a desired ideal while still maintaining a cognizance of cause without a reduction of difference. With any kind of mimetic reciprocity, whether benevolent or vengeful, there is potential for the unconditional annihilation of an obstacle as long as multiple subjects desire a similar goal. The post-victimary logic of "El vent de la nit" is still missing a braking mechanism that would maintain a cognizance of cause once mimetic desire begins to spread. That being the case, the value of self-immolation will continue to be doubted, as it is by Cruells at the end of the novel: "¿De què servirà la meva sang vessada?" (764). Sales's novel thus ends at a point of undecidability that repeats post-secularism's most serious aporia: How can two competing claims to transcendental truth exist within the same democratic sphere without succumbing to violence and exclusion?

Incerta glòria, despite Cruells's attempt to think beyond the scapegoat mechanism, ends as though Sales were unable to explicitly spell out the political implications of a post-victimary mindset. There are numerous instances where Cruells subtly insinuates, however, that his ideological adherence to love, which reclaims his faith, is not simply a religious cult centred on Christ's example. What Cruells truly desires, as evidenced by his refusal to preach in Castilian, is a regeneration of the nation for which he risked life and limb during the war. It is certainly ironic that an occasionally prolix, nearly eight-hundred page novel would leave something left unsaid, but the political difficulties of Sales's time period, even into the late 1960s, precluded a complete fleshing out of ideas. Cruells does, however, exclaim in the novel's concluding pages "¡Oh, si aparegués aquella pàtria terrenal que somiàvem, com un besllum de la celestial!" (762). He moreover concludes the work by asking that God "deixa'ns veure ni que sigui de lluny la Terra sempre Promesa i mai assolida!" (764). His belief in the possible futility of his individual sacrifice is both natural, as it stems from a fear to take up his own cross, and an insinuation that there exists a clear disconnect between embracing victimhood and restoring said victim to its humanity. If there is a clear shortcoming in *Incerta glòria* it is the novel's failure to coherently knit together the manner in which the philosophical, theological, and political are able to form a common ground.[13]

These cardinal points all appear at different intervals in Sales's work, however, and the thematic consistency found throughout the opus fortunately allows the critic to deconstruct what remains unsaid in "El vent de la nit." There are two key areas where Sales best outlines his political thought: his *Quaderns de l'exili*, a literary journal he and other Catalan ex-patriots published in Mexico during the Second World War from 1943 to 1947, and his *Cartes a Màrius Torres* (of which the *Cartes de la guerra* are a selection), which were not published until 1976. Sales returns to the ideas initially offered in Mexico in the prologue to the 1982 facsimile edition of the *Quaderns*. This is no coincidence, as Sales is in both cases outside the intellectual jurisdiction of the regime's censorship tentacles – spatially, by being in Mexico, and temporally as the aforementioned prologue and the *Cartes* are published in the first years of the Spanish Transition.

As I stated earlier, the concept of love as a producer of the sacred creates a collective association around a consecrated ideal. In Trini's section, Sales shows how deftly religious formation relies on structures of feeling in human consciousness. Political regimentation, according to Carl Schmitt, similarly rests on an affective limit point where attraction gives way to repulsion, which he calls the "friend/enemy" distinction, which is an integral component of any society that deems itself political. For Schmitt, the state, with its established set of borders, neatly provides a spatially bracketed distinction that corresponds to where friendship gives way to enmity, where the cause of one nation gives way to a political group congregated around a clearly distinct foreign ideal. The final section of *Incerta glòria* patently outlines how the initial element of Schmitt's thought functions. Love for the nation, and a faith in that singular ideal, attracts those of a like mind through friendship. The intense nature of this friendly attraction, as shown in the seminarian demonstration, is sufficiently forceful to group a community according to a friend/enemy distinction.[14]

Sales's *Cartes* and his contributions to the *Quaderns de l'exili* earnestly harp on Catalonia's inability to exist as a political entity with the right to distinction. This involves both the designation of enemies and the right to self-defence when adversarial conflict arises. As Schmitt writes, the right to distinction is critical to the establishment of a political sphere: "For as long as a people exists in the political sphere, this people must ... determine by itself the distinction of friend and enemy. Therein resides the essence of its political existence. When it no longer possesses the capacity or the will to make this distinction, it ceases to exist politically" (*Concept of the Political* 49).

Sales joined the war effort by enrolling in the Escola de Guerra in 1936 with the express conviction that it would produce an "Exèrcit de Catalunya," which he believed, had it existed, would have quelled both the fascist uprising and the anarchist exploitation of a period of lawlessness in what he calls the "sublevació anti-catalana" of July of that year (*Cartes* 15, 37).[15] Throughout the course of the war, Sales reiterates that Catalonia's failure to direct its own affairs is the root cause of the impossibility of clearly designating enmity vis-à-vis the best interests for Catalonia as a nation. The Second Republic, from its headquarters in Madrid, split graduates of the Escola between two columns, for example, with the anarchist Durruti battalion being Sales's destination. Sales decries the fact that, in lieu of forming a single army, the Republican resistance divided itself into partisan columns, each with its own specific ideology and particular cause. Sales is particularly emphatic in his rejection of partisan politics in lieu of a national defence: "Definitivament no m'agraden els partits ni la política ... Si la FAI em fa tant de fàstic no és pas perquè sigui anarquist ... com perquè, igual que els seus precursors els lerruixos, sembla tota ella una tèrbola maniobra anticatalana" (70). As long as such divisions remain, a reduction of difference that degenerates into unfettered violence where a common cause is lost is inevitable.[16]

Sales believes that partisanship is ineffective in maintaining a clear division between friendship and enmity. He writes, "En cap partit, afegí, no es troba mai aquell ideal que un busca ja que la realitat, que és bruta, els contamina" (60). Parties, it might be said, are unable to remain cognizant of a sacred ideal that the brutish contamination of reality cannot touch, leading to scandal. Only a national formation, with clearly established boundaries meant to bracket conflict, can prevent scandal by making precise objectives incorruptible and temporally stable: "Només ens hauria pogut salvar un alçament unànime del nostre poble que des del mateix juliol de 1936 hagués posat a rotllo feixistes i anarquistes i donant a la guerra que començava l'únic sentit que podia legitimar-la, el de guerra nacional per les llibertats de la nostra terra ... els catalans ens hauríem salvat com a tals fins i tot si perdíem la guerra, que no és mai del tot perduda una guerra quan es fa netament, per la pàtria" (*Cartes* 252).

Nineteenth-century Europe, in which disciplined, national armies faced off without partisan ideology compromising the purely nationalist objectives of each side, influences this interpretation of warfare's legitimacy. Sales's faith in the Escola de Guerra rests on its ability to produce a more traditional national defence with knowledge of tactics, disciplined formation, and a clear understanding of cause foregrounding calls to sacrifice. Sales, in other words, demands that Catalan soldiers be organized as a national force, which the rest of the Republican forces did not need to do, as they were unquestionably Spanish. He repeats the need for a national army in the *Quaderns de l'exili*, where he makes an important distinction between existing as a nation as such and separatism. This desire is present from the onset of the journal's creation in "Els VI punts dels *Quaderns*," which serve as a set of bylaws: "Tota llibertat és il·lusòria quan no es compta amb els mitjans de defensar-la" (*Quaderns* 30). Sales places high value on liberty, but in this context he implies that free attraction to a national ideal is the basis for social grouping. This ideal's magnetism must be sufficiently forceful that a distinction is made between friends and enemies at the extreme point where conflict is unavoidable.

Sales equates Catalonia with a crucified Christ, a nation "crucificada entre dos lladres" (*Cartes* 252), which presents the nation as the innocent lamb sacrificed between two criminals. To Sales, Catalonia did not cause or want such a war, but it was the primary victim nonetheless. One could complicate the reading by arguing that for Sales, national formation is conditioned by redeeming the victim to its humanity through a sacred ideal: the gift of love. The sacred, the consequence of the foundational violence of Christ's crucifixion, exists prior to self-immolation. The ideal of the nation is metonymically inserted into the sacred placeholder occupied by Christ's love, and any individual sacrifice thereafter only strengthens that ideal.

Schmitt stresses that the friend/enemy distinction represents a period of crisis where in order to fight for survival, one must distinguish who deserves violent retribution. He also stresses that war is hardly an ideal, but the very possibility of the political rests on the potential that violence might threaten a friendly association: "War is the existential negation of the enemy. It is the most extreme consequence of enmity. It does not have to be common, normal, something ideal, or desirable. But it must nevertheless remain a real possibility for as long as the concept of the enemy remains valid" (*Concept of the Political* 33).

A likely misunderstanding of *Incerta glòria* is the disconnect between the apparent pacifism of Cruells and the militarism put forth elsewhere by Sales, most prominently in the *Quaderns*. Echoing Schmitt, Sales stresses that violence ought to be avoided at all costs, yet the ever-present potentiality of enmity necessitates a national defence: "El pacifisme conseqüent no s'ha de limitar a protestar contra la idea d'un Exèrcit per al seu país; ha d'actuar per suprimir *tots* els exèrcits … essent així que ens és impossible suprimir els exèrcits dels altres països, i com que cap ciutadà honest no pot desitjar que sobre la seva Pàtria indefensa pesi perpètuament l'amenaça de les invasions forasteres, cal concloure que una de les condicions *sine que non* de la pacífica existència de la nostra Pàtria és un exèrcit nacional" ("Contra alguns errors" 109).

The formation of a national defence is indispensable for a political grouping organized according to a friend/enemy logic. "Pacifisme" may be even equated, on the basis of this quotation, with friendly collectivization, as it is a demonstration of docility, akin to Cruells's political protest, that decries violence. Enmity, however, precedes friendship and is friendship's precondition. The political, therefore, exists only as a result of potential enmity and is a reaction to it. For Sales this means that the nation becomes a political entity only at the point where it can field a defence against adversaries. Violence is not ideal or desired, but it exists as an extreme case and a precondition for the political by representing a social grouping's potential to make the ultimate decision, which is human sacrifice. This group is not formed by that sacrifice, but rather through the benevolent reciprocity of love.

A nation cannot universally dispel enmity, therefore the political is possible only as a result of the potential for friendly magnetism to give way to aggression. We are quite far, in other words, from a concept of the political propagated by someone such as Georges Sorel, who theorizes socialism by idealizing violence, particularly through the insurrection of workers in general strikes, as the most effective path to the destruction of a social order (171). The new order announced by the founders of the *Quaderns* is that of not only embracing victimhood but also reinserting the scapegoat into a political structure created by a founding violence. The subsequent unsettling, it is hoped, will ignite the flame of faith in an ideal that attracts adherents through friendship and love. Sales and his colleagues disallow violence as a founding mechanism, yet deem it necessary for survival. A new logic of sacrifice thus emerges that does not produce the sacred but only reaffirms its presence.

Enmity is critical in preventing scapegoating by strictly linking sacrifice and ethics. Schmitt stresses that the "enemy does not cease to be a human being" (*Concept of the Political* 54) and therefore political entities cannot engage in a war for humanity, which creates a dangerous state of exception that permits a kind of violence strikingly similar to that executed against the scapegoat.[17] Humanity is a concept that a political structure must presuppose that others possess, but "the political entity cannot by its very nature be universal in the sense of embracing all of humanity and the entire world" (53). Schmitt's notion of enmity, which

I believe strikes close to Sales's theory of the nation, is adamantly opposed to Franco's demonizing of the "Anti-España," a term that encompasses a diverse set of individuals who share one commonality: a denial of the right to historical existence. The regime denied those individuals corresponding to the "anti-Spain" their humanity in the most fundamental sense. One thinks, for example, of the fleeing Republican soldiers returned to Spain after the German occupation of France, who were executed on arrival.

When a friend/enemy distinction disappears, so does political partnership and collaboration. Humanity also ceases to be a division and is converted into a concept that a sovereign could possess absolutely. Francoist ideology promoted "Spanishness" as one such essentialist ideal that could be appropriated as the government saw fit. This is dangerous: "To confiscate the word humanity, to invoke and monopolize such a term probably has certain incalculable effects, such as denying the enemy the quality of being human and declaring him to be an outlaw of humanity" (*Concept of the Political* 54). This, in other words, is exactly what happens to the scapegoat, which is reminiscent of vainglory in *Incerta glòria* and the unconditional sacrifice for the absolute that it motivates. The scapegoat's murder exacts no reprisals precisely because its humanity has been denied through a suspension of ethics, as evidenced in Sales's novel and in Girard's theory of victim animalization.

Following Schmitt, a concept of the political that proffers the scapegoat a share of humanization through a friend/enemy distinction restores the victim to its lost personhood. Ethics, under this rubric, is embodied in a belief in the right to existence of other political entities and the refusal to participate in acts of violence without a clear cause that would legitimate sacrifice. In the 1976 prologue to the facsimile edition of the *Quaderns*, Sales reiterates that his vision of Iberia, which he draws from Jacint Verdaguer and Camões, rests on a coexistence of political entities, each of which has a right to autonomously govern itself within a federal structure: "D'altra banda, som espanyols; ja ho hem vist abans. Ho som com ho eren Camões i Verdaguer, d'aquella Espanya que és un 'niu de nacions' i que 'se engrandece' amb totes elles i amb la seva diversitat. Sempre l'expressió 'Espanya i Portugal' m'ha fet aquella tristesa que fa tot allò que atempta contra la natura" ("Paraules" 26).

Sales was not a separatist by any means and firmly believed in a nationalism within a federal structure, harkening back to Pi i Maragall and Prat de la Riba, two intellectuals he frequently cites.[18] These comments, published when the future of a post-Franco Spain was open to possibility, reiterate Sales's long-standing belief that the Iberian Peninsula exists as a geographical space inhabited by different centres of strong national feeling. None of these centres of friendly magnetism possess an absolutely unconditional right to existence over and above the others.

Peaceful order rests on the ability of these nations to harmoniously coexist within a mutually beneficial structure that is not established by an overall domination of the peninsula by sacrificing certain groups.[19] A country with multiple centres of sacred belief might exist harmoniously if it divides sovereignty equitably.

In the next chapter, Juan Goytisolo explores the apocalyptic consequences of consolidating sovereignty into a single totalitarian individual, which itself depends on symbolic mediation and indoctrination into a theological cult. When unilateral control over the state of exception is exercised, sovereignty manifests itself as a horrific, dehumanizing thrust that gains legitimacy by winning over the herd-like masses with propaganda and charisma.

4 Intimate Strife: Inside Juan Goytisolo's Sovereign Exception

What thou hast inherited from thy fathers,
acquire it to make it thine.

Goethe, *Faust*

Against Sacred Forms

The title of Juan Goytisolo's 2007 collection of essays, *Contra las sagradas formas*, neatly sums up a destructive attitude that characterizes much of his writing: the annihilation and adulteration of Spain's most iconic imagery and its most cherished literary forms. In *Contra las sagradas formas*'s introduction, the Goytisolo of the twenty-first century is referring to a process of literary creation that demands an ambivalent relationship to the past, an attitude that encapsulates both an obliteration of one's precursors and a respectful mimesis of their work. This, in Goytisolo's opinion, is Picasso's approach to *Las meninas*: "La anomalía del inventor rebelde al culto reverencial a las Sagradas Formas" (8). It could be argued, of course, that Picasso does quite the opposite: not a mimesis of Velázquez, but rather a show of respect for the precursor. Goytisolo's stance is nothing new; Harold Bloom's comparison of the birth of a new poetic voice to a Freudian primal scene particularly comes to mind.[1] The Juan Goytisolo of the 1960s and 1970s, however, whose eyes were firmly trained on Franco's Spain from his perches in Paris and Tangier, relates the profanation of the sacred to an urgent search for a linguistic and political vitalism embedded within a calcified, decadent *castiza* culture. This is clearly evident in Goytisolo's book of essays, *El furgón de cola*, published in 1967 and written between 1960 and 1966. The role of the writer, in an environment where the press "no refleja las tensiones fructuosas y contradicciones dinámicas de una sociedad," is that of a "válvula de escape" that presents "una realidad opuesta a la irrealidad de los periódicos" (*Obras completas* 2: 855). The political role fulfilled by the writer is aided by the discovery of "un lenguaje nuevo" that evades those who respect "la preceptiva literaria de nuestra tradición," which leads to "el fracaso artístico del realismo meramente formal de novelas como *La resaca*" (2: 877). For Goytisolo, a literature opposed to the "irrealismo" of the press by no means demands a realist facsimile of the external world. Goytisolo points to a novel from his own early repertoire, *La resaca*, as representative of what he perceives as an artistic failure, but he could have just as easily identified much of the social realist literature of the time period. Goytisolo, increasingly influenced by surrealism during his time in Paris,[2] describes in the essays a desire to access a subconscious Real within language that is accessible in the oneiric world of memory and fantasy. Access to the Real requires a rupture that results from the destruction of external form. Goytisolo (2: 877) attributes to the "lenguaje nuevo" he wishes to employ a creative destruction that unearths "un material virgen" from Castilian Spanish that "reproduce con fidelidad mayor la realidad de nuestra época." This line of thought approaches surrealist philosophy but concurrently bears a strong resemblance to the Mexican poet Octavio Paz's poetics: "En el vasto y sobrecargado almacén de antigüedades de nuestra lengua solo podemos crear destruyendo: una destrucción que sea a la vez creación; una creación a la par destructiva. Menos ligados que nosotros por un culto esterilizador hacia las grandes creaciones del pasado los novelistas americanos de habla castellana prueban desde hace algún tiempo la existencia de grandes riquezas latentes en las entrañas de nuestro idioma" (2: 877).

Goytisolo nowhere echoes Paz's poetry more strongly than here; in the poem "Salamandra" (1958–61), Paz writes, "No comienza la vida sin sangre / sin la brasa del sacrificio / No se mueve la rueda de los días / Xólotl se niega a consumirse" (76). The notion of a creative sacrifice, which oneirically reaches the virgin material of a reality cloaked in decadent forms, therefore appears to be borrowed by Goytisolo from both French surrealism and Paz's appropriation of Aztec mythology, which features a circular temporality, ritual destruction, and the practice of human sacrifice as a tool for social renewal.[3]

For Goytisolo, the sacred functions as a law that dictates both the imagistic and iconic inventory available to the writer, as well as the linguistic parameters, established by deified, canonical writers, within which an author must formulate a discourse. The sacred, for Goytisolo, dictates the shape of the field of cultural production and embodies a hypostatic state of immutability that is antithetical to a primordial virgin material at the heart of a shape-shifting *nuevo lenguaje*. In a discussion of his first dealings with the Communist Party in France, Goytisolo argues that consecration into a belief structure is comparable to donning an identity-defining mask: "todas las sectas religiosas poseedoras de la verdad, imprimen una suerte de carácter sacramental a sus miembros y transforman a momentos el rostro de éstos en una rígida e insondable máscara" (*En los reinos de taifa* 68). Goytisolo, as well as Jorge Semprún and Fernando Claudín, soon discovered that the Communist Party itself was one such sect that possessed a rigid conception of the truth that, when challenged, as it was by Goytisolo, Semprún, and Claudin, resulted in expulsion.[4]

Sacred law interpellates the writer in an Althusserian sense: the hegemonic cultural ideology of a sovereign state demands that attention be paid, thereby imposing the law of literary form that creates the writing subject. The politics of censorship and the kinds of literary criticism endorsed by the regime allowed the state to cultivate an ideology of literary form. For Goytisolo, we can be even more precise, since his betrayal of sacred law is performed through language – Castilian Spanish, which Goytisolo identifies as a curse for being the last, stubborn link to his native country. Except, of course, that Goytisolo was born in Catalonia, so the interpellation of the state is already at work in Goytisolo's assumption that Castilian links him like an umbilical cord to his "birthplace." At the same time, Goytisolo conceptualizes his language as an untapped source of potential whose virgin matter is yet to be revealed by Spanish authors. In a Lacanian sense, therefore, Goytisolo's interpellation is more specifically through the signifier and the imposition of the discursive law of the father, which pushes the subject into the symbolic realm and away from the sense of perceived unity and oneness characteristic of the jouissance of a primordial mirror stage. The imagistic unity of the self in the mirror stage, which proffers an ecstasy that is forever pursued, is similar to the linguistic unity represented by the "virginal material" lying within language's subconscious. Goytisolo, echoing Lacan's line of thought, specifies that certain Latin American writers, who "reproduce con fidelidad" the Real of the epoch, utilize a discourse without dissociation "entre fondo y forma" (*Obras completas* 2: 878). One can escape Althusser's hegemonic call to subjection by stepping beyond the zone where sovereign law is in effect. If Latin American writers have revealed a "nuevo lenguaje," it is because they either have no impetus, through spatial separation, to respect Spanish sacred law, thereby weakening it, or because the sacred is adulterated by intermingling with indigenous elements typical of the writers' cultural milieu.

A writer like Goytisolo, returning to Lacan, encounters a formidable *skandalon* as one cannot so easily undo the imposition of the symbolic order. The linguistic law of the father functions from both the interior and the exterior, alienating the subject from its ideal self at the very moment a proper name is imposed at birth. The very sense of oneness felt in the mirror stage is, after all, factitious, as assuming the image of another as one's own is merely one more alienating step. The interior logic of Goytisolo's celebrated novel *Reivindicación del Conde don Julián,* published just after *El furgón de cola* in 1970, hinges on whether or not this symbolic order is destroyable to the extent that the law of the father is shattered and the self discards its subjection to the law of the Other. I will argue that this transcendence never occurs, as Goytisolo's insistence on a Nietzschean eternal return wrought by circular destruction results in a metonymic shifting from one symbolic order to another. As is the case with Trini Milmany in *Incerta glòria,* transcending the *skandalon* of the symbolic order demands bad faith from *Conde Julián*'s protagonist. As with much of Goytisolo's thought, the work thinks through its contradictions by way of the sacred and the desire to cut the "amarras con el pesado lastre de la tradición" (*Obras completas* 2: 878). The novel also explicates how "el uso de la dinamita o el purgnante" that "nuestro anquilosado lenguaje castellanista exige" (878) correlates with the political function of the writer who is opposed, in a censored society, to the journalist.

The novel collapses historical linearity into a mythical zone of betrayal where the most sacred icons and literary works of Spain – or "the tribe" as Goytisolo often calls it – are desecrated through a fantastical recreation of Tariq ibn Ziyad's invasion of the peninsula recounted in Alfonso el Sabio's *Primera crónica general de España.* Goytisolo's notion of space mirrors Giorgio Agamben's chaotic state of exception where the potentiality for law exists without law being in effect. The novel takes a space, whose salient feature is the ability to commit violence without reprisal, where both the sovereign and the scapegoated *homo sacer* reside and flips their roles. The novel therefore exhibits a destructive oscillation of constitutive and constituting violence but lacks the courage to transcend the cycle by annihilating the history of a sovereign order founded on violence and exception altogether. In short, the work affirms Lacan's assertion that the death of the primal horde's father opens the path to jouissance but does not lead to a return of mirror-stage oneness and intimacy; rather, it strengthens the father's totalization by punishing transgression of the law more severely. There is no *nomos* before the death of the primal father; rather, the law emerges in Freud's work from the formation of community by the brothers. The longer the recursive chain becomes, the eternal return of the father's prohibitions stresses more acutely its most essential features, like alliteration in poetry. In the same way, Julián's new sovereign order demands the sacrifice of innocent victims through a sublimation of violence that ought to be aimed squarely at the source of authority but is deflected, instead, towards a series of scapegoats, like other iterations of authoritarian rule in Spain's past. Tariq ibn Ziyad, after all, was not the only plunderer to cross the Strait of Gibraltar to sabotage the peninsula's institutions of power – Franco and his *Convoy de la victoria* did the same in August 1936.

Conde Julián's Inclusive Exclusion

Goytisolo's transparency about the role of profanation in his work has translated to extensive critical interest in the theme of the sacred. In a 1967 interview entitled "Destrucción de la España sagrada," Goytisolo notes that his task as a writer, like that of his fictional character Álvaro Mendiola, is to undertake a "traición personal, una violación propia" (qtd in Levine, "Introduction" 19). The title of the article is indeed a citation from *Conde Julián*: "traición grandiosa, ruina de siglos: ejército cruel de Tariq, destrucción de la España sagrada" (51–2). Also well studied is Goytisolo's predilection for violence and destruction.[5] What is less known is that, in *Conde Julián*, Mendiola's betrayal of Spain implicitly relies on a theory of sovereignty that produces a political system that, in order to maintain its coherence, must maintain a zone of exception where undesirable social elements are scapegoated, stripped of citizenship, and excluded. Tangier, though technically within a separate sovereign order,[6] represents, through the kif-induced fantasies of the protagonist, this zone of indistinction and exception that strips the protagonist of *bios*, the part of his life dependent on inclusion within a specific group or nationality, to mere natural life, known to the ancient Greeks as *zoe*.[7] Tangier, more specifically, becomes the excepted nucleus of Spanish sovereignty because the narrator's theory of power underlies that of traditional Spain.

It is always a risk to argue a strong correlation between an author's personal life and his fiction, but in Goytisolo's case he is quite clear (*En los reinos de taifa* 34) that Álvaro Mendiola – whose exploits comprise the trilogy that includes *Señas de identidad*, *Conde Julián*, and *Juan sin tierra* – is his alter ego. Through an analysis of his voluntary exile from Spain alongside the reaction of Franco's censorship to his works, Goytisolo paints a picture of the author-dissident that resembles Giorgio Agamben's *homo sacer*. Agamben writes that this figure, culled from Roman law, is judged to possess a "life that cannot be sacrificed and yet may be killed" (*Homo Sacer* 82). The unsacrificability of *homo sacer* places him outside of the *ius divinum*, as he is banned from religious ritual and consecration to the gods. It is here fruitful to recall René Girard's description of the public's reversal of regard for the scapegoated victim and its transformation into a deified figure. The scapegoat, a substitute for the king who receives the brunt of anti-authoritarian violence, acquires a connection to the original father figure of the primal horde whose assassination inaugurated the tribe's first transfer of power. Refusing to sacrifice the *homo sacer* prohibits deification. As Hubert and Mauss argue, the act of sacrifice always implies a transference from priest to victim: "Sacrifice has as its purpose to affect the religious state of the sacrifier or the object of sacrifice" (51). Through sacrifice, the victim can shed the qualities that placed him at the margin of society, expiating a crime or a transgression, or the reverse may occur and he who offers the sacrifice assimilates the taint of the victim. Barring a ritual killing of *homo sacer* assures first that his dangerous qualities do not infect the general population, and second prevents the expiation of his faults and a consequent disqualification of his status as being outside the law. This ensures that the state can continue to negatively define its social coherence, and its sacred ideals, in opposition to a clear enemy who has qualities perceived as antithetical to the ideal image a governing body has of its body politic. For Franco, this meant that *la Anti-España* could never be eradicated, because the illocutionary force of a sacred image of national being depends on a threat.

In the 1960s, Goytisolo notes, along similar lines, that the regime treated a censored or banished author differently after death: "Sólo la persona u obra muerta son dignas entre vosotros [Spaniards] de lauros y recompensas" (*En los reinos de taifa* 52). He maintains this line of thought in *El furgón de cola*: "Pero si la sociedad española es dura con los rebeldes vivos, admite en cambio, generosamente en su seno a los muertos: las obras de Lorca y Hernández se editan en España y las autoridades organizan actos oficiales en honor de Juan Ramón Jiménez y Antonio Machado" (*Obras completas* 2: 841). Goytisolo is one of the "vivos," and it is not difficult to conceptualize the reasoning behind the state's denigration of subversive writers. Like the scapegoat who threatens to return and bring with him the crisis or undesirable elements with which he is associated, "las que se mantienen vivas molestan" and are destined to incite "ascos y aspavientos" (*En los reinos de taifa* 52).

At the same time, as evidence of a double exception, the sovereign also bars *homo sacer* from the *ius humanum*, or "the sphere of the profane" (*Homo Sacer* 82). This is the ontological status that Goytisolo grants to himself in his first memoir: "Pero privado por decreto de su verdadera identidad: posibilidad de escribir, publicar, expresarse en público, reunirse con los amigos sin temor a comprometerlos. Personaje de Hoffman sin sombra, menguado, espectral" (*Coto* 129). He is a spectre, in other words, that cannot be sacrificed yet is also stripped of what the Greeks would call *bios*, which links him to the individual tribe. Deprived of the protection of sovereign law, the *homo sacer* is allowed to be punished. The prohibition of sacrifice, therefore, is joined by a permission to commit homicide and other punitive measures without repercussions. Indeed the public ritual of sacrifice, and its demand for protocol, is exchanged in Franco's Spain for such things as the spontaneous police brutality administered against student protesters in the 1960s or the incarceration without public trial of perceived dissidents throughout the dictatorship, effectively sentencing thousands to death, either from outright violence or through illness contracted in the subhuman living conditions of the prisons.[8]

After a film made by Goytisolo based on his novel *La resaca* was stolen during a showing in Milan and viewed by Spanish authorities,[9] the regime attempted to paint him as a dangerous Marxist dissident. This led to a meeting with Adolfo Muñoz Alonso, Franco's director general de la Prensa, who strongly echoes Agamben's theorization of the juridical status of the *homo sacer* when warning Goytisolo that "actuando … fuera de la legalidad, no debía extrañarme de la violencia de las reacciones de condena suscitadas por mi lamentable conducta" (*En los reinos de taifa* 55). What is essential is that Muñoz Alonso never specifies the source and type of violence; the ambiguity of the statement justifies recrimination from anyone loyal to the "fatherland." The statement also demonstrates that the law is valid only insofar as there is a zone just beyond its explicit jurisdiction for those excepted from the sovereign order and stripped of their *bios*. What Franco's press secretary unwittingly reveals is that this zone of bare life is an exclusion paradoxically included within society's reach, hence the potential for Goytisolo's punishment by those offended by his "lamentable" conduct, which would be impossible if he were in Paris, for example. Of course, punishment by the government extends beyond the country's borders through excoriation in the press and menace directed at family members or colleagues sympathetic to the dissident's cause. Expressing an attitude that many other intellectuals of the time period certainly shared, Goytisolo remarks with sadness, "España simbolizará para mí, hasta bien entrada la cuarentena, no una tierra acogedora y benigna, receptiva o al menos indiferente a mi labor al servicio de su cultura y lengua sino un ámbito de hostilidad y rechazo, de un solapado, acechante amago de sanción" (*En los reinos de taifa* 19).

Goytisolo finishes his Álvaro Mendiola trilogy, not coincidentally, well into his forties. In the trilogy's first work, *Señas de identidad*, the sense of immanent punishment waiting behind every turn and lurking within every shadow is apparent in the dramatic tension of the novel, particularly through the author's inclusion of actual police reports that are adapted to reflect the vigilance of Mendiola and his subversive cohorts.

The trilogy's second work, *Conde Julián*, reinforces the link between the sacred and political theory in its construction of space, a connection that Agamben especially notes. The *homo sacer*'s locus is a zone of bare life, inclusively excluded, that serves as the founding nucleus of a sovereign order that negatively gives law its force. Agamben writes, "The particular 'force' of law consists in this capacity of law to maintain itself in relation to an exteriority. We shall give the name *relation of exception* to the extreme form of relation by which something is included soley through its exclusion" (*Homo Sacer* 18). In the previous chapter, I noted how Carl Schmitt describes the danger of denying the enemy's "humanity," which would effectively create a state of exception during armed conflict between two sovereign states that would permit unrestricted aggression. Agamben displaces Schmitt's framework of the exception from the arena of foreign policy and theorizes about its existence as a secretive nucleus of the domestic structure of the state: "The inclusion of bare life in the political realm constitutes the original – if concealed – nucleus of sovereign power" (6). Indeed Agamben homes in on the internal consequences of Schmitt's definition of the sovereign, which is "he who decides on the exception." The sovereign violently constitutes a legal order onto a state of natural chaos, but this construction requires an area of penal space in order to preserve, within the boundaries of the law, coherence and stability by preserving a place to deposit human excess: "Sovereign violence opens a zone of indistinction between law and nature, outside and inside, violence and law. And yet the sovereign is precisely the one who maintains the possibility of deciding on the two to the very degree that he renders them indistinguishable from each other" (54).

The law locates human excess within penal spaces: prisons, exile, work camps, etc. The law presupposes its own excess, which is not quite the same as a zone of indistinction. The sovereign bio-politically decides who belongs within the legal order and who is to be excluded and kept within this zone of undecidability, where the potential for law and violence exists but without codification or predictable application. The process is indeed "bio-political," as the sovereign decision determines who warrants the privilege of belonging to the *bios* of a particular body politic.

The state of exception represents a space of possibility in which the sovereign and *homo sacer* exist symmetrically, with the former defining the status of the latter. This structure makes the regulation of the sacred the original political function of the sovereign: "The production of bare life is the originary activity of sovereignty. The sacredness of life ... originally expresses precisely both life's subjection to a power over death and life's irreparable exposure in the relation of abandonment" (*Homo Sacer* 83).

Agamben links the *homo sacer*'s potential to be killed to a "relation of abandonment" with the sovereign, who presides over the legal order. In a paradox, the scapegoated *homo sacer* is both abandoned by the community and kept close enough to be vulnerable to violence. In his memoirs, Goytisolo discusses the procedure by which the Spanish press relates to an exiled writer such as himself, which is a combination of absolute silence (a relation of abandonment) and a barrage of insults and recriminations. The result of Goytisolo's film falling into the hands of Franco's authorities in Milan is exemplary in this respect. The regime's authorities were "enfrentados a la disyuntiva de detenerme o seguir tolerando una conducta cuyo ejemplo podía cundir y propagarse a otros escritores y artistas. Abrumándome con un alud de injurias y amenazas veladas, intentaban cerrarme las puertas, hacer de mí un desterrado remoto e inofensivo" (*En los reinos de taifa* 53).

The government not only placed Goytisolo into a relation of abandonment but also kept his presence "alive" by invoking his name in the press and elsewhere with insults and threats. This form of punishment, an emotional corollary to the physical abuse one might undergo in a prison, bears no connection to either the truth or to any other form of legal responsibility. The spectre of the *homo sacer* must remain within the public's collective consciousness in order to demonstrate negatively which elements deserve the protection afforded by rights that, far from inalienable, are linked to bio-political life and taken away when existence is reduced to its bare state. The sovereign exists as such only because, in a Heideggerian fashion, it "realizes itself by simply taking away its own potentiality not to be, letting itself be, giving itself to itself" (*Homo Sacer* 46). The *homo sacer*, in turn, is he who is prohibited from being anything except bare life: he cannot sacrifice his natural rights in order to enter into a social contract nor offer himself up to the gods in a sacrificial act.

In *Conde Julián*, Goytisolo sets redemption of the scapegoat in motion, which is no doubt a counter-strike at his real-life demonization at the hands of Franco's cultural authorities. The crux of the novel concerns how a betrayal within the imaginary sphere aims to decimate the symbolic realm of language and give the *homo sacer* "itself to itself" through a *nuevo lenguaje*. The novel's protagonist, Álvaro,[10] resides in Tangier and the imagery that fuels his fantasies arises from scenes witnessed in the city's streets and labyrinthine Zoco Grande in the first part of the novel, alongside Spanish television programs beamed across the Strait of Gibraltar in the second part. The space within which the betrayal occurs, however, in the second half of the novel, is neither here nor there. Álvaro fantasizes that he is infected with rabies – he is actually syphilitic – and decides to donate blood in order to infect his native country: "no estás en Tánger, sino en España, y la sangre que tan maliciosamente ofreces infectará obligatoriamente tu tribu) espiroquete no, virus de rabia" (*Reivindicación del Conde* 131).

Álvaro, existing beyond the legal order, is both geographically outside and oneirically inside Spain. He turns the tables on his countrymen by sacrificing himself and "offering" up a gift of blood that, instead of renewing the tribe, will lead to its destruction. That his betrayal is through blood-borne infection, the transmission of which is brought about by rape later in the work, alludes first to Julián's betrayal through a procedural logic of sacrifice, which is explicated partly by Hubert and Mauss in the idea of transference. Second, blood as the conduit of subversion demonstrates that the limit point, and litmus test, of sovereign power is bio-politics, the sovereign right to promote or disallow a qualification of life.[11] Julián's self-assertion as the sovereign occurs at the moment that he controls, in Agamben's words, "life's subjection to a power over death," which becomes more acute as the novel advances. In the case of Joan Sales, I argued that the right to sacrifice one's own citizens rested on establishing the state according to a distinction between friend and enemy, a decision approached only in extreme cases.

Goytisolo's Álvaro takes a step down a path towards messianically proclaiming himself the sovereign by taking away this right to exclude life from the leader of Spain when the hordes of Muslim invaders he imagines storm across the strait and desecrate the sacred. Following Agamben, he takes away his own potential "not to be" by asserting his identity through a sacrificial offering of his own blood, which by transmitting a deadly infection decides on the right to life.

This desecration, however, is a constituting violence superimposed onto a constituted order with the explicit aim of consecrating an alternative set of ideals and practices. The climax of Julián/Álvaro's invasion of Hispania occurs in a smouldering temple, naturally: "La sangre corre sin saciar su furor, la lógica de la muerte se impone: desde el vasto crucero del templo admiras el rudo y cruel espectáculo" (*Reivindicación del Conde* 232). The substitution of the sacred is symbolized in the death and resurrection of a pair of statuesque dolls that Julián/Álvaro encounters in the temple. Originally, a boy and a girl doll holding the sacrificed body of Alvarito, whom Julián/Álvaro has tortured to the point that he commits suicide, fall, putting a "punto final, con sus aullidos, al demente, fabuloso happening" (233). Alvarito, now deified, is then resurrected as a new idol: "El muñeco resucita y recobra súbitamente la vista y uso e integridad de sus miembros: vestido con blanca chilaba, ceñido de níveo turbante invoca en árabe puro el nombre de Alá, manifiesta su vivo deseo de ser musulmán" (238). Julián therefore institutes a new order as a result of sovereign violence that inserts a set of ideals, such as the speaking of Arabic, into the placeholder of the sacred within the new temple. The episode reveals that Goytisolo, at least in the early 1970s, was not unconditionally "against sacred forms," as the novel's logic prescribes a symbolic substitution of a hypostatic image of society and not transcendence over a cyclical dialectic between destruction and social codification.

What is common to *Incerta glòria* and *Conde Julián* is the idea that sovereignty based on a victimary mechanism functions like a mathematical formula of recursion where immolation and exclusion are programmed into the very reiteration of power. In this respect, Brad Epps could not be more right when he argues that Julián's conversion into a "phallic idol" who demands the prostration of Alvarito and Isabel *la católica*, novelized both as Álvaro Peranzules's daughter and Alvarito's mother by Goytisolo, is far from "a radical rejection of law, morality, and tradition[.] Julián's sexual brutality lays bare an oppressive truth of civilization beneath its mask of peace and propriety" (97). Epps intuitively sees that Julián's invasion displays its power by deflecting anti-authoritarian violence onto innocent victims. Indeed what is noteworthy about the novel's course of violence is the lack of direct displays of aggression against "el Ubicuo," Goytisolo's term for Spain's authoritarian leader (presumably Franco). My answer to Epps, whose gendered critique of the feminine submitting to and obeying the masculine through phallic violence is convincing, would be to deconstruct further the secretive truth at the nucleus of civilization. The "masks of peace and prosperity" shield from view a structure of power that consigns internal enemies to a space of exception, thereby placing the subjugation of passive bare life in the hands of the sovereign.

Recalling Hubert and Mauss, the sacrifice of Alvarito transfers – or in Goytisolo's parlance, "infects" – qualities considered dangerous to intellectuals in Spain who exclude the residual presence of Islam on the Iberian Peninsula, believing the Arabic character of the *taifas* to have been expiated through the victimization of the Moriscos during the *reconquista* and Inquisition.[12] Goytisolo's protagonist, however, also creates an order through exclusion, repeating the foundational victimary mechanism of the previous claims to sovereignty by Franco, the *Reyes católicos*, and others. Of course, how could there be order without exclusion? A society always shapes its culture through selection, so Goytisolo's critique of Europeanization merely reflects his preferences but does not in the least represent a higher critical position.

The demonizing and slaughter of those within Spain's Christian, Senecan, bullfighting, chickpea-eating order by Julián follows a victimary mechanism similar to the one that Joan Sales decried in the previous chapter. It also resembles a criticism of Spanish intellectuals found later in *Conde Julián*. The narrator notes that through scapegoating, the heaping of insincere praise onto each other by Spanish intellectuals is never interrupted by discord: "Redactando sonoros panegíricos: fuera de tono, inauténticos siempre cuando recíproca, airadamente se combaten: vieja retenida saña que generosamente se derrama sobre el outlaw y el ausente!" (*Reivindicación del Conde* 149). At the moment discord appears, these intellectuals assign blame, punishment, and insults not to the true sources of division but rather onto those who cannot respond to denigration.

On a broader, more violent scale, the dictatorship denies *bios* to those who openly refuse the sacred images, practices, and linguistic code of Spain that it propagates. Francoism denied belonging to those who, in other words, refuse to wear the dictator's civilizing mask. Exile was a punishment for those who did not comply, but a more acute zone of bare life within Franco's sovereign sphere was the prison or worker's camp. Álvaro's reversal, from *homo sacer* to sovereign, establishes exception in the consolidation of his own nucleus of power, which reasserts unmitigated violence against those who are reduced to bare life, with two key examples being *la Cava* and Isabel *la Católica*. A society of coexistence is not proposed in the novel, as the narrator remarks, after having donated his infected blood: "Todo individuo atacado de rabia será secuestrado en una habitación hasta su muerte el remedio no existe y el desenlace es fatal después del óbito" (134). Nothing survives Julián's obliteration of Spain, as his rage adopts the total consumption of resources seen in primitive festivals: "La dicha habitación y cuantos objetos hayan servido al enfermo serán rigurosamente condenados y, sin desinfección previa, nadie los volverá a usar" (134). This is an image that could not be further from the ideal coexistence proposed by Américo Castro, ironically one of Goytisolo's intellectual heroes.

Álvaro's betrayal of his homeland is, of course, a repetition of the foundational myth surrounding Julián, the eighth-century Count of Ceuta: "nuevo conde don Julián, fraguando sombrías traiciones" (*Reivindicación del Conde* 16). Julián opened Hispania to Muslim invaders in response to the Visigoth King Rodrigo's purported rape of Julián's daughter, Florinda, known throughout history and recreated in the novel as *la Cava*. The "vindicated" don Julián in the novel is, to a great extent, the feared return of the scapegoated *homo sacer* after being mythologized for over a millennium as being responsible for Iberia's eight hundred years of Islamic cultural and political presence.[13]

Turning to the subject of space, when Julian enters dreamworld where he is in both Tangier and Spain, he also symbolizes an entrance into the sovereign sphere of exception. At the beginning of the novel, the Strait of Gibraltar is transformed from being a clear delimitation of Spanish / North African space into "un lago, unido tú a la otra orilla como el feto al útero sangriento de la madre, el cordón umbilical entre los dos como una larga y ondulante serpentina" (*Reivindicación del Conde* 13). The womb symbolizes a zone of indistinction where being and becoming, actuality and potential, inner and outer are all in a nebulous process of definition. This feeling is related to the narrator's status as an exile: "Habías considerado el alejamiento como el peor de los castigos … la separación no te bastaba si no podías medirla: y el despertar ambiguo en ciudad anónima, sin saber dónde estás: dentro, fuera?" (14). The lack represented by an immeasurable separation is, through novelistic enjambment, fused with an awakening in a space where the line between being and non-being is ambiguous. A few lines later, the narrator further develops his biological conceit: "Atrapado, preso, capsulado, digerido, expulsado: el consabido ciclo vital por los pasillos y túneles del aparato digestivo-reproductor" (13). The narrator relates imagery of the reproduction of life to a process that is superfluous to vital functioning and results in digestive excretion. The narrator paints himself, therefore, as trapped within a space of potentiality, the uterus, which is both separated from and linked to the motherland, but with an ontological status that is eschatological, having been expelled, deprived of use-value, and denied the status of *bios*. Most importantly, the linking of reproduction to digestion communicates that the subject, though trapped within an inner exception, is undergoing a metamorphosis, as though the womb were also a cocoon, where identity is broken down into its most essential components – its virgin material – and reconfigured. The course of the novel, therefore, is the narrator's attempt to messianically emerge from the incubating – and incarcerating – uterus, to "realize itself by simply taking away its own potentiality not to be" (*Home Sacer* 46). The goal is to transition from being "poor in world," as Heidegger describes animal life, to becoming a being-for-itself.

Framing Tangier as an "included exclusion" maintains a separation between the narrator and the *patria*, but an umbilical connection, symbolized by the Strait of Gibraltar, allows the distance between periphery and centre to be measured. Later in the novel, the narrator criticizes recent studies by Spanish historians indicating that Seneca, whose stoic philosophy is the epicentre of don Julián's attack, was born "en el centro de la Península y no en la periferia, y hoy podemos certificar ya, sin que nadie nos contradiga, que tuvo lugar en las cumbres de la sierra de Gredos" (113). This is highly ironical, and not a direct citation of any one historiographer.[14] A similar shifting from the margin to the centre occurs in Julián's scene of betrayal through transformation of the Strait of Gibraltar into an isthmus / birth canal. At the beginning of the novel, the strait is a closed-off lake, and later an "árbitro de montañas y ribera … que separa una orilla de otra y libera su tierra de adopción de la acuciante, venenosa cicatriz" (68). At the beginning of the novel's second part, however, the narrator is not trapped within a uterus, nor is the strait understood as a closed-off lake. He stresses movement towards an internal centre: "hacia dentro, hacia dentro: en la atmósfera algodonosa y quieta" (89). A "cottony atmosphere" is similar to the description at the opening of the novel of a low-pressure weather system moving from the Azores into the Mediterranean Basin, pushing through the strait "como en un embudo entre las dos riberas hasta anular el paisaje" (12). This system, in other words, links, in a diffuse cloud of imagination, the two continents and abrogates all separation. The arrival of a front, which normally precedes severe weather, also atmospherically establishes a tone of increased tension, which of course announces the future onslaught by Julián's columns of invaders: "cruel cataclismo, dulce alivio … la niebla parece abolir la distancia" (12–13). But the metaphor of pushing into a cloud is misleading, as Julián's infection of the Spanish sacred occurs from within in a subterranean, cavernous zone.

The entrance into the peninsula from the periphery occurs by framing the opposing Spanish shore as a scar, which symbolizes a history of violence in the establishment of sovereign limits in the past and the aggression required to reopen the lesion in the future. As Julián notes, as he preaches to his squadron of North African invaders, "Contemplad la cicatriz venenosa al otro lado del mar: la riqueza magnífica al alcance de vuestro corceles" (136). He demands that they contemplate the scar, and not the land itself, as it alone provides access to Spain's sacred inner sphere of sovereignty. The atmospheric fog of Julián's delirium, which has "abolido la distancia," places the poisonous scar on the opposing shore within his soldiers' reach. The closed-off centre of the state of exception is therefore enjoined to the domestic order that once surrounded it, creating a liminal, open area of possibility that recalls the primitive function of the festival and its orgiastic and chaotic inversion of hierarchy and power.

The novel later returns to the dynamic of moving inward towards a primordial zone, presumably after the *corceles* have reached the poisonous scar, in the shockingly misogynistic rape of Don Álvaro Peranzules's daughter and the absurd excavation of her vagina. Peranzules, a lawyer, is an archetype of a Generación del '98 intellectual and the *perfecto caballero.*[15] While in Peranzules's study, listening to a harangue on the correct use of prepositions, Julián spies Peranzules's daughter, identified as Isabel *la Católica.* Isabel, dressed as a nun, begins to undress and self-flagellate with a whip, which is then taken over by Julián in a sadomasochistic display of sexual aggression that transforms into a performance witnessed by North American tourists: "Cuando le arrebatas el látigo y golpeas tú, el foco centrará su atención en el triángulo de raso situado a la altura de los ijares y la voz amena y convincente del locutor te invitará a ti y al público ahí reunido a una inolvidable, instructiva excursión por las honduras, recovecos y escondrijos del Bastión Teológico: por el interior del sancta sanctorum designado por vosotros antes de la invasión turística, el desarrollo y las bodas de plata del Ubicuo, como la Remota, Fantástica, jamás Explorada por Viajero Alguno Gruta Sagrada" (165–6).

Julián's sadistic lashing opens the scar, the Holy of Holies, the hidden and secretive ark of the covenant containing what is sacred and not to be touched. The exploration of the sacred grotto is captured on film, "el foco centrará su atención," by tourists who themselves penetrate Spain's borders in the 1960s through Franco's welcoming of consumerism and industrial development within his sovereign zone. Sadomasochism is important in Agamben's thought. He writes, "Sadomasochism is precisely the technique of sexuality by which the bare life of a sexual partner is brought to light … we also find here the symmetry between *homo sacer* and sovereign, in the complicity that ties the masochist to the sadist, the victim to the executioner" (*Homo Sacer* 134–5). Julián's lashing open the scar, which protects the sacred grotto, reduces the keeper of the sacred to the status of bare life. This essentially means that he transforms Peranzules's daughter into *homo sacer* and wills himself into being as an executioner, or sovereign, who phallically transgresses limits. Moreover, he defines himself through a symmetrical relationship with the bare life that he controls and subjugates. Maintaining Schmitt's definition, Julián acquires sovereignty by deciding on the exception. A similar display of sadomasochistic aggression is repeated later in the novel in the outrageous torturing of Alvarito on his way home from school by Julián, who is transformed into a construction site watchman.

Peranzules's daughter, an obvious symbol of *la Cava* and the manner in which her rape preceded the original betrayal of Julián in the eighth century, has no specific object within her sacred grotto. As Lacan would say about the subconscious, there is nothing there but a central emptiness or lack and is therefore the very root of desire: "Atravesando audazmente el himen penetrarás en los sombríos dominios de Plutón y buscarás en vano entre la carnosa proliferación de estalactitas la rama dorada y los toros negros destinados a aplacar la cólera de los dioses, la vaca estéril proverbialmente ofrendada a Proserpina y la oveja inmolada a la madre de las Euménides" (168).

Julián searches in vain for a precisely defined sacred object such as Aeneas's golden bough that would appease the gods, just as Lacan would say that the subconscious, understood as an alphabet, searches in vain for signifieds because only empty signifiers are available. Julián, in his final descent into the inner cavity of his motherland finds only an empty cavity: "Sin decidirte aún a depositar el óbolo y ganar por fin la tenebrosa orilla cruzarás el istmo del útero y te adentrarás en una dilatada y proterva cavidad en forma de pera" (169). What Julián encounters is the pear-shaped uterus that represents the closed centre of Spanish sovereignty that putatively contains the sacred, which, as a belief in the mythological imagination of its adherents, has no physical reality. The uterus bears a resemblance to the Strait of Gibraltar imagined as a lake earlier in the novel but transforms into a revolutionary shifting of sovereignty at the moment a scarred canal leading both outward and inward is opened up and Julián discovers its lack of contents. Julián essentially embarks on a Dante-esque descent into the subconscious and discovers its empty truth. Recalling the beginning of the novel, the uterus's emptiness indicates that Julián's abolition of the closed-off centre of exception, as well as his own cocoon-like transformation, is complete.

Gaining knowledge of the grotto's emptiness is a critical point in Julián's path to power because he reveals the sacred to be an empty signifier allowing the imputation of any meaning whatsoever, and is therefore "in play." If one thinks of the grotto as the collective subconscious of the people, the sacred becomes a structural framework of metonymically shifting signifiers that aim to give the nation a sense of oneness with its essential truth, what Ortega y Gasset calls Spain's *gema iridiscente.* To Goytisolo, such an essential truth is actually illusory but, through bad faith, is generally thought of as unquestionable. This line of thinking is a striking, but likely inadvertent, critique of discourse typical of the Generación del '98, notably Ortega y Gasset's conception of *la razón vital* and the idea that social life possesses an authentic reality vitally constructed by a community's living together. Through the free association of the imaginary, Goytisolo's surrealist approach allows access to a different oneiric reality that reveals the truth of the nation to be an empty lack.

Possession of symbolic capital and the authority it grants to ideas, images, and objects is of paramount importance in Goytisolo's novel. Pierre Bourdieu notes that production of belief is inseparable from an economy of symbolic capital, which is "a capital of consecration implying a power to consecrate objects … or persons … and therefore to give value" (*Field of Cultural Production* 75). The intimate strife that Julián effects within the sovereign exception is his path to obtaining a consecrating capital within the symbolic realm capable of granting authority to new beliefs and practices. Julián, like Franco, aspires to win control of *la gracia de Dios* by becoming *Caudillo de España*. Knowledge of the sacred grotto's emptiness is the path to acquiring symbolic capital, as it reveals that the images and figures that comprise a nation's identity are relativistic and inessential. However, by redirecting his profaning violence away from the authoritarian father figure, Julián merely ends up reaffirming the logic of *el Ubicuo*'s power. The *reivindicación* thus functions as a repetition of the manner in which "el Ubicuo" and other authority figures in the novel obtained power in the past, and this is what grants Julián the public recognition necessary to legitimate his hold on power and obtain consecrating symbolic capital. Thereafter, the arbitrariness of the sacred allows a reformulation of the essential character of Spanish identity and the creation of a new logic of exclusion that targets different individuals. The most unfortunate aspect of the narrative, therefore, is the extent to which Julián's intimate strife derives its symbolic power from the sacrifice of innocent victims.

Human, All Too Human

In *The King's Two Bodies*, published in 1953, Ernst Kantorowicz argues that during the Middle Ages sovereignty began to be thought of as divided between two entities: the *corpus naturale* of the king as a mortal, finite human being and the *corpus mysticum*, or the essential placeholder of power that could not be destroyed. The immutability of the king's mystical body protected the institution of sovereignty against the instability of the mortal being to whom it corresponded. In *Conde Julián*, one could argue that Julián is yet another *corpus naturale* who is initiated into an institution of sovereignty that binds society around consecrated sacred forms. It is important that Franco's proper name is never once uttered. Franco, "el Ubicuo," may be pushed aside, but the institution of the *todopoderoso*, another term used throughout the novel, remains. In the work's final pages, a public ritual anoints Julián into the institution of the "all-powerful," transforming the protagonist into the body politic's next *corpus naturale* but in no way eliciting a truly significant alteration in the way sovereignty is understood and exercised.

The figure of the mystical father in *Conde Julián* cannot in fact be discarded if the ritual that bestows symbolic power is to function. Bourdieu convincingly argues that any act of institution requires a ritual that predates the arrival of the one who is to be initiated into a seat of authority. Alvarito's resurrection maintains the form of a doll and along with it the mask-like plane of identity on which language, belief, and the sacred are inscribed. The content of Alvarito's language and belief structure is unimportant; rather, ritual and its public recognition are essential. To wit, the conclusion of *Conde Julián* maintains a rite of destruction couched in the consecration of an archaic logic of sovereign power. Ritual, by its very definition, embodies a reiterative historicity that is publicly known and recognized. Rites of institution, therefore, carry illocutionary force, according to Bourdieu, if the act "is guaranteed by the whole group or by a recognized institution" (*Language and Symbolic Power* 125). Julián's redemption is therefore not legitimate without the support of public opinion, which requires a set of expectations of how a leader should behave and be represented. And indeed, after Alvarito's resurrection as a doll, "los niños asisten gozosos a tu insólita epifanía: la procesión ha alcanzado la avenida de España y discurre por el andén central" (*Reivindicación del Conde* 238). Álvarito's death originally incensed and terrified "los carpetos," the term Goytisolo uses to refer to Spaniards, and they took to the streets initially to "exorcisar el peligro" (231). The women attempt to resort to sacred images and prayer: "intentan conjurar con rezos la cólera celeste: algunas depositan limosnas en los cepillos" (231). Ultimately, the masses surround the resurrected doll in a scene that resembles a presidential inauguration. Alvarito cannot become a bona fide leader solely on the basis of Julián's or Goytisolo's say-so. He is what he is only because the people's collective belief is channelled into a mystical institution of sovereignty whose rules dictate the standards to which any mortal figure of authority must conform. The institution of sovereignty, in other words, is like a religion in Durkheim's thought, as it truly exists only in the collective consciousness of a public and draws its power from the vital spirit of an interconnected populace. What dooms society to a cyclical history of violence is unawareness of, or indifference to, the fact that the body politic is the authentic source of political power, which need not be produced only through displays of aggression.

The consecration of a new *corpus naturale* requires signs and marks of authority in order to become official. As Bourdieu has it, a new leader's consecration becomes concrete "through qualifications and symbols like stripes, uniforms and other attributes" (*Language and Symbolic Power* 126). Alvarito, of course, parades through the avenues in a white djellaba and turban – a verifiable uniform – along with having other attributes such as the identification of an Islamic deity and speaking in flawless Arabic. Alvarito's suicide stresses that his resurrection represents the point in the narrative where the identities of Álvaro and the child merge into a new being through self-sacrifice. This new being is identified as Julián after the child falls into an abysm where "estamos seguros que morirá": "eres Julián / conoces el camino" (*Reivindicación del Conde* 214). The protagonist can undo his connection to Spain geographically by moving to Tangier and can change his modes of dressing and eating to conform to a different culture. However, the most difficult *seña de identidad* to undo is the one that orders the subject from within: language. And indeed, the most durable inscription that remains on Álvaro's mask of identity is language: "Feliz de olvidar por unos instantes el último lazo que, a tu pesar, te une irreductiblemente a la tribu: idioma mirífico del Poeta" (70). Acts of violence directed at his own *señas de identidad*, therefore, are an attempted assault on the symbolic realm and its inscription on his symbolic mask of Spanishness. The final part of the novel is precisely this showdown: having attacked the rest of the peninsula, all that remains to undo is Julián's own symbolic connection to that blotted-out history in order to replace it with a new symbolic order.

Disavowing an alienating mask inscribed with the symbolic order is the impetus that fuels the violence directed at Alvarito, "tú mismo un cuarto de siglo atrás" (215). The barrage of sexual assaults upon the child is an attempt to remove an outer shell in order to reach a synthesis of the "animalidad herida" (230) that the narrator identifies as existing at the core of both beings. The inscription of a language – which subjects an ego to an order imposed from outside – is what first scars consciousness by introducing a breach between essential meaning and the linguistic signifier. I linked Julián's invasion earlier in the novel to discovering the state's hidden, empty core of sovereignty. In the final part of the novel, the narrator opens another scar, which represents the closed centre of Julián's own "animalidad herida" that has been isolated by the violent imposition of an alienating linguistic identity at childhood. Indeed, Julián uses Alvarito's repeated whippings in order to open a breach that separates the subject into two parts: "la cáscara" and "la pulpa". (224). Agamben argues that sadomasochism is an exemplary instance in which an authority figure reduces his victim to the status of bare life. In the whipping of Peranzules's daughter and the assault on *Isabel la Católica* and *la Celestina*, an ontological reduction to the status of bare life was the ultimate implication of the attacks.

The impetus behind the torture of Alvarito at the end of the novel is distinct because of its sacrificial nature. Georges Bataille writes that sacrifice's ordering principle is destruction, and more specifically, the obliteration of "thingness" in the victim. Sacrifice creates what Bataille calls "immanent intimacy" between the one who sacrifices and the victim, which ultimately creates "a keen awareness of shared life grasped in its intimacy" among those who witness the execution ("Sacrifice, the Festival" 212). Goytisolo frames Alvarito's torture as a similarly sacrificial death meant to destroy the objective history of a past that cannot persist if Julián is to be given a new language and symbolic structure: "Tu odio irreductible hacia el pasado y el niño espurio que lo representa / exige los fastos de la muerte ritual y su ceremonial mágico" (213). The rite of inauguration that links Alvarito-resurrected to the mystical institution of sovereignty also demands a magical ceremony that fuses the fissures in Álvaro's identity into "a shared life grasped in its intimacy," where historical "thingness," his "cáscara," is blotted out and subtracted from the "material virgin" of the protagonist's being, or his "pulpa." The striking disconnect between the two moments of laceration, that of *la Cava* and that of Alvarito, is that the narrator believes the interior of his own identity is unlike that of Spain's sacred grotto: not hollow, but rather a central core of fleshy animality that functions as if it were a stem cell and able to produce new identifying connections. Once Álvaro and Alvarito merge into the identity of Julián, all that remains is a declaration of mastery through a new symbolic order: "Falta el lenguaje, Julián / desde estrados, iglesias, cátedras, púlpitos, academias, tribunas los carpetos reivindican con orgullo sus derechos de propiedad sobre el lenguaje" (192). The crux of Julián's redemption therefore boils down to language and the necessity of depriving the *hispanos* of their mastery over the symbolic order.

Jacques Lacan argues that the symbolic realm is the part of a subject's consciousness marked by history – a history, moreover, that is known by its metonymic shifting from one perceived ideal image of the self to another, like the series of rings on the trunk of a tree. A facile connection to Goytisolo's novel would be to argue that the historical image of Julián – his mythological reality as the governor of Ceuta who hands Iberia over to the Moors – represents for Goytisolo's narrator what Lacan calls *méconnaissance*: the speaking subject's misrecognition of itself in others who might satisfy the ego's unconscious desires. These others, known as ego-ideals, inevitably fail to live up to their promise. Desire is therefore consciously known as an unquenchable driving force precisely because the subject refuses to view itself as an empty grotto that contains no essential material that could ever be perfectly represented by a particular signifier. A logical gap in *Conde Julián*, therefore, is the narrator's failure to extrapolate the emptiness of sovereignty to the lack at the core of his own subconscious. Discovering the emptiness of *la Cava*'s sacred grotto was a crucial moment in the invasion of the Iberian peninsula; finding that the pear-shaped uterus was hollow was like eating from the tree of knowledge and becoming aware of the arbitrariness of the ideal forms around which a nation can be consolidated. For the narrator, misrecognizing Julián as an ideal ego-image denies his consciousness a similar freedom and reaffirms an enslavement to the linguistic Other as the source of a desired identity. The rebirth of Julián, and the advocation of an Arabic symbolic structure, is really the announcement of a new kind of semantic subjectivity.

Lacan, however, stresses that misrecognition is not an exact correlative of Sartre's *mauvaise foi* in the sense that the subject maintains in his or her inauthentic identification a knowledge of an unchangeable fact of reality that drives the need to act as if one were ignorant. A history of identifications makes *méconnaissance* possible, and it is therefore unlike the primary formation of the ego in the mirror stage: "Misrecognition is not ignorance. Misrecognition represents a certain organisation of affirmations and negations, to which the subject is attached. Hence it cannot be conceived without correlative knowledge. If the subject is capable of misrecognizing something, he surely must know what this function has operated upon" (*Seminar I* 167).

Julián's "lacking of a language" and the resurrection of an Alvarito speaking a pure Arabic, when compared with comments about Castilian Spanish earlier in the novel, denotes a similar "correlative knowledge" of an unchangeable fact of reality that requires a mythical substitution that is truly possible only in fiction. The narrator, on one hand, identifies Spanish as "el último lazo que, a tu pesar, te une irreductiblemente a la tribu" (*Reivindicación del Conde* 70). The imposition of a primary native language serves, therefore, as an event that is immutable in its irreducibility. Moreover, in a statement that recalls Goytisolo's praising of Latin American writers in touch with the virgin material of their language, the narrator then identifies Spanish as a "vehículo necesario de la traición, hermosa lengua tuya: instrumento indispensable del renegado y del apóstata, esplendoroso y devastador a la vez: arma aguda (insinuante) que conjura (exorcisa) la africana hueste y magnifica (potencia) su denso apetito de destrucción" (70).

In the novel's third part, in a humorous episode in which the narrator disallows all words, foods, and practices derived from Arabic and Moorish inheritance on the Iberian Peninsula, the Spanish language indeed conjures up and exorcises an Arabic presence within its own structure that profanes the possibility of a Christian, *castiza* purity. This destroys the myth that the construction of an Iberian identity can exclude all vestiges of the Muslim Other. The figure of Julián, however, transforms into a Lacanian misrecognition in the fourth part of the novel, when the narrator exchanges the previous demystification of the Spanish language for a complete substitution of symbolic register. This transition is announced at the end of the third part, after Julián has crossed the Spanish countryside inflicting a series of catastrophes. The result of the assault is pure, unmitigated silence: "Cómo en el cerco vago de su desierta arena el gran pueblo no suena?: ni un grito, ni un lamento: sólo tu risa, Julián, dueño y señor del wa-l-lah" (201). This pillaging reduces Spain to the state of an "ombligo desollado y sin voz abandonado" (201). By the third part's conclusion, the narrator eschews the blotting out of parts of the language in order to erect a new style in favour of total annihilation.

The torture of Alvarito re-enacts the silencing of Spain. At the beginning of the final part, the child is described as wont to pray "jaculatorias en latín" (207) but finishes his deific resurrection, at the end of the work, with a complete code switching. Throughout the description of Alvarito's sadomasochistic torture, he never utters a word and is reduced to a voiceless state. In a metaphorical sense, the anarchic blotting out of particular passages of the great works of Spain by crushing insects at the novel's outset gives way to a total obliteration of the library at the conclusion. One gets the impression, therefore, that the "lenguaje del mirífico Poeta" (70), referring to Góngora, and the invention of a "prosa anárquica y bárbara" (152) are inadequate for Goytisolo. Returning to the introduction of the chapter, Harold Bloom's comparison of the evolution of literary discourse to Freud's primal scene reveals a profound ambivalence in the aftermath of obliterating the father's symbolic order. Creating a new style and imputing a language with neologisms certainly displays a mastery over those who exert authority over a language's development. As with the development of totemism, however, longing and guilt inevitably give way to a "deferred obedience" to the father by re-enacting his prohibitions and structure of power. In order to impose, in a castrating fashion, a symbolic order that truly pays homage to this form of subjection, an anarchic and deconstructed Castilian Spanish gives way to a codified, rigid, and idealized form of "árabe puro" that bears a very uncanny resemblance to Álvaro Peranzules's speech and his passion for the correct usage of prepositions. The irony, of course, is that a deferred obedience to the masters of the Spanish language requires resorting to a similarly stultified Arabic. As with the king's mystical body, content is less important than the reaffirmation of a structure of symbolic subjugation. Goethe's quotation in the epigraph expresses a profound paradox that is worked out quite insidiously in Goytisolo's novel: Julián's invasion is simply a strife that reacquires a structure of law that is always-already inherited from the father.

Funnelling ideal identity images through the desires of other subjects is a never-ending source of alienation from a state Lacan calls jouissance, an unconscious state of unity born during infancy. Lacan's division of the self, known as his Schema L, places the conscious speaking subject in a relationship with the Other and his symbolic code. This alienates the self from what Lacan calls the *moi*, an unconscious ego that is formed through speculative image identification in what is called the mirror stage. Ultimately, Julián's identification with animal imagery, and the subsequent disavowal of ethics and promotion of unbound sexuality, earlier in the novel gives way by the end to a phenomenon that Lacan identifies as strictly related to the human realm: "What we have there is a first captation by the image in which the first stage of the dialectic of identifications can be discerned. It is linked to a *Gestalt* phenomenon, the child's very early perception of the human form … But what demonstrate the phenomenon of recognition, which involves subjectivity, are the signs of triumphant jubilation and playful discovery that characterize, from the sixth month, the child's encounter with his image in the mirror. This behaviour contrasts strikingly with the indifference shown even by animals that perceive this image, the chimpanzee, for example, when they have tested its objectal vanity" (*Écrits* 18).

What makes Álvaro Mendiola, in Nietzsche's words, "human, all too human," is the belief in a jouissance that results from an image identification in which one perceives no sense of alienation from the ideal self, and meaning appears immanent to external appearance. This status, typical of the imaginary realm, involves feelings of aggression and erotic passion directed towards the mother's sacred "internal empire": "Through her [Melanie Klein] we know the function of the imaginary primordial enclosure formed by the imago of the mother's body; through her we have the cartography, drawn by the children's own hands, of the mother's internal empire, the historical atlas of the intestinal divisions in which the imagos of the father and brothers (real or virtual), in which the voracious aggression of the subject himself, dispute their deleterious dominance over her sacred regions" (*Écrits* 21).

This statement greatly informs the conquest of *la Cava*'s sacred grotto and a scene later in the novel in which Julián instructs his minions to "adentraos sin cuartel en el coto / en el Coño, en el Coño, en el Coño" of *la Celestina* (*Reivindicación de Conde* 173). In the imaginary sphere, the castrating power of the father effected by the imposition of his symbolic rod is yet to be known, and therefore the dominance over the mother's sacred regions is contested by the entirety of the primal horde. One can also link the framing of the mother's body as a cartography to the centre of sovereign exception that Agamben posits in the subconscious life of the state. The feelings that Julián links to *adentrar* in the body are typical of the pleasurable pain that defines jouissance: "en mi ejército hallarás: un fuego escondido / un sabroso veneno / una dulce amargura / una deleitable dolencia" (173). The positing of a sacred essence within the grotto, however, and the symbolic capital that such an endeavour requires, means that the subject cannot remain in a relationship with the passive imago and must instead resort to the myth-making mastery of language, where the expression of power and violence is anything but ambivalent and playful. The excessive reference to Julián's erect *pinzas* and his repeated violations and sexual assaults reveal a desperate search for a lost phallus, meaning that the seminal moment of a primary identification awash in the exuberant feelings of jouissance is irretrievably consigned to the past. If society functions as a collective psychology based on the individual psyche, one has reason to doubt whether a culture, like a human subject, can truly *comenzar a cero* and act as if the cyclical lacerations of history have no bearing on structure, power, and national identity.

The torturing of Alvarito, therefore, can be read as a castrating imposition of the symbolic order that responds to the allure of deferred obedience to the father. Lacan writes that in practice the subject, when offered the possibility of experiencing jouissance by opening up a breach in consciousness, will inevitably decide to fill the gap with a new structure of desire presented by the Other. Once the imaginary realm has disappeared into the subconscious, the subject no longer assumes "the insignia of the other, but rather ... the subject has to find the constituting structure of his desire in the same gap opened up by the effect of the signifiers in those who come to represent the Other for him" (*Écrits* 264). Lacan frames the imposition of the symbolic order and the subsequent search for other constituting structures of desire as a series of "cuts," each of which creates a breach in the ego and leaves a bloody scar. The process of misrecognition in the historical development of the subject, therefore, is actually a series of self-inflicted wounds. Self-inflicted violence is what one finds at the conclusion of Goytisolo's novel. And indeed in the gap produced by Julián's lashings, which separate the *cáscara* from the *pulpa*, one finds violence being displaced onto an innocent victim. The ultimate misrecognition is therefore the belief that one can escape external subjection by becoming a master of oneself – or rather, the belief that one's internal life is autonomous and truly free of the demands of the Other: "¿Desde cuando un degenerado como tú se atreve a desafiar a Julián? ¿no sabes que mando yo?" (*Reivindicación del Conde* 227).

A New *Nomos* of the Earth?

The *Reivindicación del Conde don Julián* no doubt teaches important lessons regarding the mediation of authority through sacralization of structural authority. The truth is that religious practices and ways of thinking, whether Christian or Muslim, can bind together large swathes of people and organize the masses in a coherent fashion. This perhaps signals the importance of maintaining the sacred as a hollow placeholder around which to associate the body politic. Julián's redemption, however, also demonstrates that embedded within religious practice is a potential to resort to apocalyptic narratives of resurrection that usher in new epochs of social existence through the complete substitution of external marks of identity, such as language, the creeds or deities that serve as the centres of collective belief structures, and the symbols reflected in the clothing and gestures associated with the sovereign. A forgetful rebirth after the old law is smashed, which Nietzsche details in *Thus Spoke Zarathustra*, rejects a progressive conceptualization of history, as the ineluctable nature of society to maintain structures of thought and practice from one generation to the next refutes historicity. That Goytisolo is re-enacting a myth, moreover, denotes a historical repetition of Dionysian destruction following the gradual calcification of structure. Affirming national identity through sacred imagining thus inflects both space and time. In the next chapter, in an analysis of Juan Benet's and Mercè Rodoreda's fiction, I argue that a philosophy of oscillating time punctuated by ritual sacrifice is the logical consequence of constructing a sovereign space through scapegoating, exclusion, and violence.

Julián's disruptive violence, which acts as the means to reach apocalyptic ends, relies on false oppositions and radical alterities, such as the distinction between the sovereign and *homo sacer*, the Christian and the Muslim, the Spaniard and the African, the passive mother and authoritative father, the self and the Other. The shift in Goytisolo's novel between the third and fourth parts indicates that the author found himself in an aporetic situation. The state of jouissance and the open, playful possibility that it represents erects no barriers between where one subject ends and the other begins. In this respect, it cannot even be called purely individualistic. As Lacan argues, in the period where the human is captivated by the imago, there occurs a great degree of transitivism: "The child who strikes another says that he has been struck; the child who sees another fall, cries" (*Écrits* 19). Lacan finds in this stage of development a structural ambivalence, with "the slave being identified with the despot, the actor with the spectator, the seduced with the seducer" (19).

What Goytisolo discovers is that individuality, from a psychoanalytic perspective, comes into being at the same time one becomes a subject. And subjectivity, of course, is directly linked to the existence of external authority. From the perspective of political theory, a structural ambivalence is incompatible with the organization of a body politic where individuals are defined by both their uniqueness and their belonging to a collective nation that comprises multiple subjectivities. Goytisolo's answer to this quandary in his own life is to become an island unto himself: "El acto de desprenderme de una señas de identidad opresivas y estériles abría el camino a un espacio literario plural, sin fronteras: prohibidos por el franquismo, mis libros podían asilarse en México o Buenos Aires. En adelante el idioma y sólo el idioma sería mi patria auténtica" (*En los reinos de taifa* 72).

It is, of course, unfeasible for everyone to declare his or her independent symbolic structure to be a unique *patria*. The very possibility of completely disconnecting one's symbolic link from the primary source from which one acquired the language is disputable and has implications for understanding the third novel of the trilogy, *Juan sin tierra*. In a more important sense, however, the idea that Castilian could be a *patria* in itself is a phenomenal illusion: how could it be so without the violence that an imposed Castilian brought to Latin America, where Goytisolo's books found asylum?

That Goytisolo strictly identifies all instances of authority with a structure of cruel exception confuses violence with power. Durkheim and Bourdieu confirm that it is the vital spirit of a collective consciousness that recognizes and legitimates the connection between a sovereign and the mystical institution of power that organizes a culture and assures its continued existence. This is precisely

Hannah Arendt's definition of power: "Power always stands in need of numbers, whereas violence up to a point can manage without them because it relies on implements" (*Violence* 42). Up until the point where Alvarito parades through the streets of Madrid flanked by swarms of *hispanos*, like the Nationalist military battalion that paraded through a fallen Barcelona in 1939, he effectively possesses no sense of power but only the implements for committing violence. Arendt continues, "*Violence*, finally, as I have said, is distinguished by its instrumental character" (46; Arendt's italics). In Goytisolo's text, the narrator's identification with totemic imagery linked to the Moors is the means by which he acquires violent instrumentality that is meant to restore a phallic mastery. This identification, however, is not what grants the *power* required to become a legitimate sovereign authority. In opposition to Agamben, and by extension Schmitt, the government's ability to decide on dehumanizing exceptions and deny natural rights must not remain a publicly expected, legitimating act of institution. Reversing a "political mystery of separation," however, requires altering the institutional structure of even the most liberal democratic political bodies in the Western world.

That the mystical institution of sovereignty possesses a hollow centre that is defined by the power of collective thought, and not by a sole, violent individual, is perhaps the most important message to take from the novel. A public can become aware of its being the source of political power only if Agamben's included exclusion is undone and the sovereign's right to decide on exception is abrogated. This theory, of course, challenges the post-Westphalian monolithic structure of the state that became widespread in the eighteenth and nineteenth centuries, and demands that statehood itself become a more pluralistic concept that decentralizes sovereign power. In a world where there is a handful of singular hegemonic centres of sovereignty, an excess of "Otherness" is inevitable, as a result of a limited set of structures of national identification. The new *nomos* perhaps requires that the territorial spaces mapped out by an antiquated notion of statehood undo the consolidation of authority at the centre in favour of smaller structures of autonomy wherever feelings of cultural magnetism are strongest. This perhaps indicates that the much-feared devolution of a Europe of states into a Europe of national regions is not all that undesirable.

Tolerance and intolerance will remain embedded within each sovereign structure as a result of the sacred roots of political imagination. But a higher number of national centres of belonging assures that in the event of violence, which is not ideal but certainly inevitable, a political authority over the possibility of making the ultimate decision – human sacrifice – is more equitably distributed and placed in the hands of those whose countrymen will suffer the loss of life. As Joan Sales discovered, a friend-enemy distinction is acceptable for delineating national identity only if the Other's humanity is not denied in the process.

5 The Eternal Present of Sacred Time

In illo tempore

The works of Joan Sales and Juan Goytisolo assert the opprobrious human costs that come at the expense of sacralizing nation-space. Sales's thought sketches the relationship between metaphysics and the psychological thirst for a fixed belief structure on which to ground existence. Fixed belief structures, when disrupted, tend to employ a victimary mechanism that scapegoats innocent bystanders in an effort to quell violence, which demands a structure of the nation based on a friend/enemy distinction where the Other is never denied his humanity. *Conde Julián*, for its part, is a tragic reminder of the violence engendered by exclusion and social purification when one metaphysical ideology substitutes another, but without modifying the structural parameters of political belonging. In light of the two previous chapters, Henri Lefebvre's postulate that the concept of sovereignty "implies a space against which violence, whether latent or overt, is directed – a space established and constituted by violence" (280), comes as no surprise. The consolidation of power aggressively constitutes political space, which demands a consecrating fetishization of the country's territory at the service of the ideologies around which national unity is organized. Sacralization, and its mode of setting apart holy places, is a critical tool for such a spatial fetishism, which even secular discourse cannot avoid adopting. The physical's entrance into a sacred mode, however, also alters temporality. Is temporality therefore also something to be fetishized?

It goes without saying that the sacralization of space bears important consequences for the notion of time. Lefebvre continues, "The state crushes time by reducing differences to repetitions or circularities … it enforces a logic that puts an end to conflicts and contradictions" (23). In this chapter, I postulate that the crushing of time via repetition and circularity by the state profits from the spilling over of the sacred into secular political practice. Ritual repetition and a periodic, nonlinear philosophy of history define the shape of what could be called a sacred time. In Francoist Spain, the regime did not crush time altogether; rather, the unhistorical circularity of a sacred time of origin was interpolated within the flow of profane history. In a 1942 speech to members of the Frente de Juventudes, Franco exchanged ideological difference for a repetitive circularity of time. The great enemy of a rationalized history is chance: "las empresas de la Historia, las batallas mejor concebidas, la preparación más concienzuda y meditada, pueden ser destruidas por lo que vulgarmente se llama 'azar'" (Díaz-Plaja 117). Interpreting the validity and significance of a historical event might arrive at a variety of conclusions, depending on the metaphysical belief structure through which one filters meaning. For Franco, this filter is Roman Catholicism and its calendar of feast days: "Y es en nuestra misma Cruzada la sucesión de hechos portentosos, que coinciden en su gran mayoría con las fiestas más señaladas de nuestra Iglesia, una nueva muestra de aquella protección" (117). Franco then proceeds to give a litany of examples: the battle of Brunette took place on the feast day of Saint James; the *Convoy de la Victoria* broke through the Strait of Gibraltar on 5 August 1936, the feast day of *la patrona de Ceuta.* Under normal circumstances, these coincidences are essentially meaningless, because there is a Catholic feast day nearly every day of the year. However, Catholic metaphysics were essential for Franco to rationalize his view that Spain was "la nación predilecta de Dios" (116).[1] Collapsing profane time into ritually celebrated feast days indeed fetishizes temporality by making history an object on which to focus attention and provide meaning. Though the Virgin of Ceuta appeared centuries before the *Convoy de la victoria* crossed the Strait of Gibraltar, Franco collapses the two events into a singular moment of sacred time whose "present" is eternal.

National unity profits from historical circularity and the ritual celebration of feast days in order to maintain a cognizance of origins and reassert the logic that legitimizes the state's existence. As Lefebvre argued, a progressive time must be crushed by the state, but this does not mean that sovereign power has no use for profane temporality. The progressive nature of profane time surrounds the intermittent introduction of sacred, eternal "presents" into the calendar, creating a dialectic that appears superficially to be a mere contrast but is in reality interpenetrating. Conflating a Catholic feast day with a commemoration of the *Convoy de la victoria*, for example, slips secular history into a theological framework and offers a reminder of the state's hold on the parameters of the ideological framework of the nation, a form of control that produced a preferred ideal of Spanishness throughout Francoism. This sacred interruption of profane time, therefore, reaffirms the cultural, linguistic, and juridical structure of everyday existence within Franco's Spain. In an Althusserian sense, ritually demanding that time stop in order to pay heed to the state's business, such as the periods of mourning that followed the death of Alfonso XIII in 1941 and Manolete's goring in 1947, materialize as an interpellation where each citizen is asked to submit to an authoritarian "hey you."

Controlling the rhythm of time has as much effect on the exclusion of difference as does the purification of space. For Franco, the historical origin of Spanish unity is crystal clear, which he notes in the same speech to the Frente de Juventudes: "La unidad nacional que forjan nuestros Reyes Católicos va estrechamente unida a la unidad espiritual y la expansión de nuestra fe" (Díaz-Plaja 116). Franco may be *caudillo por la gracia de Dios*, but the *Reyes Católicos* function as his apostolic intermediaries. The *Reyes Católicos* and their immediate successors, in addition to uniting the crowns of Castile and Aragon through marriage, also achieved unity by instituting the *Santo Oficio de la Inquisición*, expelling the Jews in 1492, and later the Moriscos in 1609. Franco's merging of Spanish nationalism with a Catholic metaphysics appropriates this gateway to a sacred time of origin and inserts it into the twentieth century, which also requires directing violence towards a sovereign space left vacant by the fall of the Second Republic and excluding what he determined to be the "anti-España": liberals, Communists, Freemasons, atheists, separatists, and the like. Emphasizing an association of Catholic holidays with critical military battles is a logical step. Franco gives meaning to a coincidence of dates by appealing to historical fate, making his strident demonizing of chance unsurprising. The obsession with establishing a direct lineage between himself and *la gracia de Dios*, by way of the *Reyes Católicos*, involves revitalizing a long-completed historical moment to be used as an instrument of political sovereignty.

Franco, by equating secular military victory with Catholic feast days, makes visible a series of historical moments that affect the way the populace conceives Iberian space. Creating historical visibility, in other words, is closely linked to a community's ritual practice of sacred time and its connection with its sovereign territory. For Lefebvre, violently imposing sovereignty over a space crushes time; Reinhart Koselleck, on the other hand, notes that extracting a temporal moment from the flow of history always translates to a heightened consciousness of physical environment. As Koselleck writes, "All the examples that are intended to render historical time visible to us refer us to the space in which humans live and to the nature within which they are embedded" (102). Rituals and festivals are temporal markers that are made visible to the people by virtue of their exceptional nature. Such a visibility, however, sharpens a focus on territorial space: in Francoist Spain, the historical significance of a decisive battleground or the erection of a monument to Nationalist soldiers who fought for fascist ideals, like the Valle de los Caídos, are both excellent examples. Catholicism, in other words, provided a metaphysical framework for Francoism and a historical calendar in which secular military battles, and the Nationalist ideology they symbolized, could be inserted and linked to *la gracia de Dios* by virtue of the coincidence with holy feast days. Catholicism provided a built-in program of ritual that spilled over into the secular celebration of historical moments deemed crucial by the regime.

The equation of military history with Catholic days of commemoration, however, transcends a simple coincidence of dates. On 5 August, both the *fiesta de la Virgen de África* and the *Convoy de la Victoria* are awash in a sacred reality that stretches back to a far-off origin from which the nation's *unidad espiritual* and *expansión de su fe* erupt. This is a technique that Mircea Eliade refers to as the creation of "sacred time": "a sort of eternal mythical present that is periodically reintegrated by means of rites" and "can be homologized to eternity" (70). For Lefebvre, circularity crushes time; for Eliade, circularity represents its own unhistorical temporal dimension. The marked separation of a sacred time and its profane counterpart goes against Western philosophies of history, especially that of Hegel. World history, the exclusive realm of spirit (consciousness that possesses absolute reason), is earnestly progressive: "World history is the record of the spirit's efforts to attain knowledge of what it is in itself" (*Hegel Reader* 401). For Hegel, there are no intermittent periods of unhistorical moments homologized to eternity; spirit has traced a progressive line in its attaining knowledge, and any deviations or errors were propitious for the development of thought.

Franco's return to a sacred/profane rhythm of time is most evident in his perception of the Second Republic, which was less a learning experience or necessary historical deviation than a sharp disconnect from the nation's spiritual fount. Moreover, access to *la eterna unidad de España* required constant guardianship and openness to violence. One day after declaring the end of the Spanish Civil War, Radio Española proclaimed, "El amor y la espada mantendrán, con la unidad de mando victoriosa, la eterna unidad de España" (Díaz-Plaja 11). This dictum strongly echoes Donoso Cortés's nineteenth-century exhortation to embrace dictatorship and maintain order via the sword. The salient point is that Spain's eternal unity was an always-already concept eminently knowable and never broadened by the advancement of history, possessing, prior to the corrupting touch of profane history, the plenitude of an Aristotelian first cause. The regime thus completely erased the Second Republic from Spanish history and theorized the government as a mere profanation of the country's *bienes espirituales*, as Franco noted at the inauguration of the Valle de los Caídos: "La anti-España fue vencida y derrotada, pero no está muerta" (306). The return to sacred time occasioned by the victory of the National front replenished Spain's spiritual unity, and only by virtue of this renewal was the nation able to re-engage its inexorable crusade towards empire. As Franco noted in 1947, the Civil War was not the dawn of a new epoch, but rather a "movimiento renovador" (208).

The ongoing threat of the "anti-Spain" itself stresses a sacred-profane rhythm. Without commemoration of the heroic past through the ritual return to a sacred crushed time, the country is liable to profanation from the threatening presence of its antithesis. *La cruzada*, however, had not simply been set aside and picked up again after the Civil War. In the same inauguration speech, Franco argued that reforming to "nuestro ser" required that "bienes espirituales" be showered over Spain (306–8). The showering down of "bienes espirituales" is an apt metaphor for entrance into a sacred time that re-actualizes an unadulterated moment of origin. This re-actualization does not take place on the level of fictional myth; as Eliade notes, the regeneration of sacred time literally activates the moment, *in illo tempore*, when a society originated. An ontological replenishment of Spanish being required both a consecrated space – the Valle de los Caídos, for example – and a distinct experience of temporality, set apart from profane history, that re-actualized the founding moment of the nation.

Antonio Machado wrote in 1925 that "el concepto de lo humano no se formó de una vez para siempre, sino que cambia con la fe de cada época, con la metafísica" (279). In Franco's public speeches, a metaphysical re-establishment of a sacred time is plainly evident. It is on the level of literature, however, where one finds *el concepto de lo humano* that El Caudillo's superstructure produced. In other words, literature demonstrates how a ritual return to sacred time is felt on the level of subjectivity. Shortly after the inauguration of Franco's sovereign temple, el Valle de los Caídos, two novels were written that adeptly fictionalize the crushing effect of sacred time: Juan Benet's *Volverás a Región* (1967) and Mercè Rodoreda's unfinished work *La mort i la primavera*, which was originally submitted to the *Premi de Sant Jordi* in 1961, but not published until after the author's death in 1986. Benet's novel, alongside his 1978 short story "Numa (una leyenda)," artfully explores how the guardianship of a sacred wood by a figure named Numa translates into an existence of deadening profane time that is intermittently punctuated by the ritual expulsion of collective anxiety through violence. Numa, a woolly and savage guardian of Región's sacred wood, clearly echoes Franco's exhortations to guard Spain's *unidad espiritual* from profanation.

La mort i la primavera, which, like *Volverás a Región*, is indebted to Frazier's influential study *The Golden Bough*, centres on a small settlement next to a forest in which human remains are interred within tree trunks.[2] Rodoreda's fictional world is atemporal, where sundials leave no shadows and the village's only clock is without hands – clear symbols of a time that has been compressed to the point of not existing. The novel relates the timelessness of its space to a regimented series of rituals – such as the casting of a scapegoat down a subterranean river beneath the village every spring – that re-actualize a kind of founding violence. Unity, in both *Volverás a Región* and *La mort i la primavera*, comes about only through a call to maintain homogenous cohesion *con la espada.*

Numa's Sacred Wood

Why do you praise me? For I cut you!
I am cruel, you bleed: what means your
praise of my intoxicated cruelty?

Friedrich Nietzsche, *Thus Spoke Zarathustra*

Juan Benet's Región is a mythical province placed next to a forested mountain and patrolled by an enigmatic guardian referred to as Numa. Numa's task is simple: "Guardará el bosque, velando noche y día por toda la extensión de la finca, disparando con infalible puntería cada vez que unos pasos en la hojarasca o los suspiros de un alma cansada, turben la tranquilidad del lugar" (*Volverás* 12).

On the level of history, Benet's fictionalized guardianship of a sacred place can be placed within the context of Francoist ideology, particularly the Caudillo's justification for building the Valle de los Caídos. The monument was meant to be a persistent reminder to "montar la guardia fiel de aquello por lo que murieron [los caídos]" (Díaz-Plaja 309). In fact, *Volverás a región*'s title was originally *El guarda.*

On a mythological level, Región bears a strong resemblance to the sacred wood that Frazier depicts in his seminal anthropological work, *The Golden Bough.*[3] Frazier delves into the history of the priesthood of Nemi charged with protecting the cult of Diana. Nemi, in fact, bears a strong syntactical similarity to both Benet's Numa and the Latin *nemus*, meaning "wooded grove." Frazier writes, "In this sacred grove there grew a certain tree round which at any time of the day, and probably far into the night, a grim figure might be seen to prowl. In his hand he carried a drawn sword, and he kept peering warily about him as if at every instant he expected to be set upon by an enemy" (1).

The high priest of Nemi, like Franco, maintains spiritual unity by the sword. The priest of Nemi is also charged with the same task as Numa: to fight to the death with his *carabina* in order to protect the sacred tranquillity of an enclosed space.[4] Frazier writes that the king of the wood – the Rex Nemorensis – held his position until a runaway slave broke off a branch of the sacred tree.[5] "Success in the attempt entitled him to fight the priest in single combat, and if he slew him he reigned in his stead with the title of King of the Wood" (3). A similar battle for control of a sacred space occurs near the conclusion of Benet's short story "Numa (una leyenda)." Throughout the narrative, a *guarda del monte* patiently awaits the arrival of his adversarial successor, and near the end of the tale a battle ensues when a man with a covered face arrives on the scene unannounced. The mountain's guardian survives the skirmish, but the story ends on a cliffhanger as the narrator hears a "crujido de la hojarasca" without bothering to turn his head. The assumption, of course, is that the true successor of the sacred wood's guardianship has arrived and is about to ascend to the priesthood of Numa.[6]

In Frazier's work, the sacred wood is at once set apart and frequently susceptible to intrusions into its silent, immutable space. In *Volverás a Región* and in "Numa: una leyenda," both facets are recognizable. In the latter, the *guarda del monte* patrols territorial limits that were laid out before his arrival that determined "lo permitido y lo prohibido, lo afín y lo ajeno, lo propio y lo extraño" (69). In *Volverás a región*, a series of encroaching *viajeros* correspond to the runaway slave of Frazier's myth: "Raro es el año que el monte no cobra su tributo humano: ese excéntrico extranjero que llega a Región con un coche atestado de bultos y aparatos científicos o el desventurado e inconsciente cazador que por seguir un rastro o recuperar su gorra arrebatada por el viento va a toparse con esa tumba recién abierta por el anciano guardián" (9).

Numa goes to great pains to rebuff advancement towards modernity, which Benet symbolizes through the execution of a scientist. Another of the novel's *viajeros* is Marré Gamallo, who has returned to Región – hence the novel's title – with a wrinkled photograph of her lover, Luis Timoner, in an attempt to discover his whereabouts – or remains. Marré represents not a modern future but something far more insidious: a scarred and forgotten past. A preoccupation with history is beyond the scope of Región's existential horizon, as "la gente de Región han optado por olvidar su propia historia" (11); and any vehicle that enters into Región's consecrated, vitrified space is "extra-temporal" (13).[7]

Life in Región, suspended in a retrograde limbo, lacks actuality. Benet populates Región with people susceptible to anxiety attacks and disabused of notions of glory, and the antidote for fearful anxiety is to slow time to a crawl and discourage change. A description of Doctor Sebastián's clinic, where Marré arrives in search of Timoner, is a microcosm of the way that Spaniards experienced the Francoist "time of peace" every day. Sebastián's clinic had lost "actualidad, como esa casa del héroe que convertida en museo y defendida por un cordón de seda es conservada en el mismo estado en que la dejó" (119). The banality of profane time – symbolized by the doctor's study – is contrasted with a ritual of death that the town witnesses each time a newcomer arrives. "Un par de veces cada década el vecino arruinado de Región, de Bocentellas, o de El Salvador, despierta de su siesta ... para observar la nube de polvo en el horizonte de un camino" (13). With Numa as a protector who rebuffs change, the inhabitant of Región experiences the profane time between ritual killings as though it were protracted and sluggish. Thus the narrator notes that in comparison with other areas of the peninsula, Región moved "a un ritmo más lento" (75).

Randolph Pope has argued that a Bergsonian philosophy of change strongly informs Benet's fiction, which opposes vital energy to "the resistance offered by the body and the inertia of all matter" (115). In *Volverás a región*, Numa – who has never been seen and whose existence has never been scientifically proven – is nevertheless a required component of the collective imaginary of a lethargic people whose fears and pent-up energy need release in order to maintain the status quo. When a motor is heard on the horizon, signalling a potential infringement upon Región's hallowed space, the town congregates in the church of an abandoned town near the Mantuan forest in order to wait for "ese momento en el que los cautivos congregados para emprender un viaje común deciden … desentenderse de sus inquietudes para entregarse al descanso – el sonido del disparo llega envuelto" (14). The narrator portrays the celebration of Numa's homicides as an expulsion of vital, anxious energy to maintain a stasis resistant to historical movement. The forward compulsion of violent energy is a submerged force akin to the potential eruption of violence, which Doctor Sebastián notes is "un estado latente … que puede ponerse en erupción en cualquier momento" (126).

Granting Numa the power of homicide controls the unpredictable latency of death in Región and assures that the indifferent, sedentary nature of profane time is never unpredictably altered. The inhabitants of Región, prior to the Civil War, "llevaban mucho tiempo viviendo en emulsión: un rencor disimulado y diferido" (180). Memory, for Benet, unconsciously stores a hatred that is directly attributable to particular offences or individual relationships. Memory simply "atesora el rencor y, cuando actualiza, no busca lo que el alma guarda sino aquel sentimiento que, tras la expansión, la vuelva a llenar de cólera o coraje" (181–2). Like an inflatable balloon, memory stores rancour to a limit point that precipitates an explosion if there is no other form of release. Numa is normally the escape valve for rancour and the agent that maintains the emulsion that defines life in Región. The collective desire for violence is thus only "frenado por un guarda forestal viejo y mudo, encarnación de una voluntad que duerme a la intemperie … Pero al solo anuncio de la guerra civil la emulsión se rompe y las neutras partículas de la memoria cobran de súbito una forma y coloración violentas" (180–1). Benet's adoption of scientific discourse here works as an ideal metaphor for the deferral and ritual expulsion of violence. When the atoms of Región's emulsified social life are neutral, time decelerates and acquires the same properties of a dense, heavy neutron whose ionic movement nearly stops as absolute zero is neared. When the emulsion is broken, however, the particles become positively charged ions whose movements produce hot electrical charges. Numa's responsibility, therefore, is to ensure that the atomic social life of Región maintains a balanced, neutral charge.

The conception of rancour developed in the novel, and the way its expulsion by Numa's shots is directed at an innocent outsider, calls to mind Nietzsche's theory of *ressentiment,* a connection that has yet to be critically made.[8] The notion of rancour, of course, also references the *rencor insaciable* of Spain's enemies, a popular Francoist cliché. In *Volverás*, rancour is less a quantitative substance than an infectious condition that defines the way that each inhabitant of Región relates to the outside world. For Nietzsche, in turn, *ressentiment* creates a morality where negation becomes a creative deed through the steadfast refusal of "what is 'outside,' what is 'different,' what is 'not itself'; and *this* No is its creative deed" (*Genealogy of Morals* 36). *Ressentiment,* however, is not simply an adverse reaction to ideas or actions that contrast with an indigenous belief structure. Rather, it is a condition that hinges on scapegoating those in a more noble position, deflecting an awareness of a debased, insufficient self. "What is outside" or "what is different" is thus given evil connotations ipso facto; it is "a demand of strength that it should *not* express itself as strength" (45). *Ressentiment* functions only by viewing morality as relative, where the concepts of "superiority" and "inferiority" are fluid and determined by particular circumstances. By viewing what is superior as inferior, a consciousness full of rancorous *ressentiment* never feels compelled to ascend to a higher critical position and improve upon its weakness. In the third part of *Volverás*, the narrator attaches a strikingly similar attitude to Doctor Sebastián: "Hay una clase de deber que sólo se puede amortizar con despecho, el sacrificio no basta" (255). Progress, and the substantial change of condition that modernity represents, will always be impossible in Región as long as spite and rancour exist. As Doctor Sebastián notes, a "pasión anacrónica" allows only a progression of "ingenuidad." Real progress enters the picture only if one believes in "el fin del rencor" (219). *Ressentiment* depends on a false consciousness whereby an actor earnestly believes that his or her inferior condition is preferable to what the hostile external world presents, and it is this ingenuousness that constitutes the "enfermedad" (222) that insistently follows Región's citizenry.[9]

Syntactically, the name "Numa" also bears an uncanny resemblance to *nomos*, a term adopted by sociologists and political theorists, like Carl Schmitt, to denote the rules and regulations imposed from above in order to dictate everyday behaviour. Región's periodic congregation in and around a church belfry to witness shots of lawgiving violence also brings to mind another possible historical reference: Numa Pompilius, successor to the first king of Rome, Romulus. Numa Pompilius both founded Roman religion and legislated a law against homicide (Gaughan 329). Labanyi, in her excellent interpretation of Benet's deconstruction of myth, notes that using the name "Numa" in lieu of "Nemi" "has the advantage of linking the keeper of the sacred grove with the attributes for which King Numa was renowned: notably his championship of law and order" (96). Being responsible for law and order, however, also confers onto Numa, and any other sovereign leader, the power to issue executive orders suspending the rules. Thus Agamben specifically points out that Numa Pompilius's law against homicide is linked to *homo sacer*'s ability to be killed through the sovereign exception of kingly power in Roman law (*Homo Sacer* 85).

In Benet's novel, Numa is the result of a total transference of the people's vital energy into the person of a single guardian with the power to both impose order *and* decide on sovereign exception. This signifies that Numa, more than a mere "image of the theocratic state" (Labanyi 96), is an incarnation of sovereignty more generally. It is Numa, in the words of Lefebvre, who constitutes a space through violence, thereby crushing time. He moreover controls the constitution of everyday behaviour in Región and has the ability to classify an intruder as a *viajero*, thereby sanctioning a disruption of tranquillity. Both Numa's regard and disregard for the *nomos* of Región has profound consequences for social behaviour. To Benet, memory is the deposit place for hatred and repressed moments of failed hope and illusion. Numa can fail to keep the violent globules within Región's social emulsion suspended, thereby releasing the rancour stored in memory by allowing "la piedra" covering "un hormiguero" to be lifted. At this point, the inhabitant of Región "no sabe hacer otra cosa que correr en contradictorio frenesí, sin otra protección entre el cielo y la colonia que el miedo mutuo" (181). Numa's failure to order social activity disengages the predictable expectations of profane time. The habits of everyday existence are thus lost in a frenetic explosion of lawlessness – an uncontrollable ionic movement. The Civil War is one such explosion, and in Spain's contradictory *frenesí* what lacked was a "principio de conducta" (181). Borrowing a concept developed by Peter Berger, Numa relates to society as a "nomizing" imposition of order. Because humankind lacks "ordering mechanisms," a "nomos is imposed upon the discrete experiences and meanings of individuals" (Berger 19). As a sovereign force, however, Numa can also undo the metaphysical framework that confers meaning onto individual acts. Once Numa has lifted the stone covering the anthill's enclosure, murder also loses its power as a rite to extinguish pent-up violence. In Región, homicide is a mechanism integral to a social ordering, but in a *contradictorio frenesí* it loses its nomizing effect until the town's positively charged ions lose their electrical force and the collective thrust of *rencor* dissipates.

Criticism has at turns linked Numa specifically to the Franco dictatorship (Durán 202), classified him as a "fiction within a fiction" that is created "in an effort to shun nature" (Summerhill 52), and a guarantor of "narrative ambiguity and mystery" (Herzberger 155). In a sense, all of the above are correct.

Herzberger links the uncertainty of Numa's origin and identity to Todorov's theory of the fantastic and the structural import of enigma. What is certainly not ambiguous and enigmatic about Numa is his function – as Martínez Sarrión notes, Numa "se encarga de mantener una paz que, por sus métodos, no puede ser más decisiva, injusta, y «ruin»" (120). Región's history of intrigue and battles is indeed cloaked in mystery, in part because of the collective decision to forget the past. Numa's responsibilities as guardian, however, are blatantly evident. When a far-off motor is heard on the Macerta highway approaching Región, everyone instinctively knows to ritually congregate in the church to await the shot that is certain to come.

Franco's conception of himself as a sovereign priest anointed by God to oversee the protection of Spain's *unidad espiritual* hints at Ernst Kantorowicz's notion of the king's two bodies: one a metaphysical placeholder of sovereignty and the other kingship's temporary human occupant. Similarly, in "Numa (una leyenda)," the term "Numa" refers to the *corpus mysticum* of the Mantuan forest while the *guarda* serves as a *corpus naturale*. On the mountain, every event is "predeterminado por el numen que celaba la preservación de la propiedad" (92). The guardian, meanwhile, is only a temporary caretaker susceptible to the finitude of human existence. Once his adversary arrives, the guardian's death will be "el último acto de servicio de una carrera tan dilatada que ... debía clausurarse con un acontecimiento saturado de novedades y inéditas experiencias" (92). The mountain's noumenon is a metaphysical structure of power that prescribes a particular mode of existence, which is normally free of *novedades* and *inéditas experiencias*, but is ritually punctuated by an internecine violence – because all holders of Numa's priestly office belong to the same accursed race – that results in the transfer of power. In other words, Numa is a nomizing force, ordering society in such a way that novelties and unforeseen circumstances are impossible to realize. The finitude of the human body requires a transferal of power from one guardian to the next, symbolized by Benet's adversarial fight to the death at the conclusion of "Numa (una leyenda)," but the mystical placeholder of sovereignty – Numa – never wavers.

Returning to Durán's point, Numa does indeed apply to Franco, but he also refers diachronically to a long history of similar iterations of sovereignty along the vector of Spanish history that link the Caudillo, Felipe V, the *Reyes Católicos*, and others to *la unidad espiritual* of the nation. On a synchronic level, the consolidation of power within an authoritarian, centralizing leader such as Franco relies on the repetition of sovereignty in all corners of the state. In that respect, sovereign power extends from a single point as though it were a pyramid with a variety of surrogate *corpus naturales* stepping in for the absent leader in a repetition of his model of guardianship. For that reason, Numa is a structural myth that can be tailored, morphologically, to each individual within Región. Thus, the narrator of *Volverás a Región* posits that Numa might be an erstwhile Carlist soldier or a monk hiding out in the forest, for example. For Doctor Sebastián, it might be his mother firing those shots (144); for Marré, a number of figures have exercised over her "el peso de su desmedida censura" (276), including Adela, a member of the Región Comité de Defensa, and the innkeeper Muerte. Epps, furthermore, insinuates a link between Numa and Marré's absentee father (57).

Few critics have explored the crushing effect on time that a belief in Numa solicits. Doctor Sebastián, hypothesizing the connection between his mother and Numa, murmurs to Marré that the guardian's sovereign violence "no era una venganza sino la reanudación del ciclo crónico, la fiesta saturnal de una menta arcaica que exigía el *regressus ad uterum* para borrar los errores y descarríos de la edad presente" (144). A *regressus ad uterum*, which calls to mind Julián's excavation of *La Cava*'s vagina, mirrors the *in illo tempore* moment typical of Francoist temporality and the Caudillo's insistence on suspended moments of national purification that *la espada* guards against profanation. Thus Sebastían confers onto Numa's shots the value of a rite that can be defined as a return to sacred time – an instant homologized to eternity that resets the march of history after a period of adulterating profanation.

Another Bergsonian contribution to Benet's novel is precisely how memory functions as the nexus point between external reality and inner time. Fraser's important work on Bergsonian influence in Spain gives ample space to Benet, in particular the relational aspect of recollection in *Volverás a región*: "Memory in Benet's works is the starting point for the novelistic articulation of a nuanced philosophical approach to life in all of its temporal complexity" (122–3). In a locale such as Región, where every effort is made to stretch out the rhythm of time, the concept of duration – pure change – is frightening to people who are horrified that the "material world … is going to disintegrate, and the mind will drown in the torrent-like flow of things" (Bergson, *Creative Mind* 125). Fraser posits that space tends to be "enfolded" by time in Región, and a static description of the landscape in the first section of the novel slowly gives way to a transmutation of the external world later in the work through the introduction of multiple narrative voices (128).

Though cogent, this analysis leaves aside the resetting effect of Numa's murders, which prevents rancour from being stored up in memory that would otherwise break the temporal stasis. The rhythm that each narrator of *Volverás a región* stores up rancour may eventually transmute each person's perception of space, but the *regressus ad uterum* brought about each time Numa murders an outsider returns profane time back to zero and resets the fixed, static space described in the first section of the novel. For this reason, Labanyi (97) is quite right in arguing that regeneration is absent from Numa's mythical world. Región's homicidal ritual refuses spiritual vivification in favour of an anachronistic impulse aimed at the dispersion of anxiety. Sacred time, in other words, is regenerative only in the sense that it cyclically reproduces a moment of absolute depravity. This "resets" our own discussion back to Nietzsche, whose *ressentiment* is creative, indeed regenerative, only in its steadfast negation of difference. Benet's novel in fact concludes with such a resetting of time, as it is assumed that a far-off shot does away with Marré Gamallo, returning the reader to the opening setting of the work – a *regressus ad uterum*: "el viajero saliendo de Región" (7). Instead of directly confronting their own debasement and insecurity towards change, the inhabitants of Región ritually project *ressentiment* onto a *viajero*-scapegoat recently arrived from the external world. *Ressentiment* is thus the sickness that slowly infects anyone who spends ample time in Región, and "el Numa no es más que el pródromo" (222) of the disease. Numa is a symptom, and not a root cause, because he embodies the reactionary, infectious morality of *ressentiment* that Región's sick collective consciousness gives life. Naturally, Nietzsche treats *ressentiment* as though it were a poison (39).[10]

Labanyi has argued that Benet's novel disintegrates the separation between linear time and the mythical because both terms "attempt to repeat a lost past" (126). Lévi-Strauss's stance on myth, which in Labanyi's analysis "employs a historical linear sequence only to negate it through the use of repetition" (126), holds true only, however, in reference to Numa's ritual homicides. Interpolating linear time with repetition mirrors the dialectic between sacred and profane time, and Numa maintains his mythical ledger register only by being the agent by which the past, as a register of pain, remains irretrievably lost. Numa maintains a firm grip on the stone covering memory's rancorous anthill, signifying that on at least one level the novel refuses to erode the distinction between the linear movement of profane time and the *regressus ad uterum* that expels an anxiety brought about by the recollection of banished dreams and failure. The guardian is thus "la ficción de un movimiento abortado" (95), a legend whose presence is produced by expulsion – a creative "No."

Roland Barthes theorized that all myths are signifiers composed of two parts: a full plenitude of meaning and an empty form that invites the application of concepts. It is in the latter component, the application of a concept, that the myth merges with a singular historical moment. Thus the symbolic meaning of a myth is impoverished by the arrival of a "fully armed" concept (*Mythologies* 118). In chapter 4 of this book, Juan Goytisolo's use of the Conde Julián myth feeds off Alfonso el Sabio's biography of the eighth-century Count of Ceuta in order to empower a concept that destroys Spain's sacred forms, especially those exploited by the Francoist dictatorship in its imagining of Castilian identity. The principle function of the mythic concept is thus, in Barthes's words, "to be *appropriated* ...

the concept closely corresponds to a function, it is defined as a tendency" (119). Numa, as a myth propagated by all classes of Región's inhabitants, has his own biographical history – Frazier's *Sacred Bough*, Numa Pompilius, etc. – and also a fully armed function that impoverishes his historical concreteness. On this point, it is again critical to call to mind Summerhill's assertion that Numa is a "fiction within a fiction," and Labanyi's essential analysis of myth in the novel. Labanyi persuasively argues that the Nationalists, the older Republicans such as Doctor Sebastián, and the young idealists like Gamallo, assign to Numa different mythic concepts that all feed off – or impoverish – the myth's original signifier related to the lawful guardianship of a sacred space. "The Nationalists correspond to the custodians of the boundary, the Republicans (at least the younger ones) to the transgressors" (103), and the older liberals depend on Numa's aborted past to shield their lost hopes from view.

Numa is therefore a collective projection – a hypostatic reflection of society. The role of guardian – the *corpus naturale* linked to Numa as mystical placeholder – whether occupied by Franco or any other dominating figure, acquires symbolic capital by ideologically conforming to the metaphysical projection of a political self-imagining. Antonio Machado's dictum about the causal relationship between an epoch's metaphysics and *lo humano* conforms to Numa being "la fórmula que describe (y justifica) la composición del residuo de un cuerpo del que se sublimaron todos los deseos" (Benet, *Volverás* 221). Numa is a formula that extracts passion from the body; the residue that remains, and its placement within the ionic stasis of a society discharged of vital energy, is both justified and discursively legitimated by the myth of the guardian's metaphysical existence. Barthes, of course, links mythic rhetoric to historical discourse, which is an ideological elaboration where "the referent is aimed for as something external to the discourse, without it ever being possible to attain it outside this discourse" ("Discourse" 17–18). In Región, Numa is spoken of as though he were a signified existing beyond discourse in the Mantuan woods, but is in fact an a priori synthetic judgment whose existence cannot be empirically judged. Discourse itself becomes an ideological elaboration that determines the behaviour and subjection of anyone who utters Numa's name, a classic instance of the Lacanian symbolic order in action. Numa, as a myth, is a mode of semiotic communication, with a truth-value found not beyond language but in signification itself. Mythic meaning thus produces social facts, and not vice versa.

Benet assigns to Numa a religious function produced by a collective experience of fear. Labanyi links this to Frazier's thought (101), but I believe that Marett's elaboration of "mana" and Otto's theory of the numinous also enrich an understanding of the novel. In *El ángel del Señor abandona a Tobías*, an ekphrasis of the Rembrandt painting by the same name, Benet argues that religion is a defence against the powerful and unknown, two terms that are imbued with "mana" (104). Marett, like Frazier, argues that the term *mana*, as employed by the Melanesians, has no set meaning and stands simply for "any power that rests in whatever way upon the divine" (58). Marett diverges from Frazier in locating the origin of *mana* within individual consciousness – in "the inward experience that goes with the exercise of developed magic" (60). This stance is significant, as it presupposes that humankind is hard-wired for the sacred. Benet seems to follow this presupposition in his placement of "temor" at the heart of rationalizing religion. Because the holy is a site of pure power and unknowable mystery, humankind ritualizes religion to distance God's horror. This movement, according to Benet, is a "desviación del instinto primario y su transformación en una práctica para la cura de las almas" (102–3). In other words, religion is like all mythic thought: God is a referent located external to discourse, but without an existence verifiable outside that discourse.[11]

Rudolf Otto's theory of the numinous, a term that he extracts from the Roman numen, also presupposes that the awakening of an irrational *mysterium tremendum* within consciousness is a prelude to the rationalizing of organized religion. It is worth recalling that in "Numa (una leyenda)," Benet describes a numen that spiritually guards the mountain, which I theorized as a kind of *corpus mysticum.* Otto argues that the numinous is a "creature-consciousness" that an overwhelming encounter with the physical world awakens within the self, causing a "note of self-abasement into nothingness before an overpowering, absolute might of some kind" (10). Otto posits that humans deflect this primary instinct outside of the self and thus think of the numinous "as objective" (11). The predominance of "temor" throughout *Volverás a región*, in addition to the feelings of rancorous debasement before a numinous entity, show a clear kinship between Otto and Benet. Both thinkers also consider this primary instinct to be purely irrational and the original impulse behind the creation of religion and/or myth. Otto compares the relationship of religion's rational and irrational components to the weaving of a loom, which introduces a "moralization of the numinous" (115). In *Volverás a región*, Doctor Sebastián likewise begs Marré to not consider Numa as a "superstición; no es el capricho de una naturaleza ni el resultado de una guerra civil; quizá todo el organizado proceso de una religión, unido al crecimiento, desemboca forzosamente en ello" (221–2). On this point, Benet firmly reiterates that Numa's existence is not accidental, nor is it attributable to a single historical event; rather, the instinctual "temor" that all classes of individuals share produces a myth whose conceptual form maintains the social organization of the status quo.

The secular notion of sovereignty, particularly its manifestation in totalitarian societies, profits from a similar inculcation of fear and fascination within the enclosed space of a single individual. In Engels's words, "The essence of the state, as that of religion, is mankind's fear of itself" (qtd in Schmitt, *Political Theology* 51). From a very different philosophical perspective, Benet shares with Joan Sales, who posits an existential need for religious belief in political imagination, the notion that the sacred underpinnings of modern secularity persist because of the very structure of human consciousness. Benet's Numa thus perfectly novelizes the deviation of fear from the individual into a collective ritual around a series of *corpus naturales* – such as Franco.

Carl Schmitt, beyond his thought on nomos, sees sacred practice at the core of all significant concepts of the modern theory of the state, where "the omnipotent God became the omnipotent lawgiver" (*Political Theology* 36). The modern state, of course, shields its sacred underpinnings from view. In *Volverás a región*, however, Benet depicts a society where the transition from omnipotent God to omnipotent lawgiver is ongoing, and the sacred core of the secular modern state is also opened up to investigation. The dialectic of sacred and profane time in the novel draws attention to Numa's lawgiving nature *and* the religious cult built up around his homicidal violence. Crushing time into an instant homologized to eternity allows a *regressus ad uterum* to the moment where secularity takes leave of the theological, all the while maintaining key components of sacred imagining.

Killing Time: Ritual Death and the Origin of the Sacred

The only thing that interests me now
is the problem of circumventing the machine,
learning if the inevitable admits a loophole.

Albert Camus, *The Stranger*

In Mercè Rodoreda's novel *La mort i la primavera*, a clock atop a slaughterhouse bell tower and a sundial, the only means of telling time in the village, are without hands or style. This absence of what Henri Bergson calls "mathematical time" – time that can be measured, especially through modern apparatuses – reflects the hyper-awareness of sacred ritual in the life-world of the novel. Previously, I analyzed the periodic collapse of mathematical time into sacred ritual in Juan Benet's work. In *La mort i la primavera*, nearly all time is sacred time, with a regimented series of unending rituals providing the principal thrust of the novel's movement.[12] In such an environment, I will argue that there are no structural conditions propitious for deification and the institution of nomizing sovereignty. However, the novel depicts a society at an evolutionary crossroads in which a collective mythic consciousness is slowly gaining force, signalling that its non-metaphysical godless culture and purely sacred time are on the verge of transformation. In addition, at the conclusion of the narrative, the protagonist commits suicide and is phantasmagorically transported to an elevated position above the village. From a locus beyond society's myths and rituals, perception of the empirical world loses immanent meaning, acutely demonstrating the fundamental role that imaginative discourse and explanatory narratives exert in assigning truth-values to reality. The narrator ultimately discovers that an absolutely profane space is as stifling as a milieu awash in the circularity of sacred time, pointing towards the impossibility of banishing repetition and ritual from the linear march of secular history.

Rodoreda originally submitted the novel to the Premi de Sant Jordi competition in 1961, prior to the publication of *La plaça del diamant*, which itself was the runner-up for the award the previous year in 1960 under the title *Colometa*. In the two years following the competition, Rodoreda substantially revised the manuscript, adding characters and additional points of view.[13] In October 1963, Rodoreda wrote to her editor, Joan Sales, that "de moment he plantat *La mort i la primavera*. Ja xerro massa" (qtd in Arnau, *La mort i la primavera* 11). For nearly twenty years, *La mort i la primavera* sat unpublished before being resuscitated in the late 1970s, a few years prior to Rodoreda's death from liver cancer in 1983. Sales died later the same year. The arduous work of posthumous publication fell to Sales's widow, Núria Folch, who edited and released the different versions of the text in 1986.[14] Carme Arnau published the first critical edition of *La mort i la primavera* in 1997, yet the novel, perhaps Rodoreda's most complex and disconcerting work, has received surprisingly little scholarly attention.

At some point in the early 1960s, Rodoreda attached four unfinished fragments to the end of the novel in which the post-mortem narrator, having committed suicide, aims to recount his personal narrative free from the strictures of social customs. As I mentioned, in lieu of narrating his life history, however, the protagonist finds himself within an empty, de-historicized space where narration of the past is made impossible because of his absolute disengagement from social rituals. What ensues, in a fragment labelled as the eighth chapter of the final section of the novel, is a stream of consciousness articulated through a lengthy run-on sentence. The novel thus presents a startling separation of two spheres that normally share a dialectical relationship: on one hand, the plenitude of the village's sacred time, and on the other the entirely profane post-mortem state of the narrator. Both realms of Being are equally incarcerating, as post-mortem freedom becomes yet another form of entrapment.

Pérez classifies *La mort i la primavera* as atemporal and ambiguous in the historical time of its emplotment (183). A bevy of rituals and mechanical responses, most of which correspond to the cycle of seasons, also fend off destruction and change in the novel. The most notable example is the casting of a sacrificial scapegoat into a subterranean river underneath the village, but the entire world of the text revolves around other idiosyncratic practices, such as the locking up of children in small cabinets while the adults parade in a burial procession to a nearby forest. After the funeral rites, everyone celebrates by lighting bonfires in the stables and sacrificing pregnant horses, which are eaten, with their fetuses, in a communal meal. Other practices include culling red dust from nearby caves and painting the village's houses red every spring, killing the townspeople before they succumb to natural causes or old age, and entombing the deceased in trees with cement placed in their mouths to prevent their souls from escaping. That the souls of the deceased are precluded from an independent existence outside of the body signals a resistance to metaphysics, in which God, time, and other unchangeable "first causes" are either non-existent or being elaborated. In any event, the community is forever decaying and rebirthing, but the populace believes the decay and rebirth are always the same ahistorical repetition, a dynamic mirrored in the narrator's perception of the river that flows under the settlement: "l'aigua que venia feia la mateixa olor que l'aigua enduta. Igual, sempre igual" (81).

The ritual casting of a scapegoat underneath the village every spring reflects how the sacralization of space translates into a conception of atemporality that precludes linear advancement. The underground river is a malevolent force that threatens the community's very existence, which is apparent every spring as mountain runoff dangerously swells the water levels and threatens to flood the village. As a constant flow, the river ought to perfectly reflect, metaphorically, Henri Bergson's definition of *durée*. *Durée*, or pure change, is for Bergson the only true temporal reality and is the polar opposite of the artificiality of mathematical time. However, the narrator conceptualizes the river as a circular movement whose repetition is predictable – the water is "igual, sempre igual." The river is metaphorically inflected with a sense of stasis rather than pure change through the repeated spectacle of ritual every spring, demonstrating how a fetishization of sacred space translates into a circular marker, linked to a season, that is similarly set apart and respected. Not surprisingly, Eliade's notion of a sacred time homologized to eternity springs forth from the narrator's contact with the river: "Passava i passava la mà per damunt de la roca envescada i l'aigua feia onades grasses contra la roca i em gronxaven. Em va semblar que no hi havia temps, vull dir que el temps no era enlloc" (135).[15]

This sense of timelessness invades all sectors of the novel, including the mountain split into two, the adjoining forest of the dead, and the nearby caves from which the villagers cull red dust. Each space is linked to a ritual, which collapses the village's possibility of experiencing linear time into a long series of periodic reiterations. Returning to Lefebvre, this setting reflects a crushed time dominated by circularity and repetition. The novel does indeed reflect, in this respect, Bergson's *durée* through the total absence of a division between the past and the present in the mind of its characters. For Bergson, pure duration is "the form which the succession of our conscious states assumes when our ego lets itself *live,* when it refrains from separating its present state from its former states" (*Time and Free Will* 100).

Pérez continues that the village's refusal to mark time, alongside its destruction of the sundial and clock, indicates "an effort to halt or disguise the inexorable march of time toward the horror that is death" (181). The village's ritualistic and sacrificial rhythms, however, signal a distinct regularity of collective activity, meaning that time understood as a pure *durée*, where the past and present manifestations of consciousness are not separated, is on the verge of becoming historical. *La mort i la primavera*'s life-world may be a circular stream of repetition, but it is also broken up by a series of immobilities that are each linked to sacred ritual and tied to the passing of temporal seasons: the houses are painted red and a scapegoat is thrown into the river every spring. The Western calendar and its hourly and monthly configuration encourage the same repetition that only a running counter of years progressively advances.

Through her conceptualization of the physical space of the novel, Rodoreda also outlines the process by which the numinal character of the sacred precedes rationalization. Returning to Otto's thought, the numinous is a primary instinct that occurs before, but gives impetus to, the collective rationalization of myth and ritual. In *La mort i la primavera*, Rodoreda especially endows the subterranean river with a prima facie sentiment of fear and overwhelming power. In the fourth part of the novel, the narrator-protagonist is chosen as a sacrificial scapegoat and forced to traverse the river. While being battered against rocks and other detritus by the water's flow, the protagonist shifts his focus to a period earlier in his life, where the narrative begins, in which he is playing in the water just prior to seeing his father commit suicide in the adjoining forest of the dead. With the water rushing past, the protagonist's feet freeze, and "a dintre del pit m'hi va néixer una cosa dolenta: com si tingués un grop al mig del pit i en aquest grop s'hi arrapés la por de viure i la por de la gent i la por de tot el que no es coneix" (136). As I noted previously in connection to Benet, the admixture of horror and fear of the unknown, which is projected onto an external object, is known as "mana" by Marett and is the birth of the numinous in Otto's work. In this scene, the town's river elicits an ambivalent and sublime *mysterium tremendum* where fear and fascination intertwine.[16] Of particular note is the introduction of repetition to the second primary scene in which the narrator comes into contact with the river. When cast under the village, the narrator reaffirms that the water is "igual, sempre igual" by equating his own status as the victimized protagonist of religious ritual to his father's efforts to step beyond the strict regulation of quotidian existence through suicide. After surviving the trip beneath the village, the narrator resorts to the same escape mechanism. The father-son repetition in this case mimics the eternal present of the river: the violence "és igual, sempre igual." Thus, the division between past and present fades as the circularity of time "crushes all differences" between them, to borrow from my earlier citation of Henri Lefebvre.

This scene, which serves as the novel's bookends, harkens back to an epigraph to the text attributed to Rodoreda herself: "el misteri d'aquest pes que porto a dintre i que no em deixa respirar." In other works by Rodoreda, this sentiment would be unerringly and unproblematically linked to mystic exaltation: a metaphysical harmony beyond the novel's mirror-like reflection that exchanges realism for a closing of the space between perception and memory, between epistemological object and the self. In the prologue to *Mirall trencat,* Rodoreda notes that "darrera del mirall hi ha el somni; tots voldríem atènyer el somni, que és la nostra més profunda realitat" (21).[17] In *La mort i la primavera,* there is no room for dreaming within the highly regulated space of sacred time, where every movement corresponds to a ritual and life takes the form of a long tautology. As I will soon discuss, the society depicted in *La mort i la primavera* exists at a point where God and metaphysical thinking are just arriving on the scene. In Otto's words, Rodoreda's people have yet to totally intertwine the rational and irrational elements that constitute the holy.

As an ambivalent force that acts beyond the structures of human reason and logic, the river, as the catalyst for the numinous, resembles what precedes the sacred and might be thought of as the holy reduced of its ethical and rational elements. The numinous, Otto stresses, is a primordial religious feeling that precedes rational comprehension and is aroused at particular junctures. In *La mort i la primavera,* the *mysterium tremendum* of the numinous maintains a recalcitrant connection to materiality, which invites a number of questions: What is beyond the physical and how to explain the inexplicable? What is the origin of social order and its cosmological reference points? The novel may be a mirror held up to reality, but when reality is experienced as a noumenal phenomenon that exceeds rational thought, cognition is displaced into a mythical dreamworld that exists within discourse and the imagination. The ontic surges from the material world, but it is entirely resistant to rational confirmation and is therefore an immeasurable presence, much like Benet's Numa.

Otto stresses that the non-rational experience of numinous dread and fascination inevitably undergoes permutation with mythological or theological explanation. The numinous possesses a valence where an originally inexplicable sentiment soon attracts and appropriates "meanings derived from social and individual ideals of obligation, justice, and goodness" (Otto 114). In Benet's fiction, the moralization of numinous feeling creates *rencor,* a modality of Being treated as an ideal by the inhabitants of Región. In *La mort i la primavera,* the initial moments of mythic moralization are visible and use physical space as their point of departure. In this case, both the river and its placement next to a mountain split into two are essential: these entities elicit the overpowering affect that invites fictitious explanatory narratives. It is only natural, then, that the novel details the development of the village's founding myth, which begins with a geographical point of departure that the villagers then garnish with rationalizations.

Conceivably, this process begins with a feeling of a *mysterium tremendum* similar to what the narrator experiences when bathing in the river at the beginning of the novel. Whoever first settled in the village witnessed the marvellous sight of a tremendous river plunging into the ground in the shade of a mountain that appears split into two. Initially, the protagonist explains the town's founding site as a *baixada* where man found himself intertwined with a mountain's shadow: "I l'home amb l'ombra a la vora, va plantar la primera glicina" (36). This foundational fiction is then quickly expanded by "el vell més vell del poble" who "havia vist el naixement del tot. El poble havia nascut d'un gran malestar de la terra. I la muntanya s'havia partit i havia caigut damunt del riu, estesa" (36). The river, having been thrown throughout the countryside in the mountain's toppling, returns to its rightful place with a furious burrowing into the rock. The village, corrects *el més vell del poble*, was therefore founded "no al fons d'una baixada, sinó damunt de la terra i de les pedres estimbades, una nit la lluna hi va deixar dues ombres que van ajuntar-se per la boca" (36). Later in the novel, a man referred to as "el senyor," who lives atop a precipice overlooking the village and has an urgent desire to see the place destroyed in order to avoid being murdered and buried in the forest of the dead, adds still more wrinkles to the story: "El primer home que havia fet el poble, va matar la serp a dalt de la muntanya, i la va rebotre … la va rebotre contra la muntanya i la muntanya es fa partir … era un home que ja era mort" (111). Rodoreda's tracking of such a variegated narrative appears torn from the pages of Lévi-Strauss or Aby Warburg, suggesting that the novel offers an implicit science of how a society begins to construct a cosmological metaphysics. Each subsequent iteration of the story raises the level of the fantastic, which then requires further elaboration and disguising from memory the simple feeling of the numinous that gave birth to the entire exercise. As with any entrenchment of myth, however, there remains a preoccupation with maintaining a generational link to origins. Authority, in the second variant of the myth, is given to the oldest man in the village, whereas *el senyor* derives exegetical know-how by claiming to be a direct scion of the village's founder. Neither of the two, however, bears the symbolic capital necessary to completely consecrate any one narrative and shield the competing myths from memory.

Otto reiteratively emphasizes that even the most fantastic assertions embodied within mythological and theological fictions exhibit the mark of rationality by simply being communicatively graspable and analyzable by human intellect. In Barthes's terms, this mark of rationality is the true reality of the holy, as it exists only within discourse. Indeed any collective organized around the sacred would be unable to define itself as such, and mark for itself a definitive beginning, if such rationalizations of the numinous were not in fact intelligible to a wide swathe of human consciousness. An event external to consciousness awakens the numinous, but the myths and fictions that follow reside solely within discourse.

In light of the studies that document the passage from the numinous to the creation of an elaborate and stultified theological doctrine, we can place Rodoreda's small sliver of humanity along an interstitial point. Cortés i Orts rightly characterizes the novel's religions as godless in the sense that the appearance of a deity, if one follows the work of Durkheim, Girard, and Freud, is a later development stemming from the totemic deification of a slaughtered leader or other sacrificial victims. In order for such a deification to occur, feelings of the numinous must be exported from the body politic and inserted into the putative existence of an ancestral soul. The social collective in *La mort i la primavera* certainly folds into its rituals activities that produce such victims, but without the presence of an authoritarian, patriarchal figure regulating the process. The refusal to let the souls of its dead escape is a crucial deterrent of such totemization, as Durkheim notes: "The totem, like the ancestor, is the soul of the individual, but externalized and invested with powers superior to those it is thought to possess inside the body" (207).

Rodoreda's small slice of humanity cannot produce a sacred institution of supreme authority, such as what one finds in *Conde Julián*, without an oppressive fatherly figure who hoards for himself power and the instruments of violence and whose murder would set in motion the totemic deification that leads to the bifurcation of sovereignty: the *corpus mysticum* and *naturale*. Totemic deification, in other words, gives birth to a metaphysical sphere, beyond the finite empirical world, in which a mystical placeholder of authority eternally corresponds to whoever occupies the role of guardian below in the natural world, à la Numa and the *monte*'s guardians. The novel certainly portrays several paternal relationships – that of the protagonist, the *ferrater* and his son, and so on – but the father figures never possess the ambivalent combination of authoritarian power and affection that would both elicit murder and instil guilt thereafter. This murder, if one follows Freud, is essential in the creation of law.

Freud argues that the creation of a totem refers to a particularly traumatic event: the primal horde's assassination of the father, who hoarded power, sex, and wealth for only himself. The initial hatred for the father figure, which results in his murder, over time transforms into longing and feelings of guilt among the remaining brothers of the horde. To display reverence and allay a sense of guilt, the father is resurrected as a totemic animal and imbued with "everything that a childish imagination may expect from a father – protection, care and indulgence" (*Totem* 144). Freud calls this phenomenon "deferred obedience" and sees in it the underpinnings of the Oedipus complex. Displacing the father onto an animal ultimately was compelled by the brothers' desire to identity with – and later repeat – the prohibitions of the father. In the end, totemic thought suggests a profound ambivalence towards a seminally violent event. The sacrifice of the totemic animal first repeated the brothers' triumph and subsequent birth of society, and second worshiped the father's memory by reaffirming his prohibitions and structure of power. Through such things as myth and dreamwork, a religious group's origins are distorted and made to appear supernatural, yet the images, prohibitions, and qualities associated with the totems survive in religious practice and continue to be a sustained fidelity to the originally traumatic event. A collective attempt to deny the event its historical reality becomes increasingly transparent as religious culture develops. The replacement of a totemic animal with deities formed in the image of human beings in later religious development is, according to Freud, "the most extreme denial of the great crime which was the beginning of society and of the sense of guilt" (150).

In *La mort i la primavera*, a stable of horses – the closest thing to a totemic animal in the work – is ready to symbolize the mythical resurrection of a slain primal father. These horses are the village's only valuable possession and are already integrated into a sacrificial ritual, as the females and their fetuses are eaten on burial days. However, the victims chosen to traverse the subterranean river are always selected at random, and Freud implies that a post-mortem deification is the result of a purposeful murder directed at a singular figure. The Freudian notion of deferred obedience, and the slow disfiguring of the primal horde's founding murder, also marks the juncture at which a profane, linear movement breaks up the stranglehold of sacred time. In order to disfigure within memory a founding violence, enough time needs to elapse that the freshness of the father's mortal wounds scab over and transform into a totemic, animalistic representation. Without the appearance of a single individual hoarding a surplus of power, this founding murder cannot occur, and Rodoreda's village will continue to operate through a temporality consisting in a set series of non-dialectical sacred rituals. For the notion of the secular to enter into this ambit, a stretching out of time between the rituals would need to occur, a temporal distancing that cauterizes a transformational moment of violence.

Importantly, the shift from the purely numinous to a rational, hierarchical religion is also a precondition for the emergence of sovereignty, which Carl Schmitt describes as the institution that decides on exceptions to the law. Or, remembering my analysis of Numa, a totemized figure of authority is required for the evolution of both a deific religion and a *corpus mysticum* that might correspond to the natural body of a sovereign leader once the omnipotent God becomes an omnipotent lawgiver. The sacred, in other words, must become a rational concept before it can spill over into secular political imagination. In addition to a power-hoarding authority figure, this transition also requires a collective historical consciousness, a distancing from origins. An awareness of the past mandates that rituals be adapted to aid in remembrance of the dead, which is possible only via a profane, linear temporality.

Rodoreda thus combines the godlessness of the village with a total absence of sovereignty. The *senyor*, for example, has no nomizing responsibilities, lacks the power to enforce a state of exception, and certainly does not live both inside and outside the law like the *todopoderoso* in *Conde Julián*. In fact, he lives above the village for fear of the townspeople's death ritual, to which he eventually succumbs. With respect to the totemizing development of a primal horde, the *senyor* is significantly childless and lives alone. In this fashion, Rodoreda's novel complements Benet's Numa by depicting society at an earlier juncture of development, long before an omnipotent God could become an omnipotent lawgiver, but after a mythic consciousness has started to take shape. This also explains the aporia that the narrator encounters after his suicide; his soul escapes the finite body, but the world below pays him no heed and refuses to invest his soul with their externalized feelings of the numinous.

Thus, in Rodoreda's novel, the sacralization of space and the creation of an eternal present related to spatial consecration begin with an affect awakened by the encounter between consciousness and landscape, and not with the emergence of a sovereign leader. Arkinstall interprets in the novel a "fierce condemnation of extreme nationalisms" (166), where myth is used "to draw attention to the manner in which all nationalisms are constructed" (167). Rodoreda herself, despite being exiled in Switzerland and living apart from the regime's censorship, never attached such a modern sensibility to *La mort i la primavera*. If anything, the novel explores the primitive origins of social organization where the sacred was overtly used, through the power created by a collective belief structure, to dictate inclusion and justify the violence of exclusion. However, this does not mean that the ritual violence promoted in *La mort i la primavera* fails to resonate strongly in an analysis of modern political thought, and it gives clues to the religious preconditions for sovereignty. Moreover, the novel reveals that Koselleck's assertion at the beginning of this chapter, that making history visible always translates into an awareness of geographical placement, has deep roots. The interpenetration of humankind and its physical environment produces numinous feelings that give birth to sacred time. Moreover, the ritual "re-actualization" of sacred space within the flow of profane time cannot therefore help but return a nation to its shared history of occupying a single territory.

Like with the birth of deification and sovereignty, Rodoreda's novel thus also harkens back to the origin of time as a stabilizing force against change. Durkheim argues that religious representations are social: "Rituals are ways of acting that are generated only within assembled groups and are meant to stimulate and sustain or recreate certain mental states in these groups" (10). One such mental state already discussed is the awakening of the numinous, which presumably remerges with the yearly throwing of a villager into the river. The village treats those who survive the onslaught of the river as pariahs and exile the disfigured victims to the margins of the village, where they work at night cloaked in darkness. The appearance of the faceless men outside of their assigned ritual would awaken fear and fascination at the wrong time. The village reserves the awakening of the numinous, in other words, for a particular time of the year – in the spring – and establishes taboos to prevent a break in the cycle.

For Durkheim, tracking the procedures that a culture uses to divide, measure, and express a set duration gives birth to the notion of time. One such procedure is the performance of ritual according to the passage of seasons. Time can be comprehended only through the repetition of objective signs, which primitively begin as a "recurring cycle of rituals, holidays, and public ceremonies. A calendar expresses the rhythm of collective activity while ensuring its regularity" (12). Rodoreda's denizens therefore do not destroy the sundial and the clock in order to rebuff time; the objects simply have no use-value in such a regimented culture. Yearly sacrifice, alongside such practices as the painting of the village's buildings with red dust every spring, are themselves temporal markers.

It is important to conclude with a return to the narrator's post-mortem transition from the sacred time of his village to the pure profanity of a limbo state disconnected from ritual and myth. This indeterminate space is purely secular, infused with sacrilegious knowledge, and bereft of ritual. But in the total absence of the mythic structures of culture, individual freedom transforms, beyond the social, into an aporia. The narrator-protagonist of *La mort i la primavera* lacks a clearly defined rite of passage beyond death and beyond time in his post-mortem limbo. His soul, in other words, has escaped its cement entrapment, but conferring onto the dead a post-mortem value is the work of the living, who are indifferent to his metaphysical state.

In terms of Rodoreda's literary oeuvre, the existential crisis that completes Adrià Guinart's experience of freedom in *Quanta, quanta guerra* (1980) bears a logical consistency with the narrator's unfettered potential to recast his own fictive narrative at the conclusion of *La mort i la primavera.* Both characters begin their journeys with a fierce desire for liberation but end up back home in a state of utter alienation and disenchantment. In *La mort i la primavera*, the narrator remains tied to his former village, observing the ongoing rituals from above. Despite the freedom to narrate and think, origin, in the words of Karl Kraus, remains the obstinate goal.

Prior to the narrator's death, individual identity was muted by the force of collective behaviour; society and its rituals hypostatically offered a collective image to which each individual citizen identified. In death, Rodoreda's protagonist cannot rebuff the urge to return home – like Guinart – but the impossibility of subscribing to a ready-made identity-image compromises all advancement: "Tornar. Deixar-me voltar per les coses … tornar per refer per afegir per canviar" (169). In such a state, however, natural phenomena that were previously explainable through myth revert to a mysterious state: "De vegades i cada dia més les coses vénen no sé, com vénen, com les fulles quan només en queda el que les fa" (168). *Quanta, quanta guerra*, a novel replete with angels, gives way to a listless phantasm in *La mort i la primavera* that silently haunts a home made totally inaccessible, where the simplest of movements lose meaning outside of the rhythms of social practice. *La mort i la primavera*'s narrator thus enters into a kind of homogenous empty time that is devoid of historicity. In storytelling, being embedded within the discursivity of culture is highly significant. From the narrator's suspended, alienated position, *començar per on vull* is a more difficult proposition than it seems at first glance. "Tornar per refer, per afegir" is complicated, if not made entirely impossible, when one's life is complete – "tancada" (169) – and still suffering "en alguna banda … Jo no sóc enlloc m'he esborrat d'uns camins i d'uns arbres … Però perquè hi havia estat alguna cosa queda" (169). This paradox – of being both nowhere and everywhere at once – creates a narrativistic aporia that resists a definitive conclusion. Hence, the narrator exasperatingly asks a rhetorical question: "Començar què?" (170).

Pure secularity is thus as ineffective, by itself, as a crushed time that is entirely awash in the light of the sacred. In Benet's Región, a morality centred on *rencor* creates an atmosphere hospitable to directing violence towards scapegoats, in a desperate hope to expel accumulated anxiety. When awash in Numa's sacred time, the inhabitants of Región lack the willpower to recalibrate the historical thrust of their fossilized social structure. In Rodoreda's fiction, the narrator does ultimately manage to step outside a sacred temporality into a zone devoid of ritual and myth, yet lacks the ability to reconcile the two spheres into a stable dialectic. The protagonist's inability to disinvest himself from his past mode of Being – with all the horror of his village's rituals open to observation from his post-mortem limbo – leaves unanswered the manner in which a new, more equitable sacred-profane time might be constituted.

In the next chapter, Luis Martín-Santos attacks both problems through his dialectic of de-sacralization and sacro-genesis. Borrowing heavily from Continental philosophy, Martín-Santos applies a psycho-therapeutic approach to Spain, as though the country were an infirm patient. This process involves first stepping outside the flow of time – much like the narrator's actions at the end of *La mort i la primavera* – and second the production of a new reality founded on a counterset of morals, transcending the previous dialectic of existence.

6 "De-sacralization" and "Sacro-genesis," or How to Step Outside of Sacred Time

Absence is the highest form of presence

James Joyce

In evasion itself is the there disclosed

Martin Heidegger

Sacred Dialectics

As a literary evaluator for Gallimard in the 1960s, Juan Goytisolo was charged with selecting which post-war Spanish novels were to be translated and published by the French editorial house. Joan Sales's *Incerta glòria* was one such choice. The most glaring omission from the series, according to Goytisolo, was Luis Martín-Santos's *Tiempo de silencio*: "La única ausencia significativa y lamentable del cuadro es la de Martín-Santos: su novela me llegó con retraso" (qtd in Lázaro 291). Goytisolo, in any case, was undoubtedly familiar with the work prior to publishing his Mendiola trilogy, so familiar that it may have been his "inspiration" for novelistically undertaking a systematic annihilation of the sacred. In an article published in 1965 by *Las Langues Modernes*, Alain Rouquié, the French translator of *Tiempo de silencio*, asserts that Martín-Santos's untimely death in an automobile accident the previous year "Le impidió terminar las otras dos partes de una suma prodigiosa de la que sólo conocemos algunos fragmentos y que se hubiese titulado *La destrucción de la España sagrada*" (qtd in Lázaro 291). *Tiempo de silencio*, in other words, was purportedly the first entry of a trilogy dedicated to the question of the sacred and its destructibility, a concept that has mostly eluded serious attention in criticism of Martín-Santos's work but was very famously used by Goytisolo to construct an entire literary career.

And of course, to conscientious observers who are familiar with Goytisolo's opus the title Rouquié attributes to Martín-Santos's proposed trilogy is quite uncanny. When pressed years later by José Lázaro, Martín-Santos's biographer, Rouquié reiterates that the source of the phrase was Martín-Santos and not a self-made invention or erroneous attribution taken from Goytisolo: "Sí, sí, esa expresión de «La destrucción de la España sagrada» es de Martín-Santos, por supuesto, yo no me la inventé. Además, ¿en qué fecha decías que está publicado mi artículo? Enero-febrero de 1965, no hay ninguna duda, es de Luis Martín-Santos. Cuando la utilizó Juan Goytisolo yo pensé que él conocía ese título de Luis y que lo había adoptado" (Lázaro 291). The object of the present inquiry is not to point fingers at Goytisolo or anyone else for borrowing phrases. The resonance that the concept of the sacred projected onto a disparate collection of writers such as Sales, Goytisolo, Benet, and Martín-Santos during the 1960s and 1970s is, however, very provocative.

A more relevant question is perhaps why destroying the sacred had such magnetic attraction. Lázaro asserts that Goytisolo's embrace of the destruction of sacred forms functions as a "complicidad," which in a certain sense is a non-starter. The role of the sacred in Martín-Santos's thought – let alone a comparison of the way he destroys and resurrects a logic of sacred forms within the functioning of Spanish society to another author such as Goytisolo – has never been investigated. Or, in other words, the farthest literary criticism has gotten is to the stumbling block of complicity, which if transcended, reveals a very different approach to sacral annihilation and genesis in both *Tiempo de silencio* and in Martín-Santos's unfinished second novel, *Tiempo de destrucción*, which José Carlos Mainer released in fragmentary form for Seix Barral in 1975.[1] The very notion of complicity in fact biases one towards looking for similarities, when it is the departures from Goytisolo's appropriation of the sacred that make Martín-Santos's treatment of the subject so appealing. In fact, the way the sacred functions in each writer's work boils down to the distinct intellectual currents that structure both Goytisolo's and Martín-Santos's notions of being and time. While Goytisolo's dealings with French surrealism and post-Freudian psychoanalysis undoubtedly shaped the psychological comportment of Álvaro Mendiola, Martín-Santos's intellectual upbringing and psychiatric practice borrowed heavily from what he calls "existential psychoanalysis," which is significantly informed by the philosophy of disciples of Edmund Husserl, particularly twentieth-century theories of existentialism found in the work of Jean-Paul Sartre and Martin Heidegger.

In an oft-cited epistolary exchange with Janet Winecoff in 1962, Martín-Santos situates the sacred as the fulcrum on which the function of the novelist pivots.[2] To a question about the ends of a writer's mission, Martín-Santos rather blandly responds that he aims to "modificar la realidad española" (237), which seems to point to rejecting an objective mirroring of reality in favour of privileging a literature that re-imagines society through the transcendent machinations of the novelist's free subjectivity. In light of the then prevailing current in Spain of *objetivismo* within social realist literature and the dehumanizing aesthetics of Ortega y Gasset, Martín-Santos is undoubtedly trying to create a measure of artistic and philosophical distancing from his predecessors and contemporaries. However, a far more interesting answer comes shortly thereafter in the questionnaire when Martín-Santos insinuates that an objective understanding of the cultural myths of a society is a preparatory step for the de-sacralization of myth. In answering how he perceives the function of the novelist, he replies, "Su función es la que llamo desacralizadora-sacrogenética: Desacralizadora – destruye mediante una crítica aguda de lo injusto. Sacrogenética – al mismo tiempo colabora a la edificación de los nuevos mitos que pasan a formar las Sagradas Escrituras del mañana" (237).

If one considers *Tiempo de silencio* as the starting point for an unfinished trilogy aiming to destroy the sacred in order to reinsert into reality a new set of scriptures, the novel transforms into an objective account, or a "crítica aguda," of the unjust structures that regulate the narratives informing the self-imagining of the vital projects of the Spanish populace. What is noteworthy is that sacrogenesis and de-sacralization (which I translate directly from Martín-Santos in lieu of saying "sacrilege") occur at once in the same gesture.

Winecoff, in a short critical analysis prior to the interview, classifies *Tiempo de silencio* as a new novel, both formally and thematically, that strives to "*create* reality rather than copy it" (233). However, sacrilege first requires a critical understanding of what is sacred, and in that vein much of *Tiempo de silencio* is similar to such *objetivista* masterpieces as Cela's *La colmena*, Sánchez Ferlosio's *El Jarama*, or a precursor to the social realism movement and one of Martín-Santos's models, the work of Pío Baroja. The key difference is that Martín-Santos fails to accept the external world's mirror image as completely adequate for critical contemplation and the end point of what constitutes the real. For Martín-Santos the normal experiencing of the external world is closed off to reflection and therefore known only partially. Unlike Lacan, however, Martín-Santos's "real," though invisible, is certainly knowable and never fatalistically chased after in a series of mis-recognitions. Following the heavy influence of phenomenology on Martín-Santos's thought, there is always a "there" there that is not buried within a collective subconscious. But a simple mirror reflection of the world as apprehended in everyday experience always falls short of passing a reality test if one thinks of a totality on two levels: what is sensually there and the inner contradictions such a system hides within itself. In a lecture presented in 1963 on the distinction between realism and reality, Martín-Santos criticizes the obsessive search of Spanish social realist literature for the visible: "Muchos novelistas españoles piensan que la realidad que ellos necesitan cambiar es visible y muy visible. En tales condiciones, el diálogo hubo de resultar difícil" ("Realismo" 142). Reality distances itself from realism and is open to critical reflection only when contextualized within a temporal structure that passes through the testing of dialectical processes.

Philological hang-ups over *Tiempo de silencio*'s place in the canon distract from Martín-Santos's psycho-pathological and philosophical appropriation of realism. This approach, which the author imports from his training as a psychiatrist and his doctoral dissertation completed under the direction of Juan José López Ibor and Pedro Laín Entralgo, novelizes social reality as though it were a sick patient, capturing the external world not through a reflective mimesis but by plucking a concrete situation in its wholeness from the current of time and distilling it, through a phenomenology of understanding, into intelligible lived experiences. In an interview that explored his psychological approach, Martín-Santos defines the first step in a psychiatric diagnosis as being capable of "captar la «forma» como el enfermo vive sus contenidos mentales" (*El análisis existencial* 119). *Tiempo de silencio* first captures the totality of experience, or *Erfahrungen*, of 1940s Madrid and alchemically converts the data into *Erlebnisse* accessible to reflection. It is at this point that an understanding of experience permits a reconfiguration of reality without ever stepping into a strictly subjective, imaginative sphere, a modality that is prima facie incongruent with Juan Goytisolo's work.

Even in its very earliest reviews, critics frequently compared *Tiempo de silencio* to Joyce's *Ulysses*, as readers inevitably homed in on the stylistic stream of consciousness emanating from Pedro, the novel's protagonist, throughout the text.[3] However, the novel's chaotic and seemingly contingent barrage of happenings also have great bearing on the first concept expressed in the book's title: time. The notion of a life-world defined as a vital flux that agglomerates life experiences (*Erfahrungen*) that are never adequately theorized owes a great deal to the Husserlian phenomenology that informs the work of Wilhelm Dilthey and Karl Jasper, who were both the titular subjects of Martín-Santos's doctoral dissertation.[4]

Everyday life, without second-order observation, is thought of as a barrage of presents and therefore not experienced as temporal, though it always is. For Martín-Santos, creating a temporal consciousness is part of a psychiatric cure: "El ser del hombre es la cura. La cura se nos resuelve en tiempo. El tiempo ... ha de ser el concepto existenciario fundamental de vuestra labor" (*El análisis existencial* 84). In other words, *Dasein* is thought of as not simply "being there" but also as a being whose involvement in the there is structured by a temporal thrownness. However, in Martín-Santos's work entire national groupings and cities are thought through as collective facticities unyieldingly projected by the past that are enigmatic and resistant to cogitation. *Tiempo de silencio*, in particular, describes Madrid as a city with a lack of "sustancia histórica" that is dragged and carried along by "gobernantes arbitrarios" who privilege and reward certain modalities of being without knowing "a ciencia cierta por qué sino de un modo elemental y físico" (*Tiempo de silencio* 15). Life experienced at its most primal, sensual level denies the possibility of reflection, which in this case precludes a transcendent consciousness, or understanding, that would serve as the foundation of historical truth. Dilthey would argue that such an elemental stream of life is utterly bereft of an awareness of time. Life, however, is capable of being "fixed by attention which arrests what is essentially flow … When we want to observe time the very observation destroys it because it fixes our attention" (*Selected Writings* 210–11).

Arresting time and objectifying its contents is a form of destruction, and this is crucial to understanding Martín Santos's conception of the function of literature and of a realism founded on dialectics. A "time of silence" is in reality a time of blindness when life passes by without critical reflection. Curing Spain's illness, however, requires that the readers of Martín-Santos – in the words of Antonio Machado – lose "la fe en su propia ceguera" (281).[5]

Lázaro very thoroughly documents several instances in which Martín-Santos characterized his work as "realismo dialéctico," though the author "no dejó muchas pistas sobre su concepción" (274). In fact, Vilanova's early review of the novel already attaches the term to Martín-Santos's thought, though he never discusses the precise meaning of *dialectical* at length. What was generally understood, however, was that Martín-Santos approached realism in a manner very different from that of his contemporaries. In an interview with Lázaro, Ricardo Doménech attributes the importance of dialectics to Martín-Santos's shift, shortly prior to his death, from existentialism to a Marxist politics (273). If one is being precise, however, and thinking through the term in reference to sacrogenesis and desacralization, a clearly Hegelian process emerges that frames the identification of internal contradictions as the pathway to speculative transcendence.[6] However, the thought of Marx and Engel remains patent in the notion that social consciousness determines the horizon of ontological possibility.

Martín-Santos first proposes in a psychiatric essay that a dialectical process can become available to comprehension only by "captarlo en su total transparencia" (*Apólogos* 137). This is the project behind *Tiempo de silencio* and reflects the novel's significance as the first entrant in a trilogy. *Tiempo de silencio* emerges with intent to document every sphere of Madrid's social structure, from its most destitute *chabolas* to the upper registers of its aristocracy, but with an awareness of the regulating forces that keep the city's structure intact. As a transparent totality, the novel is a light shed onto the darkness of a silent, ominous time. Silence shares an important relationship with darkness – *captar* what is hidden from view allows the reader to relinquish his or her blindness. Once again, similarities between *Tiempo de silencio* and other objective works of Spanish mid-century literature are explained in this *captación*. As Hegel writes in the preface to the *Phenomenology of Spirit*, to get culture to emerge from "the immediacy of substantial life," one must start from both "*general* principles and points of view" (3). Martín-Santos similarly distils the immediacy of substantial life in 1940s Madrid in an effort to glean an objective understanding of a uniquely Spanish point of view, or world view – a term greatly developed by Dilthey – that the author then fits into a broader matrix of culture.

As a first step towards making the city's history visible, Martín-Santos abstracts Madrid into the totalizing form of *Tiempo de silencio*. However, this type of abstraction occurs only after the flow of the novel acquires sufficient historical sediment. In the same introductory passage describing the "elemental" way that one experiences cities such as Madrid, the narrator of *Tiempo de silencio* comments, "Es preciso, ante estas ciudades, suspender el juicio hasta un día, hasta que repentinamente – o quizá poco a poco aunque esto apenas es creíble – tome forma una cosa que adivinamos que está presente y que no vemos, hasta que esa sustancia que se arrastra ahora por el suelo se solidifique, hasta que lo que ahora ríen tristemente aprendan a mirar cara a cara a un destino mediocre y dejen vacías las grandes construcciones redondas o elípticas de cemento armado para recogerse en la intimidad estrecha de sus casas" (17).

Decades prior to Alain Badiou's *Being and Event*, Martín-Santos here offers an evental understanding of history where truth, though always already "there," is graspable in moments of rupture. The sudden appearance of the sediment of history occasions the judgment of a place – here a city – that solidifies into a form that one may call the novel. This solidified form is transported into the intimacy of the domestic sphere where the reader is transformed into a second-order observer of his or her mediocre destiny. In a Marxist fashion, this is how the reader becomes aware of the typologies of social consciousness assigned to each sphere of being within a culture.

Martín-Santos's *Tiempo de silencio* and *Tiempo de destrucción* are created by a product – the novelist – of the effluvial course of the city's temporal flow: "La única posibilidad de captar la realidad dialéctica en su devenir constituyente la logra el hombre cuando él mismo va incluido en el proceso" (*Apólogos* 138). Authorial agency thus functions as an internal contradiction of the object of study where the arresting of time is a form of destruction. About this point, J.M. Castellet paraphrases a talk in which Martín-Santos theorized that "el realismo en la literatura sólo podía servir como detonante: era la bomba que desacralizaba un mundo caduco y represivo, petrificado" (qtd in Lázaro 283). The novelist, by detonating the bomb, opposes the enigma of a culture's sterile facticity through objectification and irony, a tone that certainly permeates Martín Santos's first novel. This arresting of the life-world of the *pueblo* allows direct contemplation and returns one to Dilthey and the relationship between cognition and the distillation of experience into something that can be analyzed.

The novelist's assumption of agency is alluded to in *Tiempo de silencio* as an evental rupture capable of changing an existential project. In a conversation between Amador and Similiano, the detective in charge of searching for Pedro, the "toma" of existence is compared to "la primera vivencia. ¡El instante! La crisis a partir de la cual cambia el proyecto del existente. La elección. La libertad encarnada" (195). Freedom, which is always already present within the subject but denied through bad faith, is literally incarnated and results in a critical rupture – "la crítica aguda de lo injusto" – that is ultimately capable of deflecting the effluvial flow of history. This constitutes the first "vivencia" or lived experience, that reveals how one is and is an antidote to an existential quandary referred to by Amador: "nadie piensa que uno es lo que es" (195). In this vein, Martín-Santos reveals his indebtedness to Sartre, who writes, "Consciousness is not what it is" (*Being and Nothingness* 105). It *is*, of course, a nothingness endowed with absolute freedom.

Arresting Madrid's life-world permits the next step in Martín-Santos's dialectical process, where one "piensa que es lo que es": *la concienciación*. In Machado's words, this is the point where the patient loses faith in his or her blindness and begins to believe in an alternative way of being. The novelist is the conduit, much like the psychotherapist with a patient, to the birth of reflection that can grasp a historical temporality comprising lived experiences: "Al ser vividas por el hombre, por un grupo, por un pueblo, éstos llegan a ser ejecutores de la historia y creadores de una nueva realidad" (*Apólogos* 139). The sick city, like the infirm analysand, steps to the side of its subjectivity and observes itself through the abstraction of its case history by the novelist-analyst. *Tiempo de silencio*'s elaboration is preceded by the author taking the first step of the dialectical process, which is recognition of his own being as a contradiction inextricably related to and determined by its opposite, which is the world view that a culture imposes. Dialectical realism, in this sense, requires that understanding not be limited to one side of the thesis-antithesis spectrum, as an awareness of contradiction can arise only by viewing past experiences with an awareness of opposition. Thus in a very Hegelian sense, history is overcome by creating a new speculative reality within literature that hopefully takes root through the collective reception of art, which a reader absorbs in the intimacy of *la casa*.

Hegel argues in his *Logic* that every finite object possesses the possibility of sublating itself and turning into its opposite. This turning into an opposite, however, is not the result of an external circumstance: "Life as such bears the germ of death within itself ... the finite sublates itself because it contradicts itself inwardly" (*Hegel Reader* 171). The novelist, capable of destroying historical temporality by objectification, becomes the germ of death within the finite cultural situation he or she aestheticizes, and therefore resembles, in Castellet's words, a *bomba detonante*. Hegel continues that working out a dialectical process is similar to transcending understanding by pure reason, which is mystical without being mysterious: "The rational as such is rational precisely because it contains both of the opposites as ideal moments within itself. Thus, everything rational can equally be called 'mystical'" (173). Hegel, in turn, refers to the totality of opposition as the speculative or positively rational.

Martín-Santos thinks through a *concienciación* as both "sacro-genética" and "desacralizadora" in that is creates a transcendent sublation beyond history. Martín-Santos therefore understands the sacred and the profane to be two opposite yet mutually determinant parts of a whole. A *concienciación* promotes the profane to the status of a sacred ideal, creating an ideology that analyzes, in a transcendent gesture, the ordering of the world. One can now understand that the two terms enclosed within the very title of *Tiempo de silencio* themselves function as a thesis and antithesis. And indeed the two opposites are mutually dependent: the darkness of silence normally submerges time, yet its moment of cognition is the agent that destroys existential muteness. The very preposition *de* implies that time springs from and belongs to silence. But a separation remains: the notion of time, following Dilthey, implies an awakening of historical consciousness by an agent opposed to the castrating silence of a culture lacking "sustancia histórica."

Once again, Martín-Santos takes leave of Goytisolo's use of the sacred in *Conde Julián*. Álvaro/Julián's maintenance of the sacred as a symbolic placeholder surrounds its *homo sacer* within a mysterious enclosure of sovereignty, in a process that is antithetical to the possibility of historical transcendence in a dialectical sense. Goytisolo's novel silences contradiction; Spain is left "desollado y sin voz" in order to seem as if the sovereign sphere were defined purely by a single, sacred ideal. Goytisolo's novel proposes an infinite cycle of symbolic determinations within an unchanging sacred relation of power, which constitutes what Hegel calls "taking captive of reason," where what is understood to be true turns into "a constant sublating itself and an overturning into its opposite" (*Hegel Reader* 173). Hence there appears a repetition of the eighth-century count of Ceuta's betrayal at the conclusion of *Conde Julián*. This extends to the previous chapter, where Numa's cyclical homicides reset profane time by re-actualizing a sacred origin, and to the village of Rodoreda's novel as well, where enslavement to ritual repetition precludes rational thought and transcendental historical movement. Wherever thinking is absent, an irrational acceptance of temporal thrownness forces humankind to make and remake the same structures of relation, whether they are political, legal, or religious.

In reference to sacro-genesis and de-sacralization, thinking becomes possible when the sacred and its opposites – the profane – are consciously known to be two ideal moments of a single finite object. Hegel, once again, pinpoints in the preface to the *Phenomenology of Spirit* that consciousness, the "immediate existence of Spirit," comprises two such dialectical moments: "the two moments of knowing and the objectivity negative to knowing" (*Phenomenology* 21). The instant that sacralization occurs is simultaneously the birth of profanation, because opposition to the sacred arises only once an object is set apart, consecrated, and given definition. Sacrogenesis and de-sacralization thus constitute a classical dialectic, as the sacred always implicitly carries within it the seeds of its own undoing, and knowledge of the profane is required for one to understand the inclusions *and* exclusions determined by a relational social structure.

Tiempo de silencio itself is first a sacralization in the most basic sense. In order to create an abstracted transparency that grants access to reflection, an author must extract a parcel of time from a culture's vital flow and set it apart within the formal delimitations of the novel. This is closely related to Heidegger's interpretation of time, which works as a historical propulsion that sweeps up the subject. As Heidegger explains in *Being and Time*, "Dasein simultaneously falls prey to the tradition of which it has more or less explicitly taken hold. This tradition keeps it from providing its own guidance, whether in inquiring or in choosing" (46). The subject, in other words, does not possess the agency to redirect the thrust of tradition that pushes toward the future. Martín-Santos's mission in *Tiempo de silencio* is to pluck a moment from the thrust of tradition to provide those who are subject to this propulsion – the Spanish body politic – the opportunity to amend the direction of their historical flow. Heidegger, however, falls short of adequately explaining the erotic nature of "falling prey" to tradition, a topic that Sartre later tackled.

In the next section, I will thus argue that the subjection of consciousness to cultural symbols in *Tiempo de silencio* is successfully analyzed through Sartre's theory of love and *l'être-pour-autrui*. In the final section, I investigate how working through dialectical tension produces a transcendental metaphysics tied to the objectification of symbols in *Tiempo de destrucción*. If the mission of *Tiempo de silencio* is to produce a *concienciación*, *Tiempo de destrucción* adopts sacrogenesis in the transcendental appearance of a new reality founded on the sacred oath of unflinching justice taken by Agustín, the novel's protagonist, upon donning a judge's robe and resisting a judicial system within *un estado sin derecho*.

Le regard d'autrui: The State's Loving Embrace

In an essay on love and eroticism, Martín-Santos points out that the "continua desenajenación" of humankind is directly related to "la progresiva desacralización del ámbito cultural y la disolución de los dogmatismos" (*El análisis existencial* 115). In *Tiempo de silencio*, time works as the relational mediator between the petrified, sacred determinants of being rooted in a culture's world view, and individual subjects who adopt the poses assigned to them on the basis of social positioning.

In Martín-Santos's thought, the manner in which a subject becomes alienated through the sacred bears a strong relationship to Sartre's notion of love, especially what is referred to as "el amor del pueblo" in *Tiempo de silencio*. The fundamental problem to be explored is how precisely a centripetal pull towards the sacred occurs when a subject freely sacrifices personal freedom by perceiving an external manifestation of subjectivity as the limit point of being. I have previously touched on the influence of Jean-Paul Sartre upon the thought of Martín-Santos. And on the point of love the novel owes much to the third section of *Being and Nothingness*, where Sartre describes Being-for-Others in detail.

In previous chapters, the sacred was related to political love in Joan Sales's thought, as an ideal that is gainfully placed within a symbolic shell in order to bind members of a community together. In Goytisolo, the sacred also bound a community together, but only through forceful acquisition of symbolic capital by the sovereign, who dictates the ideational content within the symbolic tabernacle of the sacred. In Benet's novel, this tabernacle was endowed not with love but with *rencor*, demonstrating that a metaphysical morality can *negatively* forge relational bonds among social classes. In Martín-Santos, the sacred maintains its relational character; however, the resonance of Sartrean philosophy, particularly the notion of consciousness's reliance on bad faith, replaces the imposed national allegiance to sovereign power with a collective deceit inherent in the body politic's desire to belong to a national tradition. In Heidegger's *Being and Time*, tradition is a projection of *Dasein*'s possibilities and is thought of as something to which one falls prey. By precluding *Dasein* from inquiry and choice, tradition also proscribes a rational understanding of Being and any possibility of existential transcendence. In Sartre's philosophy, this dynamic is whittled down to the primary encounter of the self with the Other, though Martín-Santos elevates this microcosm to a general conception of the political and relates it to symbols projected within the cultural realm.

At the conclusion of *Tiempo de silencio* as Pedro makes his way to the Príncipe Pío train station en route to the countryside, he reaches the fatalist conclusion that being a country doctor is the ontological limit of his historical thrownness. This serves as a limit point where Pedro thinks of himself as "yo a quien en nombre del destino se me dijo: 'Basta' y se me mandó para el Príncipe Pío con unas recomendaciones" (289). Shortly thereafter, once on his way to the provinces, the protagonist vocalizes an onomatopoeia of the train's movement: "tracatracatraca-tracatraca … se puede formar un ritmo, es cuestión de darle forma, una estructura gestáltica" (292). On one hand, the onomatopoeia symbolizes the re-engagement of Spain's stream of silent time with its rhythmical flow in the wake of a disturbance. Pedro's doubt is here founded on the absence of a totalizing rational form that might explain the rhythm's meaning. The irony, of course, is that by the novel's conclusion, the gestalt of a totalized *captación* of Madrid has indeed been realized through the very structure of *Tiempo de silencio*, which at its start lacked an agglomeration of historical sedimentation but by its conclusion has grouped a collection of fragments into an objectified account of time.

Pedro's flight along the vector of the motor of time motor is encapsulated in the name of another of the novel's central figures, Cartucho. Cartucho is romantically involved with Florita, the guardian of rats that her father stole from Pedro's lab. In the work's final denouement, Cartucho enters the scene of an open-air festival to take his revenge on the doctor who, in his mind, killed his girlfriend after her failed abortion. In a flash, Cartucho darts onto the dance floor where he "se fijó precisamente en la que tenía que fijarse" (279).[7] What he *had* to focus on was Dorita, Pedro's fiancée, in a vengeful tit for tat. However, Martín-Santos reserves a modicum of innocence for Cartucho by depriving him of agency and free decision-making. He behaves like a missile, in other words, whose fuse was lit some time ago and whose trajectory is preordained and immutable. Although the abortionist and Muecas have been taken into custody, Cartucho's particular "tradition" – his thrownness – constitutes a spool of time proper to Madrid's lowest social sphere that demands that justice remains in the hands of the one who has been wronged. Muecas and the abortionist's consignment to the Spanish justice system therefore cannot deflect the thrust of Cartucho's destiny. In a Sartrean fashion, Cartucho feels no anguish because there is no alternative possibility.

Pedro's alienation from his idealized vision of the future is not the result of a single event, that is, his expulsion from the *sacerdocio* of cancer researchers. Readers of the novel will recall a night of debauchery, prior to the failed abortion in the *chabola*, when Pedro arrives at his boarding house and rapes Dorita, the granddaughter of the *pensionista*. Pedro's expected social pose, which is projected at the beginning of the novel by the girl's family and described as if it were a fact, is to be Dorita's suitor: "El trío femenino estaba demasiado sensibilizado al dato objetivo *hombre joven* para que fuera, en ningún momento, durante su estancia en la pensión, confundido con cualquier otra especie de semoviente" (42). As though he were a farm animal programmed to copulate with any unclaimed female of the species, Pedro is consigned to a species of social expectation, which he rationally resists, knowing that his aspirations lie outside the city. However, on an elemental, physical level – which is precisely how Martín-Santos describes how one experiences reality without rationally understanding one's being – Pedro cannot help but be struck by the girl's beauty, which hits him "tan violentamente que … podía Pedro quedar en silencio simple" (46). Social dictums, which in the absence of critical awareness remain unexplained and appear obligatory, reduce experience to a primal drive, which Cartucho embodies as though he were an automaton. Martín-Santos is thus suggesting that what humankind might take to be an animalistic drive rooted in a stage prior to rational development may originate in myths regarding suitable gender roles or the appropriate way to respond to a personal injustice (Cartucho).

Although the rational part of Pedro's mind protests his attraction to Dorita, an elemental pull towards her slowly takes root, which the narrator frames as the presence of a distinct project of being to be chosen over and against his preferred image of himself. By the end of Pedro's *tertulia* at the beginning of the novel with the three generations of *pensionistas*, he feels "una angustia ligera mientras iba cediendo poco a poco a la tentación" (49). In Sartre's parlance, if a culture's facticity forced one to embark on a particular path, there would be no anxiety, because the future would appear to be predetermined and therefore not be a choice at all. The very problem of the nature of consciousness, "which is to be what it is not and not to be what it is" (*Being and Nothingness* 116), is that one always feels pulled between separate destinies, and the realization of responsibility for this freedom is profoundly agonizing. Pedro, by virtue of his birth and cultural upbringing, *is* a Spanish man whose behaviour is influenced by modes of cultural discourse, but this is a social role he wishes to transcend.

Shortly before to forcing his way into Dorita's room, Pedro's "angustia ligera" becomes a full-blown existential crisis. Referring to himself in the third person, he notes, "Queda aparte la construcción de una vida más importante, el proyecto de ir más lejos, la pretensión de no ser idéntico a la chata realidad de la ciudad, del país y de la hora. Él es distinto" (116). Falling into the historical thrownness of what is socially expected of Pedro does not itself cause anguish, nor does his attraction to Dorita sacrifice his freedom to choose. Rather, her very presence makes Pedro aware of multiple destinies and forces him to come face-to-face with his innate freedom. At the work's conclusion, once Pedro's freedom is dispelled and his options are reduced to being a country doctor, all anguish disappears. In *Tiempo de silencio*, time's march recommences in the wake of an explosive event whose unfolding reconfigures the conditions of Pedro's existential possibility, leaving him, in his words, castrated, which is another way to say that he is deprived of authority over his actions: "¿Y por qué no estoy más desesperado? Es cómodo ser eunuco, es tranquilo, estar desprovisto de testículos" (293).

How can one fall into history's movement if consciousness has at its core a distressing liberty of choice? Similarly, in a culture dragged along by time's silent vector, without rational comprehension of society's visceral workings, how do individual subjects like Pedro *not* perceive their innate freedom? In *Tiempo de silencio*, the answer is love and the distinct ways in which a human subject ascribes to cultural models that a society considers sacred. Pedro and Dorita's sexual exchange is a microcosm of how love functions in national culture, or at least how that national culture functions within Martín-Santos's Madrid. In Sartre's philosophy of love, the lover sacrifices subjectivity in order to become an object in which "the Other's freedom consents to lose itself, the object in which the Other consents to find his being and his *raison d'être*" (*Being and Nothingness* 479). The beloved, in other words, denies his or her freedom to "be" in order to perceive the lover as an object representing the limit point of subjectivity. By the same token, the beloved also becomes an object for the lover. Unlike in Hegel's master/slave dialectic, however, love must not consist in a forceful abrogation of the other's freedom. A modicum of freedom is preserved, but this liberty possesses an end point that the beloved believes the or she has chosen without coercion. The lover "does not want to *act* on the Other's freedom but to exist *a priori* as the objective limit of this freedom" (480). The lover and the beloved, therefore, each believe that the other is the chosen end of their respective subjectivities, which are each permitted to continue existing – but without absolute freedom.

Through Pedro's character, Martín-Santos focuses on the essential objectification of the Other that Sartre describes in *Being and Nothingness*. What is curious about Pedro's intrusion into Dorita's room is the nearly immediate declaration of love each makes to the other. While vacillating about whether or not he should enter Dorita's room, Pedro notes that the boarding house "insiste en su silencio macizo como un estuche" (114), which refers both to the lack of light in the flat and to the forces that propel him to make a decision that conflicts with his rational mind, which is incapacitated after a night of drinking. Silence and darkness once again intersect. As he slowly succumbs to the pull towards Dorita's room, Pedro asks a series of exasperated questions about the nature of love: "¿Es acaso el amor una colección apresurada de significaciones? ¿Es acaso el amor la unificación del mundo en torno a un ser simbólico? ¿Es acaso el amor esta aniquilación de lo individual más propio?" (115–16). Pedro's inner eye perceives Dorita lying on her bed for the taking, an action that corresponds to a path of self-identity that his rational mind rejects: "Él vive en otro mundo en el que no entra una muchacha solamente por ser lánguida y jugosa" (116). Despite these protestations, the same impulse towards the girl that provoked his initial "angustia ligera" also leads him to turn the knob to Dorita's room, as if a "demonio" were making decisions for him. Within a small part of his consciousness, however, there remains a small space occupied by "lo más libre de su espíritu [que] se defiende todavía un momento para entregar luego … inevitablemente la libertad y caer rendido" (117). Dorita thus transforms into an objectified love object and the limit point of Pedro's subjectivity. His objectification of her is where Pedro finds his reason for being, which is sealed the moment he responds to Dorita's demand to declare his love for her, and this determinism constitutes a sacrificing of "lo más libre de su espíritu."

It would be too simplistic to say that what pushes Pedro is only an instinctual impulse when his idealization of Dorita and his own conception of masculinity come filtered through the cultural symbols that populate *Tiempo de silencio*. When he imagines Dorita sleeping, she becomes "la imagen inmóvil de lo que él nunca ha visto, el cuerpo desnudo con su forma de capullo, con su arquetipo de exactitud. Como sirena silenciosa la llamada de este cuerpo resuena tras la literatura siempre erótica del mundo" (115). This points one towards the emphasis Sartre places on objectification when viewing another person as one's beloved. This demands that the Other be an idealized limit point, or "arquetipo de exactitud," that is assimilated phenomenologically into one's consciousness through the projection of an external symbol that is often unrelated to the beloved herself. Such external sources are the property of the cultural realm in *Tiempo de silencio*, where Dorita's idealization into an archetypal form is embodied in popular works of theatre and art. At the novel's conclusion, for example, Pedro and Dorita attend a sentimental comedy prior to the latter's murder. There, the "buen pueblo acumulado ... desea la triunfal entronización de la imagen policromada de la mujer" (272). This idealization of the actress is rooted in the *buen pueblo*'s shared cultural history, which feeds an impulse that matches the woman on stage with "las populacheras infantas abanicadoras de sí mismas y de las duquesas desnudas ante las paletas de los pintores plebeyos" (273). As for the *supervedette* onstage, the public wants assurance that she "es la misma hembra tan taurinamente perseguida" (273). Through the projection of such symbols, Pedro's declaration of love after intercourse constitutes an affection that indeed consolidates around a symbolic being whose objectivity completely effaces the uniquely subjective elements of Dorita's existence and inserts in her place an elevated feminine image that the society of the spectacle projects outward.

Love is difficult when only one of the two subjects is an object for the other, a point that is made in the Martín-Santos short story "Tauromaquia" by the story's protagonist, Juanito Reyes. In *Tiempo de silencio*, Dorita, rather than rejecting Pedro's aggressive advances, welcomes him with open arms and makes a similar declaration of love. In Reyes's case, he is seeing a foreign woman named Nora, who loves him not only for the bullfighter's physical qualities but also for his "cualidades espirituales, coraje ante el peligro, decisión rápida, posibilidad continua de desprecio hacia la hembra" (76). This line of thought mirrors the theatre audience's approval, in *Tiempo de silencio*, of a man who "taurinamente" pursues the woman. In Nora's case, whether or not one is born into a Spanish world view is irrelevant to the acquisition of perspectives dictated by cultural models of thought. What is essential is an environment where cultural symbols affirm and repeat such qualities.

Martín-Santos's treatment of cultural symbols replicates the departure he makes from Freudian psychoanalysis in his medical writings. There he writes that "el símbolo no puede interpretarse sólo al modo freudiano, como *traducción* de un dinamismo psíquico subyacente" (*El análisis existencial* 162). In a sense, Martín Santos's departure from Freud mirrors Sartre's philosophy, which itself denies the existence of a dynamic subconscious featuring elemental drives. A symbol, returning to Martín-Santos, is also "la forma como el hombre deviene el ser que él ha proyectado ser" (162). What is not fleshed out in this psychiatric writing is that this projected symbol does not emerge from consciousness, which starts out as nothingness, but is instead adopted from another source. In light of *Tiempo de silencio*, an external symbol is potentially understood as the formal realization of one's existential project and the point towards which one directs purposeful action.[8]

In *Tiempo de silencio*, an ekphrasis of Goya's *El Aquelarre* embodies such a model of exhibiting power and virility over the female members of the species, which perhaps forms part of the network of symbols through which Dorita objectifies her loving image of Pedro. "El gran buco" is interpreted not as "el cabrón expiatorio" but as possessing a horn that is a "signo de glorioso dominio fálico" (155). He who possesses phallic power is equated with the bull, and not the bullfighter, whose horn is a symbol loaded with potency. Just as the desire of the theatre-going public is centripetally pulled towards the *supervedette*, "la muchedumbre femelle" expresses "en súplica sincera la posible revitalización por el contacto de quien ... se complace en depositar la pezuña izquierda" (155–6). The notion of revitalization through physical contact returns one to the notion of the sacred and the mystical power with which it transforms mere objects into consecrated symbols. And like a sacred idol, the *gran buco* persists in "el usufruto de la adoración centrípeta" (155), which pulls the women closer to the figure, all curious to discover its truth: "las mujeres se precipitan; son las mujeres las que se precipitan a escuchar la verdad. Precisamente aquellas a quienes la verdad deja completamente indiferentes" (156). The allure of an objectified image of masculinity becomes the centre of truth for a group of women who previously exhibited existential inertia. The "gran buco" therefore serves as a model of power, a magnetic lure in possession of a sacred truth that calls out to those in need of revitalization, and a symbol to adore.[9]

Both the *supervedette*, who reminds the public of monarchical greatness, and the virulent bull, who reminds the *buen pueblo acumulado* that they are descendants of "el águila de la guerra" (274), shield the public from awareness of Spain's decadence and propose – as the highest point of Spanish subjectivity – models that are rooted in a distant past that maintains a connection to present reality only through a mythology promulgated by collective belief. "Que esta imagen de la que fue, que triunfó con las mismas artes ... conforte y regocije y haga sentirse vengado al vencido pueblo" (274). Though the public certainly is free to choose any modality of being, the images projected within the Spanish cultural realm provoke, "haga *sentirse*," a somatic response of feeling that supersedes rational thought, which would inspire only feelings of inferiority. The body politic adopts cultural symbols in a very visceral manner, which is far more magnetic than empirical observation: "¿Para qué intentar buscarle cuatro pies al gato madrileño si la copla explicativa y lúcida que canta la supervedette va derramando historias y grandeza?" (273). It is unnecessary to take stock of one's mediocre destiny when the symbols projected within the cultural field provide a readymade limit point of subjectivity that proposes a national "truth" comprising feelings of greatness and redemption. In any case, knowledge of the self's multiple possible destinies produces such anguish that it is simply easier to fall into the historical vector of time pertaining to one's national tradition. This tradition is often arbitrarily determined by the images and creeds a central authority projects both onto its own populace and to the external world through such things as tourism pamphlets.

However, the majority of the characters in *Tiempo de silencio* never experience the anguish that comes with infinite possibility, meaning that the ease with which one falls into a culture's thrownness may be related to the alternative ways that consciousness assimilates cultural models. Symbols may draw in consciousness through both cognition and somatic attraction. Why examine Madrid's objective reality when the ideals projected by the *supervedette*'s couplets provoke *feelings* that are taken to be an objective limit of one's subjectivity? If one follows Kant's distinction between a judgment of critical reason and of aesthetic taste, the latter is unique in its avoidance of cognition and empirical reflection. Pedro's perception of Dorita as a cultural archetype and the audience's approval of "taurinamente" pursuing the *supervedette* are indeed capable of being rationalized by an outside observer. In contrast, Martín-Santos asserts that the everyday experience of a culture's facticity predisposes one to accepting symbols based on the aesthetic response that they provoke without ever reaching the point of critical reason.

I have compared a time of silence to a time of the sacred, meaning an environment where the sacred dogmatism of culture and politics pushes one on an elemental level to think and act in certain ways. The trajectory of *Tiempo de silencio* suggests that one tends to "love" culturally consecrated symbols that become instrumental in the definition of identity. The valence of the sacred, or its ability to form social bonds, is highly effective in part because a consecrated object often appeals not to the rational mind but to aesthetic feeling, especially what Kant would call the sublime, which projects feelings of both awe and of terror – like the numinous in Otto's thought. In the previous chapter, for Benet and Rodoreda a sacred object or deific figure assimilates externalized feelings of the numinous, which is itself an admixture of terror and awe. In all cases, the sacred can provoke automatic responses of feeling when one nears, touches, or profanes an object that is set apart. Both the presence of the sacred and its profanation provoke feelings that precede the activation of all rational thought, whether these sensations are reverence, horror, or adoration.[10] The sublime mixture of awe and unrelenting adoration that the sacred demands always requires that the adherent suspend rational doubt, and it is extremely difficult to disengage from an object or symbol once one has experienced it on such a strongly sensational level.

Martín-Santos's Madrid is a city broken into a dioceses populated with priests who re-enact the cultural models endorsed by the country's seat of authority. Muecas, for example, mimics the power relationship represented by *el viejo derecho* of an omnipotent paternal figure. A government has the capability to rhetorically and financially endorse certain cultural activities over others, thereby giving an activity like bullfighting a sacred character that draws on centuries of exhibiting a public spectacle of control over the flesh of another being. This, in reference to Franco's Spain, illuminates the importance of converting Manolete's death into an extended period of mourning. A sentimental comedy, another cultural form endorsed by the government, remains relevant through the regime's consecration of an intellectual elite who argue that such works pertain to a canon of performing arts. The list goes on.

By attracting the public's adoration through the sacralization of symbols, a state exploits the innate desire of the body politic to belong to a national structure. This offers a theory of the political where the *pueblo* enters into what it believes to be a loving relationship with the state. And indeed, capturing "el amor del pueblo" through the desire of the body politic to be loved is a very effective way of acquiring power because the transaction never appears forced or obligatory: "El amor del pueblo, para quienes lo quieren y comprenden, es amor no comprado … no es amor prostituido, sino amor matrimoniable, instituido sobre antiquísimas instituciones, bendecido por el necesario número de varones tonsurados y expuesto como ejemplo de coincidencia y de decoro, de equilibrio y paz no conturbada" (*Tiempo de silencio* 273).

Those in power not only want the public's love but they *understand* it, meaning that they are able to exploit the matrimonial dependence between the body politic and the institutions that regulate social life. The *pueblo* never escapes its subjection to the consecrated "antiquísimas instituciones" with which it is lovingly involved. The symbols that a government culturally endorses highly influence the behaviour of the general population towards itself and towards figures of authority, which is perhaps alluded to through Pedro's identification with San Lorenzo at the conclusion of *Tiempo de silencio*.

In Martín-Santos's Madrid, the error of the body politic in contracting into a loving relationship with such symbols is to believe that the *amor del gobierno* sacrifices its own liberty in an objectification of the *pueblo*. Once the beloved becomes an objectified centre of signification, as the state does when the public subscribes to its sacred models of culture, it becomes a certain and factual part of reality whose objectivity appears immutable by being independent of the existence of the self. This is of course quite powerful, as it discourages a general belief in the potential to change the symbols embedded within reality, although these images determine and regulate one's national identification. Moreover, this explains how one might be dragged along by history without attempting to step aside from the current of time and take stock of the bonds that hold society together. In Martín-Santos's novel, those who want *and* understand the public's love also, more importantly, comprehend its desire to hypostatically revolve its collective love around an elevated cultural symbol. The priestly "gobernantes arbitrarios" (*Tiempo de silencio* 15) who hold political sway in *Tiempo de silencio* never sacrifice their freedom to modify and endorse the values or ideals are thought to be the ideal limit of the body politic's self-identification.

Rerouting Sacred Time: *Tiempo de destrucción*

If Martín-Santos is thought of as a psychiatrist-cum-novelist mediating the neuroses of an ill Spanish society, it becomes important to pinpoint exactly how the author defines a "cure." As is indicated in Martín-Santos's psychiatric writings, a "desajenación" from the sacred dogmatism of culture restores a patient's freedom. However, this newfound freedom still requires a new vital project. Martín-Santos argues that such a project combines an objective understanding of the reality of one's symptoms with an ethical attitude towards the future. The decision to repetitively enact an ideal image of one's being and leave behind the recollection of the temporal circumstances that compelled the neurosis in the first place leads to a definition of the ethical that appears Kierkegaardian: "El paciente ha de reconocer como real la imagen favorecida de sí mismo ... El neurótico debe reconocer que no son admisibles las grandes discrepancias entre conducta concreta y actitud ética" (*El análisis existencial* 197). An ethical orientation towards the future requires closing the gap between a patient's actuality and his or her ideal image of the self.

In a psychiatric cure, a *concienciación* frees the patient from his or her automaton state, which then permits the patient to act "en el plano de las actitudes éticas merced a una lucidez" (*El análisis existencial* 198). Martín-Santos's notion of *concienciación*, which views the distillation of time into lived experience as a foregrounding for the members of the *pueblo* to become "ejecutores de la historia y creadores de una nueva realidad," is undoubtedly influenced by the second protagonist in his doctoral dissertation, Karl Jaspers. Jaspers writes, "Transcendence, as historic appearance in an objectified symbol, establishes a community that is unique in kind" (304). Metaphysics, therefore, appears symbolically and is historic without being cloaked in a mythological idealism whose distancing from the community is mysterious and resistant to cognition. Unlike in Sartre's relationship of love, Martín-Santos's theory of existential analysis proposes an intersubjective encounter where the lover does not snatch away the freedom of the beloved. This is precisely the principle limitation that he finds in Sartre's philosophy: "Sartre no ve el «amor» en su plenitud y de aquí nacen sus más esenciales limitaciones ... no alcanza a ver la decisiva eficacia del psicoterapeuta" (63–4). Love in its plenitude, which the analyst-analysand encounter epitomizes, permits the psychotherapist to provoke, not annihilate, freedom in the patient by assisting in the objectification of symptoms. Martín-Santos points to Jaspers on this point, arguing that "para Jaspers el médico puede ... provocar la curación. Sartre cree que es sólo el enfermo el que puede convertirse" (64). Jaspers, as we will shortly see, is instrumental in the conceptualization of *Tiempo de silencio* as a sacred cipher that opens up the possibility of an alternative destiny to the reader. This literary object, whose encounter with the reader constitutes a complicity, refuses to be the limit point of the Other's subjectivity.

The novelist, through a dialectics of sacrogenesis and de-sacralization, produces an objective symbol, the novel, whose contours are filled by the sedimentation of history. The knowledge that this object produces frees the community depicted within the work from its *normas objetales* and the unconscious propulsion of national tradition. The awareness produced by such a rupture bears many similarities to Jasper's notion of a cipher-text. This text is the site where "Being is grasped" and its reader is given both the gift of his or her historically determined nature and an awareness of freedom: "It is only the cipher-script which speaks to me, if I am ready for it. Philosophizing, I remain suspended between harnessing my possibility and being given my actuality as a gift. It is an associating with myself and with transcendence but it seems only rarely as if an eye looked at me out of the dark" (311).

And indeed it is the novelist who, out of a dark time of silence, meets the reader's subjectivity in the intimacy of his or her home, as though the meeting between literature and its audience were a private loving embrace.

The subject receiving the novel-cipher is confronted by a double exposure. First, the cipher creates an awareness of the reader being an object, or, an actuality. But at the same time, in an existential sense, it also exposes the subject to its innate, alienated freedom. Martín-Santos's definition of cure thus strongly resembles the desired effect of Jasper's cipher: "En el psicótico, la libertad está totalmente enajenada ... la cura consiste precisamente en la suscitación de un nuevo proyecto que substituya al proyecto neurótico. Y para ello, en la liberación de las trabas que, a lo largo de su vida, han ido limitando la libertad del neurótico" (*El análisis existencial* 184).

The dialectical process of obtaining a psychotic cure – whether for a sick patient or an infirm city – involves an auto-awareness of alienated freedom and a "harnessing of possibility." Jasper's cipher-script mediates this process, and in the case of Martín-Santos, a cipher is represented in existential psychoanalysis by the analyst's narrativization of a patient's case history and in literature by the novelist's totalizing, transparent *captación* of a time of silence.

Tiempo de silencio functions as a cipher that first assigns an awareness of actuality, where one relates a depiction of 1949 Madrid to the time of the text's readerly reception, which itself is regulated by the same projection of the past depicted in the novel. Beyond an awareness of actuality, the novel-cum-cipher also harnesses possibility through a "toma de conciencia," which is synonymous with, in psychiatric terms, a *concienciación*. On this point it is tempting, and even logical, to think of Florita's mother as the hero of *Tiempo de silencio*, because, unlike Pedro, she refuses to be silent and does not fall back into poses indicative of her assigned social position. The mistake is to think of her report of Muecas's guilt to the police as an ethical gesture, at least with respect to how ethics functions in Martín-Santos's thought. The narrator offers only a litany of reasons why the mother does *not* decide to support Pedro's innocence: "Y repetir obstinadamente: 'Él no fue.' No por amor a la verdad, ni por amor a la decencia, ni porque pensara que al hablar así cumplía con su deber, ni porque creyera que al decirlo se elevaba ligeramente sobre la costra terráquea en la que seguía estando hundida sin ser capaz nunca de llegar a hablar propiamente, sino sólo a emitir gemidos y algunas palabras aproximadamente interpretables. 'Él no fue'" (249).

In order to act in accordance with a universal truth or a duty defined by her being a witness to the crime and closely related to the victim, Florita's mother would have already needed to "flee time" by establishing a vital project incongruent with the robotic phrases and gestures that define her dragged-along-in-time existence. As the narrator of the novel puts it shortly before her confession at the police station, she is still a character "determinada al dolor y a la miseria por su origen" (248). What occurs, ultimately, is a classic awakening of the woman's consciousness, which is to say an awakening of the freedom to opt for a destiny that resolves the situation in a way markedly different from Cartucho, who is from the same social sphere and *longue durée* as the mother.

But Florita's mother's consciousness emerges from an essential nothingness without an a priori conception of moral duty or ethical behaviour. What marks her character up to this point in the novel is that she knows nothing about anything: "No saber nada. No saber que la tierra es redonda. No saber que el sol está inmóvil" (248), and so on. *Tiempo de silencio* ends, in other words, at the point where the heroine's freedom is *desajenada*, which incidentally coincides with her husband, Muecas, exiting the picture and becoming subject to the legal system. But being given an actuality is only half the story, and for an ethical sensibility to emerge, Florita's mother would thereafter need to harness her possibility and substitute the symptoms of an alienated freedom with a transcendent vital project. As the quotation above notes, her move towards consciousness itself is not meant to elevate her "ligeramente sobre la costra terráquea en la que seguía estando." This is the work of the future.

The future comes in the follow-up to the novel through Agustín in *Tiempo de destrucción*.[11] *Tiempo de silencio* best resembles a novel moulded through the trope of descending into the abyss, à la Dante's *Inferno*, which is also the structural shape of Joyce's *Ulysses*. In this case, Madrid's *chabolas* represent the abyss. In *Tiempo de destrucción*, of which only two of the four sections were close to completion at the time of the Martín-Santos's untimely death, the name Agustín must be read in reference to the saint of the same name, who experiences his own *concienciación* upon being asked by God to "take up and read." In that vein, the novel, which recounts the protagonist's voyage to the university in Salamanca to become a jurist in the first section and his investigation of a murder in Tolosa in the second, best resembles a Bildungsroman. In biblical terms, of course, Pedro is to Job what Agustín is to St Paul. We ultimately do not know Agustín's fate because the novel was unfinished, which ironically places him even closer to Paul, whose death is not documented by scripture.

Like Florita's mother, Agustín begins the novel being projected by a temporality indicative of where he is born on the peninsula and the city to which he emigrates. Mainer writes ("Prólogo" 37) that one of the unfinished fragments destined to form part of the novel's third section entitled "Canción de Águeda" reveals that Agustín's birthplace is Villaflores, near Salamanca. The novel's narrator, in turn, notes that "los muchachos que van para Juez suelen ser en su inmensa mayoría provenientes de las planicies de la Iberia árida. Solamente algunos vienen de la húmeda Galicia" (180). Villaflores, of course, is located in the heart of the arid *meseta* of Castile and León. The narrator also implies that the interpretation of law in Spain is kept generally within the hands of a homogenously conservative group, as no judge "por el contrario [viene] de las regiones que se consideran más progresivas de la nación, de las industrializadas Cataluña y Vasconia" (180). In the 1950s and 1960s, this statement was fairly objective, just as there were very few *militares* from these regions. In the context of Agustín's trajectory, however, the narrator is implying that his choice to become a judge has a historical thrownness rooted in geography that carries with it a predetermined modality of maintaining the "aparato institucional del Estado": "Así se sigue haciendo la historia en el mismo sentido con que se empezó doce siglos antes. Mediante el ariete de la lengua y la perfección del juicio escueto de los castellanos" (180). The judicial system is an institutional extension of the state's central seat of authority and wields the power to punish those who "flee time" and are deemed delinquents.

In this respect, a judge is to the Francoist state what a Catholic priest would be to the Vatican: a representative of a primary, papal figure of authority. A state consecrates a select group of individuals – a *sacerdocio* – with the power to discipline and punish in order to maintain the regulations made possible through an institutionalization of society. Legality and judicial authority are not inherently undesirable constructs and are essential components of social contract theory. However, thinking of a society's interpretation of justice as a publicly agreed upon iteration of "fairness," as John Rawls would argue, *is* unreasonably utopian. Rawls, who proposes a theory of justice modelled on social construct philosophy, argues that principles of justice are the "outcome of an agreement, citizens have a knowledge of the principles that others follow. It is characteristic of contract theories to stress the public nature of political principles" (*Theory of Justice* 16). Rawls's theory was highly disputed, most famously by Jürgen Habermas, and even Rawls himself reconsiders his original position in a follow-up work, *Political Liberalism*.[12]

Without wanting to belabour the point, I would agree with Rawls that stripping justice from those elements that subjectively benefit select parts of the polis with an eye towards a universal moral principles is a valiant end point. In Martín-Santos's Madrid (and Tolosa), however, just punishment for the select few who are permitted to enter into the polis and participate in the construction of the *civitas dei* are not equally subject to the law's application, and the law itself is an ever-evolving subjective notion. In *Tiempo de silencio*, for example, it is implied that had Florita's abortion been performed within the confines of a higher social class, the law might have turned a blind eye. In *Tiempo de destrucción*'s Tolosa, murder is legally prohibited for all citizens, but when the primary suspect is a member of the local industrial oligarchy, the police close the investigation without a resolution. The problem, therefore, is not necessarily the law itself. In *Tiempo de destrucción*, Martín-Santos homes in on those who treat the law as a subjective concept and on judges – those in charge of the penal code's institutional application.

With respect to the sacred dogmatism that assures the seamless continuation of time's thrownness, the law complements cultural symbols in its abrogation of the body politic's freedom as a being-for-itself. Unlike the choice of a loved object, which does not appear forced, the distribution of justice in *Tiempo de destrucción* is a way to undo the complicities of others and assign punishment to those the state identifies as stepping outside of the flow of national tradition. The narrator writes that children who decide to become judges will be those who "determinen las penas que deben afligir a los delincuentes, desde la muerte, hasta los arrestos apenas justificados por el derecho preventivo de la Ley de Vagos" (179). The "Ley de Vagos" is a clear instance of the arbitrariness of law based on the state's regulation of behaviour. During the Second Republic, the law's application was limited specifically to transients but ambiguously could be applied to anyone posing potential harm to social order, meaning that throughout the life of the legislation there remained a subjective opening completely dependent on the state's arbitrary definition of delinquency.[13]

In 1954, Franco attached homosexuality to the measure, specifying that punishment included internment in a work camp or special institution, with the only real requirement being isolation from the general population. Homosexuality plays a role in *Tiempo de destrucción*'s plot, as it is supposed that the engineer-foreman of the factory was romantically involved with the watchman, a fact gleaned through Agustín's dealings with a transvestite he meets by chance at an *iñauteria*, or Basque carnival. The suggestion that judges are in part attracted to the position through a desire to inflict punishment appears to be an indirect reference to Franco's heavy reliance on the prison system and worker camps to discourage ideological opposition through the use of the death penalty and brutal sentencing. While analyzing the character of those attracted to a judgeship, the narrator questions whether "hay quizá una cierta satisfacción instintual en ejercer el derecho a juzgar. Hay quizá una cierta gratificación sádica al infligir con plena legalidad sufrimiento al prójimo" (180). Inflicting suffering onto one's "prójimo" resonates in a country where the victors of a civil war continued, throughout a "time of peace," a violent crusade to rid the country of elements that profaned the regime's sacred notion of the nation. Ultimately, the narrator's uncertainty about a primal drive towards punishment is inconsistent with the general theory of Being promulgated throughout Martín-Santos's two novels. Innate drives are substituted for the assimilation of external models of comportment whose attraction is based on the subject's inner lack as a being-for-itself. However, questioning whether or not Agustín acts on the basis of a primal impulse does create dramatic tension by placing in doubt his potential for conversion later in the work.

Michel Foucault argues that the carceral system includes the "cloister, prison, school, regiment" (*Discipline and Punish* 293), implying that each segment uses similar mechanisms of punishment and regimentation to mould behaviour. In discussing the Mettray Penal Colony, which resembles the same punitive institutions in the modified "Ley de Vagos," Foucault argues that the officers "had to be not exactly judges, or teachers, or foremen … but something of all these things in a quite specific mode of intervention. They were in a sense technicians of behaviour: engineers of conduct" (294). Foucault marks a clearly defined point in the nineteenth century where the carceral system is completed, at which point the religious, political, educational, or judicial sectors collapse their unique functions into a "specific mode of intervention" meant to impose sets of behaviours. The ultimate goal of such a carceral mindset is to reduce one to a malleable state upon which any previous claims of selfhood antithetical to the sacred law of the institution are tossed asunder. The "technicians of behaviour" were thus tasked with producing "bodies that were both docile and capable" (294). In *Tiempo de silencio*, the malleability of "materia viva" echoes Foucault's thought: "¡Oh cuán plástica la materia viva; siempre nuevas sorpresas alumbra para quien las sepa ver!" (34). In this context, the "materia viva" refers specifically to Muecas's daughters, but existentially it has a bearing on Pedro as well, whose ideal image of himself as a researcher is replaced, through a punitive measure taken by his doctoral advisor, with becoming a country doctor, which he accepts with outright resignation ("Se puede cazar. Cazar es sano.").

An analysis of cultural symbolism in *Tiempo de silencio* and the manner in which the law functions in *Tiempo de destrucción* offers a complete picture of how a sacred dogmatism regulates the flow of time. On one hand, exposure to the aesthetic draw of long-established symbols such as *el aquelarre* pushes a subject away from adopting comportment inconsistent with the inscription of culture. On the other end of the spectrum, the justice system functions as a protective watchdog that interprets the law, which itself is thought of as an objective limit point of subjectivity, in a way that justifies the punishment of those who would rupture time's unconscious flow through *concienciaciones*. Punishment, which comes at the hands of a *sacerdocio* of judges consecrated with the authority to mediate and inflect sacred dogmatisms, in turn sacralizes those who profane the ideology of the state. This returns us again to the process by which Agamben theorizes the creation of *homo sacer*, whose fate is particularly spelled out in the "Ley de vagos" through the complete separation of the delinquent from society. Once touched by the law, a prisoner is set apart from his or her profane everyday existence and a kind of sacrifice is then carried out by the carceral system that reduces one to a malleable *materia viva*, or in Agamben's parlance, bare life.[14]

Prior to Agustín's *concienciación* – when he takes an active interest in the watchman's murder – the novel spends a great amount of time defining the peripheral social role of a judge. Agustín, like a priest preaching from a pulpit, observes society through a distanced perspective and avoids all subjective complicity with others. He defines complicity as "el cemento social" (196), and becoming a judge attracts him precisely because "la complicidad es la máxima fórmula social y por horror de la complicidad estoy dispuesto a ponerme fuera de ella: esto es, *a ser juez*" (196). Agustín's initial reaction to the Tolosan *iñauteria* is a key moment that reveals the sacred character of the judge. In his eyes, the agglomeration of the town's 18,000 citizens forms a "liturgia rítmica" (309), but the hierarchy of the congregation is broken by the liminal nature of the carnival, which represents a moment where the sacred is no longer set apart and protected. The *iñauteria* operates as a rupture where social divisions are removed in a unification of desire, class distinction, and *longue durée*, as the carnival coalesces "tan disparejas trayectorias" (311). Even the set-apart and exclusive character of the town's casino is suspended. The carnival "rompía toda posibilidad discriminativa y la única marea golpeaba en los salones del Casino con la misma violencia con que rompía en las tabernas de las calles estrechas y con la que había presidido horas antes la congregación y desfile de comparsas en la plaza pueblerina, momento inicial en que todos los sujetos … dejaron en suspenso sus deudas, sus nóminas y hasta sus fidelidades de noviazgo siempre sacrosantas" (314).

The event temporarily postpones liturgical rituals that regulate the congregation's behaviour and silences the dogma assigned to each social class. After entering a casino, the crowd even mocks Agustín's role as a sanctified judge, which marks a turning point in the novel by forcing the protagonist to step down from the pulpit and become complicit with others.

Agustín learns of the watchman's murder after being approached by a Bilbaoan transvestite in the casino, who says sardonically, "¡Mascarita-juez, no sabes nada!" before whispering, "Te están engañando. No sabes nada del crimen del sereno" (317). Similar to how St Augustine reacts to the singing voices of children, Agustín at this moment feels "el sobresalto de legalidad," and through his complicity with another individual "sintió una alegría vaga … le había aceptado el reino multitudinario: había sido reconocido y convocado: era cierto que existía" (319–20). The upsurge of legality coincides with a profaning encounter with a member of the congregation, which points Agustín towards the freedom to unravel the truth of a murder with far-reaching consequences. Agustín's *concienciación*, in other words, mimics the plenitude of love that Martín-Santos finds absent in Sartre, whereby complicity with the Other is not a mandatory annihilation of freedom.

Agustín's conversion, after his *concienciación* during the carnival, allows the judge to enact an ethical comportment more closely integrated with a universal morality. The narrator compares Agustín's time in the casino to climbing Jacob's ladder (315), which can be thought of as a progressive climbing towards a more virtuous and egalitarian model of applying justice. The judicial system is transformed from a machine calibrated to the interests of a small minority to an objective witness that unearths time's sedimented layers, where a judge assumes the role of the analyst who mediates the creation of a cipher-script that documents the *normas objetales* of the analysand. Interjected into the middle of Agustín's methodical unravelling of the murder's truth is a contemplation of time, where the narrator remarks that the past "tuvo a su paso una realidad total, una verdad total … una inmodificabilidad" (343). Similar to the framing of Madrid as a city without "sustancia histórica" dragged along by time in *Tiempo de silencio*, the narrator notes that "el sedimento residual" of the past's immutable total truth normally "se hunde incesantemente en el abismo del tiempo" (343). The challenge in resurrecting the truth of the watchman's murder is heightened by the fact that the residual fragments of time are conserved only in "algunas mentes confusas," and from this "incesante proceso de modificación … el juez intentará elevar la efigie del *castigo justo*" (344).

Agustín functions as the ethical repetition of the ideal image Martín-Santos sees of himself as a psychiatrist-cum-novelist whose *captaciones* open up an awareness of consciousness in the reader. For Agustín, just punishment not only represents unearthing the true murderer of the watchman but also "el instrumento extraordinario" that captures "la piedra que se iba hundiendo" and modifies it so that "la imagen del crimen quede indisolublemente unida a la del castigo, de modo que el criminal nunca gane y el universo moral sea, una vez más, confirmado en su verdad inconmovible" (344). Essentially, Agustín recalibrates justice through a moral matrix that creates a distinct relationship with the past. Before, the law maintained the mystery of time's thrownness by removing from public view those who exposed the arbitrariness of traditional Iberian modalities, whereas Agustín's evasion discloses the "there" that lies beneath the surface of reality.[15] A society in which interpretation of the law that does not reflect the will of the people is not, in an Aristotelian sense, political at all; a political partnership "aims at the most authoritative good of all" (*Politics* 35). Agustín's integration into the vital horde of the carnival, in stark contrast with the strict regimentation of Franco's Spain, is propitious for the creation of a political consensus that makes the law objectively applicable to all and protects one's *prójimos* from unchecked violence.

A time of the sacred is undone the moment its mystery is dispelled, and what this mystery hides are the alternative parts of history sunken into a temporal abyss. Previous investigations of the watchman's murder not only covered up a connection to a powerful member of the Tolosan oligarchy, but also buried the homosexual relationship between the engineer and the watchman on an even deeper plane. While interviewing the engineer and his family, Agustín responds to being shown a two-dimensional plane of the city with a question about the factory's connection to a gothic cathedral: "Debajo de toda iglesia gótica y bajo las fachadas barrocas añadidas posteriormente, suele haber una basílica romana aún reconocible. Y cuando el lugar es verdaderamente sagrado, debajo están los fundamentos del templo romano y más profundos algunos residuos megalíticos" (339–40).

Linking Agustín's notion of sacred places to a conception of sacred time confers powerful meaning to the relationship between justice and the resurrection of history's *verdad total*. Reconstituting the truth of the plenitude of time is a "de-sacralizing" gesture that reveals the official mapping of history as a false, two-dimensional account that obscures the unconsciously hidden foundations of the past, which continue to exist in the same way that Bergson's memory is never truly "forgotten." Moreover, a sacred edifice becomes visible only through the illusion of being set apart from structures that had been considered centres of authority. In truth, what sinks into the abyss and is thought to be absent is the highest form of presence; what lies beneath the surface provides a foundation and has the dangerous potential to become visible once again and propose a competing interpretation of history.

In summary, Agustín's detailed report of the watchman's death at the conclusion of the novel's second part deepens an understanding of how the speculative transcendence that emerges from a "sacrogenesis–de-sacralization" dialectic creates a cipher that argues against what had been sacred and set-apart models of behaviour. Agustín's complicity with the society in which he adjudicates law produces a text that caters to the good of society and not to cronyistic power relationships, rejecting the way Spanish institutions of law normally functioned during Francoism. The novel proposes a model for using the freedom created by a *concienciación* to change one's vital project, as the detailed report unveiling the truth of the murder is the result of Agustín's dedication to enacting his ideal image of "judgeness." And as mentioned before, Agustín represents Martín-Santos's own repetition of the ideal result of loving complicity between two beings-for-themselves, where neither participant abrogates the freedom of the other to be free. In the end, Martín-Santos's two novels together argue against unification of the body politic around sacred, symbolic beings without empirical thought and awareness of alternative possibilities. Similar to how Joan Sales's novel thinks through the exemplarity of Catalonia's victimization as a means to undo the victimary mechanism, Martín-Santos's unfinished trilogy produces a "sacred scripture of tomorrow" that argues against the sacred of Francoist Spain.

The specific *concienciación* that Martín-Santos carries out is an awakening of the political animal that lies beneath the oppressive *mascaritas* of identity that the regime promotes. Martín-Santos's 1963 speech on realism and reality is telling: "En la actualidad, la única arma con que el escritor español cuenta para la modificación de una realidad insoportable es precisamente la de escribir una novela suficientemente hábil para que pase la censura o suficientemente real para que preocupe políticamente al lector. No hay que olvidar que el escritor español oculta, generalmente, bajo su caparazón de hombre de pluma, un animal político en trance de ser definitivamente emasculado" ("Realismo y realidad" 141–2).

Martín-Santos's attempts to integrate his political sensibility into the partisan framework of the Partido Socialista Obrero Español resulted only in repeated detainments and closed doors. Turning to literature required creating a formal style that avoided the censors. A literature conceived as a sacred text denouncing the dogmatism of the regime's ideology concomitantly participates in a new conception of the political founded on the collective reception of literature within the intimacy of the home.

In the next chapter, I will argue that Salvador Espriu, like Martín-Santos, uses literature as a tool for de-legitimizing the illocutionary force of Spain's most cherished symbols and marks of identity. In lieu of thinking through sacrogenesis as a one-to-one encounter between the novelist-analyst and reader-analysand, Espriu constructs a poetics in his collection *La pell de brau* that endows the writer with the priestly function of congregating a sacred communion of national belonging. By the end of the 1960s, Espriu's priestly poetic voice transforms into a universal singularity – a mediating space through which Iberia's lost religiousness might be re-established. Unlike in Goytisolo's work, Espriu constructs a new Iberian temple that fundamentally alters the state's structure, enacting Habermas's idealistic notion of a public sphere where cultural centres each endorse their own particular symbols but with a conscious acceptance of plurality.

7 Espriu's Sepharad and the Equitable Restoration of Sacred Sovereignty

Once we open ourselves to a dialogue
we become caught up in its embrace.

Jürgen Habermas

Sacrifice and the Poetic Expulsion of Self

The notion of sacrifice permeates the entirety of Salvador Espriu's opus, most explicitly beginning with his rewriting of the Greek tragedies *Phaedra*, in novelistic form, in 1937, and *Antigone* in 1939.[1] Taking a long view of Espriu's literary progression reveals a series of critical moments where personal loss translates into a poetics that takes on an increasingly universal tone.[2] Like Dante's traveller into the inferno, Espriu's poetic persona, with each death that it encounters, slowly aggregates the stories of other and then must lose himself in order to create space. Espriu's duty is reflected by Tiresias in his adaptation of the Antigone tragedy: "El meu do és ben miserable. He d'escoltar i revelar tothora les calamitats dels altres" (47).[3] This dynamic acquires greater complexity in the poetic collection *El caminant i el mur* in "Just abans de laudes." While sinking into the underworld, "guiat enllà del vell origen de les aigües," the poetic voice announces its sacrifice: "Jo, que moro i sé / la solitud del mur i el caminant, / et demano que em recordis avui / mentre te'n vas amb les sagrades hores." The poetic voice here confronts a *tu dialèctic*, a rare moment of interpersonal exchange in the work, which is otherwise populated by the narrator's hermetic and solitary contemplation. As in Dante, shades deposit their stories with the solitary traveller, the *caminant*, who fosters a kinship with the dead in Hades. At the same time, the poem stresses that it is the poetic voice that demands that we, the readers, recognize his last moment of lucidity before floating down into the ether, which is the cost that the poetic traveller pays for forging a kinship with the dead.

The demand to remember takes on an ethical element that would be absent without the sacrificial dimension of the poetic speaker's death, which points to a truth tied to the role of remembrance in the constitution of a national community. The sacralization of death is the work of the living, the only ones who can mobilize around and grant meaning to a life dedicated to "la contínua font" of the *poble*. In Espriu's *El caminant i el mur*, poetic space is vacated when the poet lends part of himself to another's voice, which also demonstrates strong mystical overtones.[4] In Espriu's case, the call to remembrance signals the fact that sacrifice has implications that reach far beyond literary tradition.[5] More concretely, the arc of Espriu's post-war literature begins with a cosmologically abandoned time of destitution – the Spanish Civil War – and arrives at a transcendent Iberianism where the sacred communion of each nation on the peninsula connects with a universal project of coexistence in 1960s *La pell de brau*. Throughout Espriu's work, one finds a meditation on the relationship between a sacrificial vision of reparation and the restoration of sacral community, which culminates with the motif of building Sepharad's temple in *La pell de brau*.

Immolation in Espriu's work, as a conduit by which one identifies with the victim, nears the stance of Georges Bataille. Bataille's thought, as well as the study of sacrifice in primitive groups by anthropologists such as Hubert and Mauss, expands on the expiating nature of victimization.[6] In times of discord, death, or sin, sacrifice is a symbolic representation of a culture's self-mutilation and the expulsion of a malignant aspect of itself. More concretely, Bataille writes that sacrifice is "the rejection of what had been appropriated by a person or by a group" ("Sacrifice, Mutilation" 70). Bataille thus equates sacrifice to vomiting, and he who sacrifices participates in a "disgorging, free, continuously identifying with the victim, to vomit his own being just as he has vomited a piece of himself … in other words to throw himself suddenly *outside of himself*" (70). In Espriu's case, a repeated meditation on the poet's paying of the ultimate price, which comes to a head at the conclusion of *El caminant i el mur*, concerns victim identification, which is possible only by mutilating a previous practice of poetics that, in the wake of the Civil War's violence, only constructs imprisoning walls. Being thrown outside of oneself leaves behind a mediating poetic structure whose purpose responds to Martin Heidegger's post-*kehre* questioning of what poets are for: to provide the lyrical space through which to elevate the other's discourse to the status of a *cançó*.[7]

Espriu's political stance on Iberianism harkens back to Jacint Verdaguer and Joan Maragall and reflects a federalist structure. For Espriu, Sepharad, an ancient Hebrew term for the Iberian Peninsula, refers to the entirety of Hispania, a concept traditionally thought through by intellectuals such as Ortega y Gasset as a project excluding the periphery: "La meva concepció de la Península, el meu ideal d'organització social i política de l'Estat espanyol ... contempla una Espanya federal composta per quatre nacions: la nació castellana, la portuguesa ... la basca i la catalana" (cited in *Obres completes* 12: 243).[8]

However, with each successive prologue of *La pell de brau*, Espriu seems to lose more of the optimism he once used to distance himself from Carles Riba, his poetic mentor. In 1968, Espriu notes that the bilingual edition of the work "és un indici – un petit senyal, és clar, – que encara hi ha qui adopta valentament una esperançada actitud" (*Obres completes* 1: 241). The tone of the message insinuates that the numbers of those willing to adopt a hopeful disposition are dwindling. By August 1976, a few months before the Spanish parliament would declare democracy and a moment fraught with questions about dismantling Franco's governmental infrastructure and the devolution of power to regions such as Catalonia, Espriu's tone is even darker. He notes that *La pell de brau* was originally a response to "unes paraules d'Ortega, que també els homes de la perifèria peninsular érem capaços d'entendre el complexíssim conjunt dels essencials problemes ibèrics" (243). The next paragraph, however, reads, "Aviat em vaig preguntar, i continuo preguntant-me, si l'esforç valia la pena" (243).[9] On a poetic register, much of Espriu's work prior to his disenchantment in the late 1960s and 1970s links the edification of Sepharad to the sacrificial effort of a voice that extinguishes its own personality in order to become a mediating space. What truly seems tragic is that someone who worked tirelessly for cultural salvation in the belief of a greater Iberian coexistence would be reduced to such doubt in his old age.

Ironically, Espriu's first literary works, a series of short stories written in his early twenties, also question the validity of self-sacrifice in the resurrection of a dying culture that appears indifferent to its fate. "El país moribund" was first written between 1934 and 1935 and published in *Ariadna al laberint grotesc*. The story protagonizes a country that "havia perdut la seva ànima" by virtue of a literature that is "raquítica, amorfa, grisa, sense personalitat ni entusiasme" (*Narracions* 39). The narrator comes across the personified moribund country alongside a port, a not so subtle geographical indexing of Barcelona, which Espriu fictionalizes using the term Lavínia elsewhere. The mid-1930s, politically speaking, found Catalonia and its bourgeois intellectual establishment in disarray. Francesc Macià's death in 1933 and the Confederación Española de Derechas Autónomas victory in the 1933 elections left the Esquerra Republicana Catalana increasingly at odds with leftist anarcho-syndicalism. The October 1934 revolt by a Lluís Companys–led coalition as a response to the central government's limiting of the Generalitat's autonomy was a further blow. Within the cultural realm, it was clear by the 1930s, especially to a new generation of writers such as Espriu, that the classical, perfectionist vision of the *noucentistes* and the desire to resurrect a Mediterraneanism with Barcelona as a seat of authority was untenable. Both Espriu and Riba adopted Ancient Greece in their adaptations of *Antigone* and *Phaedra*, respectively. The poets' representation of a decadent, ruinous civilization is at least partly a response to the *noucentistes*' tarnished political program, in addition to being a commentary on the mythological import of fratricidal conflict in the case of *Antigone* and internecine strife in *Phaedra*.

"El país moribund" reinforces the notion of a country that wrests its glory from an antiquated past, as the country comments, "Sóc tan sols una anacrònica silueta medieval" (39). The narrator then invokes a series of voices in an attempt to make the country reconsider its position. This parade of characters introduces the reader to mythological personalities from Sinera, a backwards spelling of Arenys de mar, Espriu's birthplace, that reappear later, such as Pulcre Trompel·li and Ecolampadi Miravitlles. Espriu's creation of archetypical characters so early in his career suggests that he had a mythologizing intent from the start. Espriu, in the incipient stages of his self-fashioning as an artist, adopts a myth-making stance but roots the ironical turn of his fiction in a definite cultural context that would have been easily recognizable to his readers. This effort begins on a scale limited to Catalonia in "El país moribund" but slowly opens itself up to an Iberian metaphysics later in Espriu's opus.

The narrator's rebuttal of the moribund country's cynicism also opens a window into Espriu's incipient self-fashioning as an intellectual, with references to Nikolai Berdiaev and Oswald Spengler. The narrator references Spengler in order to convince the moribund country that its decadence is merely temporary. Spengler, and his work *The Decline of the West*, views European grandeur at or past its apogee, and also endorses the use of external myths and historical experience in order to understand one's own cultural milieu. He writes, on the relations between world cultures, that there is a "wealth of psychology" in between "Cultures which immediately touch one another … but also as between a living Culture and the form-world of a dead one whose remains still stand visible in the landscape" (*Decline of the West* 2: 55). This latter exercise typifies much of Espriu's post–Civil War work, which delves into Hebrew mythology, Egyptology, Ancient Greek thought, and biblical motifs as all part of a prism through which to refract a discourse on Iberia. Indeed many of these traditions figure prominently in Sepharad's history, which in Spengler's words constitute "remains" that stand visible on Iberia's landscape.

Espriu partly owes Spengler for the adoption of mythologies from outside his cultural heritage as a tool for understanding twentieth-century Iberia, but Francoist censorship also played its part by mandating an indirect and veiled criticism. By pooling together sacred motifs from other sources, Espriu constructs a metaphysics of Iberia by cognizing, and thereby profaning, consecrated myths from other milieus and the communities that gave such narratives a vital force. The mysterious origins of a sacred narrative are unveiled by applying myth to a historical situation, which places the very real spilling of blood as the motivator for the creation of a new mythology within Espriu's own opus. With respect to Spengler's influence on Espriu, it is useful to compare the development of Iberian civilization with a connectedness to religion, where the autumn/winter phase of a culture's decadence is related to a loss of sacred belief.[10] Spengler relates a springtime renewal to a religious upswing, and he calls a "second religiousness" a moment that appears "in all Civilizations as soon as they have fully formed themselves as such and are beginning to pass, slowly and imperceptibly, into the non-historical state in which time-periods cease to mean anything" (310). Western Civilization, to Spengler, was beginning to show signs of reaching this point within a handful of generations. A culture's second religiousness, the rediscovery of an early sacred force, consists in a "deep piety that fills the waking-consciousness ... Nothing is built up, no idea unfolds itself – it is only as if a mist cleared off the land and revealed the old forms" (310).

Though not evident in "El país moribund," Espriu's initial collection of poetic works unerringly symbolize objects denoting a lost religiousness, such as sunken temples, false idols, and public losses of faith. This is quite evident in "Una vella resposta que t'haurà de servir" in *El caminant i el mur*. "Abandonant la llei / us heu alçat morts ídols enfront del vostre Déu." The vitalism of a deity, which when translated to a Spenglerian notion of civilization, is akin to the return of the primary sacred forces of a culture's first religiousness, is hidden by dead gods in the destitute period of the autumn of civilization. Espriu conceives of a poetic sacrifice that demands the soul's descent towards the dead, an emptying out that reverses Teresa de Ávila's *grados de oración*. The final poem reflects this turn: "Baixats amb mancament tots els graons, / m'endinsen pel domini de la nit." This is a descent to Hades, to the dead, which implies a sacrifice of the self quite distinct from the unification with God of both John of the Cross and Teresa by relinquishing subjectivity. On this point, Espriu reveals that his kinship with the *Antigone* tragedy is not only with Tiresias, but also with the play's eponymous main character. In Sophocles's version of the play, Antigone notes to her sister Ismene, who wishes to join in the former's sacrifice, "You are alive, but my own soul / has long since died, that I may bring help to the dead" (56). A plummeting into the ground of Being is akin to removing the false idols shielding a civilization's sacred roots from view by "clearing a mist off the land," which means that the temple built at the conclusion of *La pell de brau* is less a new construction than a revelation of the useful detritus from the ruined places of worship.

In 1934, the spectre of a poetic sacrifice was beyond Espriu's horizon of experience, as the conclusion of "El país moribund" details the narrator's refusal to save the country from its own suicide. Despite the narrator's argument for the possibility of cultural resurrection, the moribund country acts according to its moniker and leaps into the sea: "El cos queia amb clapoteig a les aigües encalmades, en un solitari indret, i jo n'era l'únic testimoni" (41). The story's conclusion diverts a focus on the narrator and places attention squarely on the indifference and ignorance of those whose country has plunged into the sea. The narrator decides to "telegrafiar la notícia, és més essencial que intentar salvar-lo," but the people's response is a telling portrait of the society of Espriu's time: "Té, el país es va morir, visca! Fins tenim un país que se'ns mor" (41). However, the conclusion is ambiguous. Has the country already died and is the populace unaware that its nation has sunk to the bottom of the port? Or does the story comment on the critical state of all European countries and the absence of a Continental project of cultural resuscitation, especially among the nations of the Iberian Peninsula?

The Sacred Bonds of Kinship

Living through the Civil War, which halted Espriu's studies in Egyptology, reconfigured the poet's consideration of sacrifice. Espriu's post–Civil War poetry endorses a solitary kinship with the dead rather than merely telegraphing signs of decadence to the apathetic living. Returning to Spengler, Espriu decided to reach into the cultural depths of the past to rediscover a deeply rooted sacred communion that, in a prophetic motion, could lead to a second religiosity. This turn mirrors Pablo Ibbieta's change of perspective in Jean-Paul Sartre's story "The Wall," which did not play a role in Espriu's own adoption of *el mur* as a literary sign, although that may be hard to fathom. In Sartre's story, Ibbieta, while trapped in a cell awaiting death by firing squad the next morning, remarks, "I'd never thought about death because I'd never had any reason to, but now I did have a reason, and there was nothing else to do but think about it" (7). In 1939, the Civil War was Espriu's reason to think about death, and there was nothing else to do but think about it.

Espriu's *Antígona* is initially dated 8 March 1939, a few weeks before the Nationalist takeover of Madrid and a month before the Republic's unconditional surrender.[11] Though written a few years after "El país moribund," the works are worlds apart in their cultural gravity. The role of sacrifice, embodied by Antigone in her steadfast dedication to the sacred rites of kinship demanding that she bury her brother Polyneices, is stressed by Espriu in the work's 1947 prologue: "Mai no pararíem de mostrar el sacrifici de la princesa, la lliçó del seu alt exemple" (18). However, Espriu adopts Aeschylus's *Seven against Thebes*, not Sophocles's version of the tragedy, and several observations can be gleaned from this changing of *muthos*. Rather than beginning the story after the two brothers' battle for the city, Espriu dramatizes Polyneices and Eteocles and their civil war. This decision expands the scope of the tragedy, emphasizing Antigone's propulsion to both her own death and that of her family line, which is shared by the city itself, whose downward momentum towards more conflict and auto-destruction is equally immutable.

Espriu's version also presents a very different version of central authority – Kreon – by insisting on his subjection to his inner council and incapacity for autonomous thought. More importantly, Sophocles's version of the play ultimately argues against an innate moral fault in Kreon's character by subscribing his actions to *hamartia* and allowing for discovery, or *anagnorisis*. Aristotle's *Poetics* defines *hamartia* as "error," but it is a substantial error and leads to "a disastrous choice of action: a choice which arouses our pity because it is both catastrophic and made deliberately but not out of wickedness" (*Poetics* 17). Kreon, in Sophocles's work, is neither totally innocent nor totally guilty as he steadfastly adheres to the legal code of Thebes and to the demands of Eteocles, who bestowed his power on him. Of course, Kreon's moment of *anagnorisis* comes too late, after both his son and his wife have committed suicide, leaving him, in his own words, "dissolved in wretched anguish" (*Theban Plays* 87). In Espriu's rendition of the tragedy, there is never a moment of correction or realization by the sovereign. Kreon's final words, "Què aconselleu? Us exigeixo una clara resposta," deprive the leader of total agency, and therefore the critical reason to analyze the effects of a situation and foresee its tragic consequences. The tyrant's moral flaws are not merely missteps, and Kreon's lack of awareness in Espriu's rendition of the play precludes his ever assuming responsibility for the city's demise and move beyond his innate wickedness.

However, Espriu's *Antigone* concludes with the onus of responsibility placed not on the tyrant, who is a clear stand-in for Franco, but on the people. In a long monologue, "el Lúcid Conseller" describes Antigone's death as "impolític" for not having attracted a single witness: "Sovint les pitjors crueltats no alteren la nostra indiferència" (*Antígona* 73). Antigone's sacrifice has no productive potential and is limited to the extirpation of her familial lineage. The silence surrounding her death, and its incapacity to draw together the collective force of the city, prevents her sacrifice from translating into a sacred gesture: "No varen col·locar Antígona en un inaccessible cim, amb els hipotètics déus, sinó, com a tu i com a mi, a nivell de la confusa vida, és a dir, a nivell del sofriment" (73). Antigone's isolated final resting place symbolizes the aborted potential of her sacrifice. Earlier in the play, when Antigone is presented before Kreon for illegally burying Polineices, the public surrounded the palace in protest, but fear of sovereign retribution maintains a veil of silence around her death and precludes her sacralization as a deific figure. The gods, in the lucid councillor's words, are merely "hypothetical," because the deification of an innocent victim is achieved only through the outward expression of the collective's will. In truth, Antigone never becomes a transcendent *corpus mysticum*, like Numa does in Benet's fiction, with the potential to be politically represented by a living *corpus naturale*. As a consequence, she – like the rest of the community – is resigned to her most basic human fate, which is to suffer.

With respect to post-war Spanish society, Espriu is asking a fundamental question about civic life and, in the councillor's words, "la responsabilitat … del nostre silenci," which is in part born of a "temor de desplaure al nou rei" (73). In Francoist Spain, the public's fear of protest was well founded, considering the reprisals one could expect from the state carceral system. However, on a more abstract level, I believe one can return to Arendt's distinction between power and violence and consider Espriu's commentary as a reminder of the political potential of the body politic's collective vital force. But it is difficult to read Espriu's repeated assertions of Sepharad's cowardice throughout his poetry as anything but criticism of the public's submission to the regime.

Antígona presents competing claims to sacred truth, placing the bonds of kinship and loyalty to the state in conflict. The different interpretations of the tragedy frequently play out this division. Hegel's thought is perhaps most well known, and is summarized succinctly by Judith Butler in *Antigone's Claim*: "Hegel claims that Antigone represents the law of the household gods … and that Creon represents the law of the state. He insists that the conflict between them is one in which kinship must give way to state authority as the final arbiter of justice" (4–5). Butler deconstructs the state/kinship binary by interpreting instances of destabilized gender throughout the play, as kinship and the state forge an opposed representation only "by each becoming implicated in the idiom of the other" (10). Butler reflects a theme developed throughout my own study, which is the manner in which sacred discourse tends to spill over into the secular conception of sovereignty, precluding the capacity of the two spheres to maintain a separation between their respective idioms.

The centralizing brand of Iberianism criticized by Espriu, as evidenced in Ortega y Gasset's thought and in Franco's sacralization of Spain, presents an image of the state that finds legitimacy in a claim to sacred truth, which is purified by excluding alternative narratives of national heritage often located at the peninsula's periphery. In Espriu's *Antigone*, Kreon represents multiple Francoist impulses: the adjudication of who can take part in the sacred rituals of the polity, the sovereign right to scapegoat, and a conversion of the sovereign into a priestly consecrator of martyrdom. In the wake of the Theban civil war, Kreon effectively leaves Polineices as an unburied *homo sacer* barred from sacred ritual and therefore prohibited from being transformed into a divinized object of worship around which his former allies might organize. Also, in a clear reference to mass

Republican exile in the wake of the Spanish Civil War, Kreon declares, "Desterraré el culpable de fomentar divergències contràries a la unió i al ressorgiment de la ciutat" (62). The notion of scapegoating is here evident, as it is in many other works studied in this book, through the justification of victimary exclusion in order to end discord and mimetic violence. "Union," in this case, is a misnomer. Kreon places responsibility for conflict exclusively on the losing side, and the alternative to exile is silent submission. In opposition to Polineices and his forces, the city recognizes heroism in those who perished fighting for Eteocles. Kreon's line, "aquesta és un diada de dol i d'homenatge als nostres herois. Seria avinent de dedicar-la a meditar en un greu i religiós silenci," demonstrates how a sacred idiom of martyrdom spills over into the secular sphere of heroism. National mourning involves a religious silence that gives meaning to the deaths of those loyal to the state, thereby converting their loss into sacrifice. The line drawn between those whose deaths reflect heroism and those whose bodies are left above ground at the mercy of vultures also defines the boundaries of citizenship and membership in the state's sacred communion, a dynamic Franco played out in his construction of the Valle de los Caídos. As a final subtext, the Antigone tragedy is a reminder that the sacrificial dimension that Espriu later confers onto his poetic voice is a gesture of protest – a claim to an alternative sacredness whose purpose is derived from a duty to his perished kin. The political resonance of this gesture, regardless of how hermetic much of Espriu's poetic work might be, always remains tied to a socio-historical context.

Antigone, returning to Butler's thesis, adopts a legal idiom, normally assigned to the secular functioning of the polis, in her competing claim to sacred truth based on kinship. When brought before Kreon's court, Antigone claims innocence – in a discourse belonging to jurisdictional process – and argues that "la meva sang m'ordenava d'arrencar aquell cos de la profanació" (71). She frames her death, moreover, as a sacrifice made not for the benefit of a subjective belonging to a familial heritage, but as a necessary step for the good of the polis. Her final words in Espriu's version of the play indicate as much: "Que la maledicció s'acabi amb mi i que el poble, oblidant el que el divideix, pugui treballar" (72). Antigone, in her last statement, adopts the king's idiom with respect to scapegoating, prohibiting the city's resurgence from being framed as an autonomous act of the sovereign. Moreover, she links her behaviour, which responds to "els nostres antics preceptes" (53), to the well-being of the polity. This resolution has consequences that reverberate throughout Espriu's subsequent meditations on the sacred.

In political terms, Antigone is an instance in which a peripheral component of a political structure contributes to greater civic health through fidelity to its own ancient sacred patrimony and codes of action. In terms of federalist intellectual history, this stance harkens back to the nineteenth-century champion of *particularisme*, Valentí Almirall. Almirall postulates that "particularism," a movement that argues for a federalist restructuring of the Spanish state, is "un remei" (23) to the poverty of the nation and not a veiled argument in favour of Catalan separatism. For Almirall, the Catalan *renaixença* is a peripheral answer to a Spanish problematic, which would "augmentar lo patrimoni nacional d'idees" (23). In contrast, Kreon, a symbol of the unitary state, is the continuation of a centralizing force that imposes a top-down vision of sovereignty in which power is hoarded by the centre. This variation of political structure tends to engender cyclical violence, as when Eteocles's dismisses his father's edict and Polineices is exiled beyond the walls of Thebes. Espriu's version of Antigone thus presents two competing ways of using the sacred to organize the state and its components: one, federalist and based on a kinship that is conscious of pluralism, and another based on a centralizing authority that is exclusive and victimizing.

Death by the Pen: *Les hores*

Espriu famously writes in poem XLVI of *La pell de brau* that "a vegades és necessari i forçós / que un home mori per un poble." The poet, far from simply speaking in generalities, is referring to his own lyrical transformation that commences with the onset of the Spanish Civil War in 1936. Beginning in 1946 and up until the publication of *Final del laberint* in 1956, Espriu moves from the deeply personal hermeticism linked to his first poetic works to the capacity to embody and thereafter project a collective voice in *La pell de brau*, published in 1960. This shift is evident in Espriu's grammar. The first-person singular is predominant throughout *El caminant i el mur* and *Final del laberint*, only to be replaced by the first-person plural in many of *La pell de brau*'s fifty-four poems. Alongside this transition is a corollary movement beginning with an obsessive meditation on death, which Espriu identifies as a principal theme of *El caminant i el mur* in the collection's first prologue, to a movement of redemption and of hope in the rebuilding of Sepharad's sacred temple in *La pell de brau*, which itself depends on unmasking false idols.

Espriu's first major poetic works feature a perspective turned inward towards a past that avoids disappearance through lyrical recollection. Espriu's birthplace of Arenys de Mar, poetically known as Sinera, protagonizes his first collection, *Cementiri de Sinera* (1946). The first two sections of *Les hores* (1952/1955) are dedicated, respectively, to the deaths of his mother and the Mallorcan poet Bartomeu Roselló-Pòrcel. Memories of infancy and of his mother return in *El caminant i el mur* (1954) in the first section entitled "Les ombres, el riu, el somni perdut." Of great interest, however, is the third part of *Les hores*, which was written after the initial two sections and is dedicated to the death of Salom, a heteronymic creation that Espriu uses to refer to himself. Salom is an avatar that also makes an early appearance in Espriu's work, most notably in the short story "El meu amic Salom," published in *Ariadna al laberint grotesc.* The story debuts the term *Konilòsia,* a mythological term referring to Barcelona, and in Spenglerian fashion construes Catalonian society as out of touch with its first religiousness. Konilòsians "tracten el patrimoni col·lectiu, tant l'espiritual com el material, amb la més grossa de les indiferències" (*Narracions* 17). The story attaches several autobiographical markers to Salom, including a decision to study law, which Espriu himself had done at the Universitat de Barcelona in 1930. As in "El país moribund," Konilòsia is framed as a country on the downward slope to death and in need of a redeemer. Salom, naturally, declares himself a saviour: "Em vaig ensorrar, jo, el redemptor" (18).

The third section of *Les hores* is dedicated to "Recordant allunyadament Salom (18-VII-1936)," implying that the horrific conflict that erupts in July 1936 sacrifices a part of the poet's voice. The death of "Salom," a term that is normally translated into Romance languages from Hebrew as "peace," also signals an outbreak of violence and a long-departed sense of wholeness and well-being. In the poem "Pontos," the poetic voice links a recollection of Salom to a sacred temple that has sunk into the sea: "Al fons dels ulls tranquils del mar / he vist el somni / caigut, romput, del temple / d'un déu antic" (*Cementiri / Les Hores* 89). Pontos himself is an ancient god who is supplanted by Poseidon in Greek mythology as the deity of the sea. Pontos is also a locality of the Alt Empordà, near an archaeological site containing vestiges of Iberian and Roman settlements from the Bronze Age, and was also the site of a battle against the French in 1795. In this poem, the disappearance of Pontos resonates with the myth of Atlantis – which indexes the epic poem *L'Atlàntida* by Jacint Verdaguer, signalling that the sinking of a decadent Mediterranean civilization accompanies Salom's violent passing, which poetically serves as Espriu's own heteronymic sacrifice. As a site of cyclical grandeur and decadence, Pontos betrays a sacred character by virtue of the layering of its history, similar to what occurs in Martín-Santos's *Tiempo de destrucción.* The poet, who witnesses without indifference the residue of the temple, remains cognizant of a cultural patrimony, unlike other Konilòsians.

In an epoch of lost religiousness, Salom becomes untethered from his congregation and his temple of lyrical expression, which loses visibility because of the destructive force of a divisive past event. The sacred, a unifying social force that represents the transcendent reality of a united people, is declared null and void. The contrast between Pontos's violent past and the tranquil *ulls del mar* is striking, and perhaps references Spain's "time of peace" of the 1940s and 1950s when a persistent confrontation with death mutes explicit violence, as though the always-present reminder of one's mortality itself dulled the sharpness of experience. Espriu's repeated references to Sepharad's famine and thirst in *La pell de brau* lend credence to this notion, and it is difficult to imagine how death would *not* be a central preoccupation for Espriu. Not only was the remembrance of conflict constant, in part because of the regime's incessant sacralization of the martyrs of the winning side, but life within the country was marked by the constant spectre of mortality – famine, poor living conditions, and government oppression. The prohibition against honouring the dead on the losing side made it Espriu's duty to break official dictums, like Antigone, and obey the precepts of kinship in search of a religiousness that had been lost. The charged symbolism of "Pontos" bears references to a history of violence, the fleeing of the gods, and millennial degradation, traits that become more explicit in Espriu's next work, *El caminant i el mur*.

Coming eye-to-eye with mortality arrives with the outbreak of combat. Whenever the poet looks into the eyes of the sea, which preserves the memory of what was destroyed, what unfolds in his consciousness is a reminder of a sunken civilization, the painful losses etched into the temple's walls, and the absence of collective, congregational experience. The trope of melancholic loss linked to the sea recalls other Iberian cultural itineraries, most prominently the *cantigas d'amigo* and the notion of *saudade* in early Galician-Portuguese lyric. The first section of *El caminant i el mur*, not surprisingly, commences with an epigraph by Rosalia de Castro, "Quero quedar ond'os meus dôres foron." Espriu's initial poetic works following the war, up through the first two sections of *El caminant i el mur*, find the poet stranded alone on an island, immobile, and staring into the depths of his pain through the reflection of the past by the sea's iridescent waters.

The structural effects of such an environment affect the kind of poetic language within Espriu's reach. "Pontos" stresses that the resonance of language, through the experience of pain, loses its hopeful lyricism, and conceptualizes death as an isolated and carceral state that disengages the poet from previously certain points of reference. The poet's words themselves become calcified and distanced from the flexible musicality of song:

> Ah, marbre fred del temps, la meva vida
> que perdo contra el glaç de les paraules!
> Damunt la roca nua de la mort,
> puc ja només alçar l'alta columna
> d'aquest dolor, un aspre, solitari
> crit sense cant.

Time is as cold and immutable as marble, qualities that also invade language itself. For Espriu, poetic language loses its warm musicality and assumes an icy facade, assisting in the poet's entrapment by forming part of an incarcerating wall. Later in the collection, this sentiment is repeated in "Ofrenat a Cèrber," where the poetic voice arrives at the gates of Hades after having sunk his hands into "l'or misteriós / del meu vell català i te les mostro / avui, sense cap guany, blanques de cendra / del meu foc d'encenalls." The poet's delving into the mystery of language was a flash in the pan, a bolt of light that leaves nothing but white ash in its wake. Moreover, language has been transformed from being vitalistic into hardened ice and is a threat to the poet's very existence, which is implied in the violence of "losing one's life against the words." In this poem, it is impossible to avoid consideration of Francoist language politics and the penalization – even auto-mutilation – of an innate part of Espriu's daily existence, to speak nothing of his poetic vitality. The energy of language is directly related to the viability of the poet's own existence, and yet, despite the word's lost warmth, the poetic voice of "Pontos" refuses to be subject to a different linguistic code and sacrifices himself against "el glaç de les paraules."

Espriu's *Kehre: El caminant i el mur*

"Pontos" and "Ofrenat a Cèrber" foreshadow the underworld that characterizes many of the settings in *El caminant i el mur*. The collection's second poem immediately highlights Espriu's curious take on mysticism, where the "camins del meu pensament" function as the River Styx and the pathway towards a "record de mortes." Consumed by solitude and in possession of a language disconnected from others, the poet's response is to construct a wall – an "alta columna" of pain. The regime removed the poet's contact with formerly dependable fields of cultural production, inserting a breach between author and public. Without the possibility of linguistic and cultural transmission, one can speak of both an external exile – as many Catalan intellectuals fled the country – and an internal exile in the death of private life, a fact corroborated by the confiscation of even private correspondence in Catalan in Spain's postal system. This is, to be sure, a destitute time, to borrow a phrase from Heidegger, as the poet experiences a schism between himself and a reading public that no longer listens. The poet would desperately like to flee his "covarda, vella, tan salvatge terra" towards greener pastures in the north, as he writes in "Assaig de càntic en el temple," but the only escape route available is a passage to the underworld via inner consciousness.

Espriu, both here and in *La pell de brau*, reiteratively refers to Sepharad's cowardice, which links directly to the councillor's meditation on the silence of Thebes at the conclusion of *Antígona*. Espriu, somewhat controversially, critiques the public's refusal – rather than its incapacity – to listen to and value a cultural patrimony that protests the laws of a tyrannical king and its victimizing use of the sacred. The poet's plea that his readers remember him, after he slips away from *les sagrades hores*, is more than simple desperation; it also embodies a healthy dose of frustration with his country's indifference. Driven to hermeticism, Espriu's response, in *El caminant i el mur*, is to make a turn that theoretically resembles Martin Heidegger's own *kehre*. After the Second World War, Heidegger turned his attention from a strict understanding of how *Dasein* apprehends *Sein* and "turned" the perspective around, from the self to Being. An unconcealment of Being depends on human subjectivity, which leads to a meditation on language, particularly poetic language, and the function of the poet as a sleuth tracking the footsteps of the gods. In Espriu's case, *El caminant i el mur* resembles a long sacrificial process in which the poet negotiates how to move beyond entrenchment within a geographical and cultural history. Espriu's goal is to arrive at a point where the poet might function as a universal mediator of the stories and histories of others. *El caminant i el mur*, in other words, negotiates how to transition from Sinera – the site of the poet's own familial deaths – to Sepharad, a territory balanced between national sacred communions. Espriu's contemplative sinking into a Hades populated by the deaths of others thus negotiates the relationship between the singularity of a poetic *Dasein* with the mediation of a multifarious Iberian reality and its optimal organization.

In philosophical language, Espriu's task, at the point where he is poetically placed up against a "wall" and given the choice between betrayal and literary death, is to direct his poetological transmission towards a kind of open, indefinable origin of Being, which in this case is the origin of his own irreducible personal history. As indicated earlier, Sartre's Civil War narration "The Wall" resonates with the existential quandary presented to the poetic voice developed throughout *El caminant i el mur*. Ibbieta is placed in a situation without exit where sacrifice for his comrade, Ramón Gris, is impossible. Offered the opportunity to salvage his life if he gives up Gris's location, Ibbieta sends his captors on a wild goose chase to a local cemetery, believing that his associate is elsewhere. As the result of circumstances beyond Ibbieta's comprehension, Gris had actually relocated to the cemetery, is captured, and is killed. Ibbieta's "betrayal" is effected by his own words betraying *him*. It would seem, therefore, that the only possible way for Ibbieta to adopt a sacrificial vision of his own death would be to say nothing and remain silent. The crux of the issue, however, is that heroism is nullified not by the contingency of Gris's movement but rather by how the omnipresence of death neutralizes any transcendent meaning towards which to direct human action. By the time Ibbieta is brought before the Fascists, he "couldn't give a shit about Spain and anarchy: nothing had any importance anymore" (23). Under these auspices, preserving his own life, or extinguishing it for the sake of Gris's importance to the anarchist cause, cannot hope to be perceived through a sacrificial vision. To Ibbieta, the entire quandary appears "comical." In the words of Espriu's *lúcid conseller*, what is the "omnipresence of death" but the enchainment of humanity to "la confusa vida, és a dir, a nivell de sofriment" (*Antígona* 73)?

Ensconced in an environment in which the sacred symbols of kinship have sunk into ruin, Espriu's poetics fight to find a transcendent truth that would help to bestow a sacrificial dimension onto the lyrical treatment of death. In Sophocles's *Antigone*, returning to the conceptual nearness between Espriu and Tiresias, the latter's prophetic potential is neutralized in Sophocles's version of the play by failed augury and sacrifice. Instead of fire leaping forth from Tiresias's burnt offerings, "a putrid liquid" oozes out from the immolated animal, and its gallbladder explodes. This phenomenon, coupled with a vision of birds tearing at each other rather than announcing an augury, leads to the prophet declaring to Kreon that the gods no longer listen because Thebes has been mismanaged. Moreover, the explosion of the gallbladder directs the audience's attention to the correlation between the outbreak of violence and the disintegration of sacred rites.

Espriu's quest to revalidate the potential of sacrificial ritual demands re-sacralization, which reinstitutes a bond between earth and firmament. This intent, of course, is also comparable to *Antigone*. Franco's incessant sacralization of Spain, from the pulpit of the state, contrasts with Espriu's own counter-sacralization based on the deep bonds of kinship. The course of *El caminant i el mur* navigates this dilemma, which comes to a head in the work's final two poems, "Escrit a la manera de Salom" and "Sentit a la manera de Salvador Espriu." A close analysis of the two shows that the best manner to pass beyond the poet's imprisoning wall and return to the living is to dig downward "ond'os meus dôres foron." The poems also indicate something far more substantial about the closure between Espriu's fictional persona – Salom – and his connection to a painful personal history of loss.

Salom, Espriu's avatar and writerly identity, comes face-to-face with the poet himself – his maker, if you will – in the collection's final two poems. Stranded on an isolated island of death in "Escrit a la manera de Salom," in the poem's opening lines Salom questions what it is that his pain constructs: "Alçarà a poc a poc el meu dolor / la bona casa en els dies de l'erm?" However, the poet's pain only builds his wall higher. The icy words against which the poet flings himself are in the second stanza specified as "tots els noms de la mort," which imprison him in "una lenta cançó." Salom, and the ontological position of Espriu as a writer, here reach a limit point where the nature of the wall that impedes movement is finally understood. In terms of poetic progression, the movement towards "feeling" (*sentir*) things in the manner of Salvador Espriu in the next poem begins a poetic traversal beyond Salom's death and a release from the imposed exile of a destitute time. Salom's death is finally granted a sacrificial nature; sacrifice is solicited in order to transcend *el mur*.

The transition from "escrit" to "sentit" in the final two poems of *El caminant i el mur*'s points to a movement beyond spoken discourse that hinges on the ineffability of something felt, heard, or sensed. Unlike the Castilian *sentido, sentit* in

Catalan implies that something is both heard and felt. Espriu, in his own genuine manner, calls the reader's attention first to prosody, rhythm, and poetic recitation. This is a critical reminder that the poet is first and foremost a responder to the aural appeal of language, which mirrors Heidegger's study of the Romantic poet Friedrich Hölderlin: "The more poetic a poet is – the freer (that is, the more open and ready for the unforeseen) his saying – the greater is the purity with which he submits what he says to an ever more painstaking listening" (*Poetry, Language, Thought* 214). In being "sentit a la manera de Salvador Espriu," the poetic voice in this work recollectively gestures towards an openness to the revelation of language's appeal, at the same time inciting the reader-listener's anticipation of the forthcoming poetic recitation. The poem is thus a meta-poetical meditation that ruminates on the originary hearth of Espriu's literary craft.

The opening line of "Sentit a la manera de Salvador Espriu," "He de pagar el meu vell preu, la mort," indicates that Espriu's solution for escaping his imprisonment is self-immolation. Though *Final del laberint* is still to come, the poem foreshadows the stylistic shift that comes about with the emergence of *La pell de brau.* Escaping the hold of the dead requires an offering, and the sacrifice is Salom and the poetics associated with that avatar. Recalling the thought of Georges Bataille, identification with the regime's victims demands an auto-immolation – a thrownness outside of the self – which leads to a rupture of personal homogeneity in the intermingling of others within the poetic voice. This, in a sense, is precisely how the poet transforms into the mediator of the stories of others. Having jettisoned Salom's manner of writing, Espriu's poetic persona is now "silenciós." "Sentir," however, requires active understanding for salvation to take place. This is the condition of leaving Salom behind in the poem's penultimate verse: "Però sentir només, sense comprendre, no em salvarà del vell furor del vent." Espriu's concept of understanding implies that hearing is perhaps the most critical of the senses, which also harkens back to collecting the stories of others throughout the wanderings of the poetic voice.

By abandoning an antiquated form of poetics associated with Salom, and the violence of the Spanish Civil War, Espriu's turning from the dead to the living takes place in the poem's second stanza: "Silenciós, m'alço rei de la nit / i em sé servent dels homes de dolor." A condition of being *rei de la nit* is to be a servant "dels homes de dolor," or more specifically, those who have been subjected to a violent silencing and require a mediator for their words. Language remains problematic, as the conclusion of the second stanza openly questions how to recover a verse that might bring closure to the destitute time: "Ai, com guiar aquest immens dolor / al clos de les paraules de la nit?" This quandary remains unresolved at the conclusion of the poem, as the poet is "sense missatge, sol, enllà del cant." On another level, this signals the completion of Salom's sacrifice and the ambiguity of writing in the manner of Salvador Espriu, a style yet to be defined. *Sentir*, for the moment, is the limit point of poetic ontology.

The poet's payment of the ultimate price – death – points to the importance of auto-sacrifice in the poem and the shedding of authorial subjectivity in preparation for a redefined mission. A descent into the world of the dead once again invites references to *The Divine Comedy*.[12] Another comparison, one that is also fairly well known to critics, is Espriu's use of symbolism from the Ancient Egyptian philosophical and religious text, the papyrus of Ani, also known as *The Egyptian Book of the Dead*. The work is a guide to the afterlife, narrating the voyage from a first-person perspective. A glance at the work shows immediately why Espriu felt drawn to the imagery. In the protagonist's search for the great gods, the narrative voice must pass by a "House of the Night-bark; it is the wasp which fetches me to see the great gods who are in the God's Domain" (Goelet 112). From this, one cannot help but think of language tending to be a house of Being, with poetry being understood as the foundational ground upon which the edifices appear that enable truth events, those moments that permit a greater understanding of one's Being, to occur. As Heidegger writes on Hölderlin's work, "Poetry is the sustaining ground of history ... our existence is poetic in its ground" (*Elucidations* 60). The notion of a poetic ground propitious for construction or edification becomes important later in the chapter, as a temple is built at the conclusion of *La pell de brau*. The topology of the Egyptian afterlife demonstrates why Espriu's poetic voice must not only emanate from his home, but also first descend into the afterlife in order to confront death in the pursuit of fleeing gods. Espriu thus recaptures a lost religiousness, pursuing a lost sacrality and connection to the metaphysical forces guaranteeing and legitimating the ontological Being of a public that no longer listens.

Espriu does not think of poetic movement as a linear progression into a transcendent future; rather, a descent into the afterlife to remember history is the only method that can recover the proportioning of meaning and the balancing principle that disappeared from Spain with the advent of a destitute time. Remembering Heidegger's approach to Rilke's *Urgrund* is fruitful: "What Rilke calls Nature is not contrasted with history. Above all, it is not intended as the subject matter of natural science. Nor is Nature opposed to art. It is the ground for history and art and nature in the narrower sense ... Rilke calls Nature the *Urgrund*, the pristine ground, because it is the ground of those beings that we ourselves are. This suggests that man reaches more deeply into the ground of beings than do other beings. The ground of beings has since ancient times been called Being" (*Poetry, Language, Thought* 99).

Espriu's human poetic subject, already the creature most capable of reaching deeply into the ground of Being and therefore most able to achieve intimacy and knowledge of his own finite nature, ventures downward in "Sentit a la manera de Salvador Espriu" in order to reach the outer limit of life: death, "el meu vell preu." With eyes that are tired of the light of day, the poet becomes ensconced in the destitute darkness of the world's night in a downward motion, "amb mancaments," which implies an emptied interiority already voided of its contents. The immense pain that the poet guides down into the abyss in the second stanza of the poem accentuates the difficulty in confronting death and dwelling on it poetically. But like Tiresias in *Antigone*, the capacity to listen passively opens consciousness to an awareness of the plenitude of Being, which is akin to a vision of clarity within a flash of lightning – what Heidegger calls a clearing. This is intimated earlier in *El caminant i el mur* in "Cançó de la plenitud del matí": "Llum de retorn de barca: / la solitud guanyada / A l'or caminat del dia, / llum de retorn de barca."

"Cançó de la plenitud del matí," with its maritime imagery, harkens back to the mystical involution of perspective that metaphorically equates recollection with a boat on the Styx at the beginning of *El caminant i el mur*. In "Cançó de la plenitud del matí," a matinal plenitude reaches its apogee and the cusp of its dissolution, in a Nietzschean noontime moment where the sun leaves no shadows.[13] As in the case of Tiresias, this prophetic opening gains access to a set of truths that are inconsistent with the accounts of violence endorsed by governmental historicization of conflict. Espriu's poetic resuscitation and commitment to the sacred remembrance of the *vençuts* contrasts with a countermovement of consecration, which is epitomized by Kreon: "Aquesta és una diada de dol i d'homenatge als nostres herois. Seria avinent de dedicar-la a meditar en un greu i religiós silenci." The sacrality of filial connection reaches deeper into the ground of history – Anthony Smith's vertical, national, sacred communion – and is inconsistent with the artificial Francoist dictum on silence, imposed on a divided territory, that makes heroes of those affiliated with the state in its present structure of power.

"El meu vell preu": the poetic self is destined to a death that confronts and fulfils a state of debt firmly rooted in bygone times. To be sure, death is understood here as trans-subjective. What requires payment is a universal human law; as Heidegger writes, "Death is what touches mortals in their nature" (*Poetry, Language, Thought* 123). Death, in other words, is the laying down of the ultimate law, and knowing its inevitability produces the *Stimmung* of anxiety that Heidegger, in *Being and Time*, attaches to the most basic nature of *Dasein*. In Heidegger's post-*kehre* thought, however, an encounter with death translates into knowing the breadth of all possible human experience – the absolute limits of mortality. This, of course, is a kind of measuring. Heidegger posits that "to write poetry is measure-taking, understood in the strict sense of the word, by which man first receives the measure for the breadth of his being" (219). To take this measure of the breadth of being, the poet must discover the outer boundary of life – *el mur* – that death constitutes. Knowing death, then, means partaking in an authentic life; experiencing death as death means to dwell poetically. As Espriu descends and discovers the breadth of being, he must step beyond the limits of his individual subjectivity towards the death of his heteronym, Salom, in order to "guanyar" solitude before re-experiencing the plenitude of the *matí*.

Acknowledging death, however, is not understood as an end point in "Sentit a la manera de Salvador Espriu." Espriu poeticizes a confrontation with one's mortality as an event that is followed by a turning, or a *kehre*. Near the end of the poem, after lowering himself into the dominion of the night, Espriu's poetic voice reverses the downward trend: "Silenciós, m'alço rei de la nit." Reaching into the abyss, being marked by the universal law of mortality, and turned "toward and into" his nature (*Poetry, Language, Thought* 123) allows Espriu's poetic voice to discover that an intimacy with the trans-subjective law of death and the weight of humankind's collective pain is accompanied by a withdrawal of language. This phenomenon is detailed earlier in the collection in the final stanza of "Cançó de la mort callada." The turn beyond death is also a turn beyond the sayable; death not only deprives one of speech, but is inaccessible in and of itself. For Espriu, death is not a privation but is an opening up, an invitation to listening, and that is why the poetic voice links Salom's offering to *sentir*. The pain of experience transforms into pure silence, thereby opening up space for the ascension of the sacred, universal, and recuperated speech of the dead. The first two lines of the third stanza of "Sentit a la manera de Salvador Espriu" are therefore an answer to the question posed at the end of the second:

> Ai, com guiar aquest immens dolor
> al clos de les paraules de la nit?
>
> Passen el vent, el triomf, el repòs
> per rengles d'altes flames d'arquer

The poet cannot progress with the instrumental, wilful use of his own language to passively capture the triumphant draft of the night that is endangered by shooting flames. In this context, death is indeed accessible, as it sends the venturing poet onto the other side of life's orbit. Above all, death is not a linguistic predicament; it is the solution to an ontological dilemma that only poets can extract in the darkness of a time of violence and silence.

Espriu's poetic turning induces a stepping outside of the self: "Presoner dels meus morts i del meu nom, esdevinc mur, jo caminat per mi." On one hand, a connection to the proper name and to its filial connections constructs the wall and functions as an entrapment. Climbing beyond the wall of subjectivity is achieved only through a division between the self and the proper name. Being a prisoner of his deaths and of his name, the poetic voice interprets his existence as both a function and a fiction of the past. This existential fiction is written by experience built up in the name. "Jo caminat per mi": the ambiguity of the preposition "per" is significant, and a translation into English is challenging. One could write, "I walked because of me; walked by me; walked through me." Eschewing the incarcerating function of the name requires physically traversing his past, walking over and beyond the self. The poet walks through himself by inverting his gaze towards the ambit of the forgotten by participating in recollection. In *Final del laberint*, walking through oneself, through one's *wall*, is achieved only after having paid respects to *els meus morts*. This settling of personal accounts leads to an emptying out of poetic subjectivity and a transformation of the white space of the page into a confluence of voices – the *diverses parles* of *La pell de brau*. Unlike Salom, who claimed to be a redeemer, Espriu's later openness to mediating a censored collective voice opens up the possibility of restoring a lost religiosity linked to the roots of the nation.

Final del laberint: Redeeming a Lost Religiousness

Shedding an antiquated lyricism through sacrifice in "Escrit a la manera de Salom" and "Sentit a la manera de Salvador Espriu" precedes a thematic and stylistic maturation in Espriu's oeuvre soon after writing *El caminant i el mur* in 1954. In the opening remarks to Espriu's complete works, J.M. Castellet stresses that *Final del laberint* (1955) concludes the second lyrical stage of Espriu's authorial evolution. With the publication of *La pell del brau* in 1960, Espriu begins a period of social compromise, where in Castellet's words, "el poeta se encarna en el tiempo histórico que le ha tocado vivir y, desde dentro del mismo, presenta el drama de Sepharad" (*Iniciación* 73). *Final del laberint* and *La pell del brau* certainly mark a *kehre* for Espriu as he finds a new poetics, a reformed *cant*, to describe the problematic and recurring presence of violence on the Iberian Peninsula (Sepharad) and the collective effort required to resurrect a "second religiosity" through restoration of the sacred bonds of kinship. Espriu's post-*kehre* civic address can be understood only in terms of his prior meditation on his mortality and that of his people. Having measured the breadth of being of humankind by encountering death, Espriu can then return to the living, ascending through the vertical draft as "king of the night" fully imbued with the wholeness of existence, which the poet measures by reaching into the *Urgrund* of Iberian being.

The beginning of *Final del laberint* bears a strong thematic consistency with the point at which *El caminant i el mur* concludes. In the first poem, the notion of palatial glory being reduced to a painful darkness harkens back to the Iberian destitute time that was poeticized in *El caminant i el mur*. "Amb lent dolor esdevé somni fosc / aquella llum dels altíssims palaus." The poem marks a past event and offers a reminder of the *caminant*'s voyage into the abyss. Transgressing *el mur* required digging downward, following the serpentine paths of inner consciousness in order to establish contact with the atavistic forces at the heart of the peninsula's collective Being. Poem I of *Final del laberint* then sketches a domination of the wall that cloistered Salom in *El caminant i el mur*, which the poet's elevated perspective reflects: "Miro tota la nit i sento el cor / vastíssim de la terra, el maternal respir fangós que guarda el vinent blat." From a greater height, like a priest above in a pulpit, one can view the night in its plenitude, which harkens back to the beginning of *El caminant i el mur* and Nietzsche's noontime moment, making this a *cançó de la plenitud de la nit* and a sign that darkness is on the cusp of receding into a new dawn. Being, within the abyss of poetic consciousness, unfurls its plenitude through a revelation that is first felt. Even at this juncture, sight and speech remain inaccessible, as the heart of the earth and its maternal breath are only felt and not open to lyricism. From a declaration of history at the beginning of the poem, Espriu in line seven announces a future event notable for its potential. The mute, prophetic poet envisions a harvest and acquires wisdom through a cognizance of the land's latency, which is known through the literal sensation of its palpitations.

The end of poem I reiterates the past trials of the poet in *El caminant i el mur*, as the imprisonment of the poetic voice is reprised but without a clear answer to the essential question, "Com obriré camins al meu retorn?" One might suppose that, with language as a house of Being, these *camins* are linguistic in nature. In an indication that *Final del laberint* ought to be read as a continuation of Espriu's earlier work, the poem concludes, "Vaig davallar per esglaons de pedra / al clos recinte de llises parets / i avanço sol a l'esglai del llarg crit / que deia per les voltes el meu nom." Poem II specifies that the only exit from such a crypt, without "finestres" and "cap porta," are "paraules de cançó." Words finally return to the poet's lips through a transformation that has sacrificial overtones, as the poetic voice notes just prior to restoring a redemptive language: "quan la sang és escampada amb ira per la roja tenebra / esdevinc justificat, home sencer." Importing the deaths of others, including that of his own heteronym, Salom, into a mission of salvation justifies the poet's future purpose and invents a new, accessible lyric.

Obviously this strongly resonates with Christianity, most notably Saul's transformation into Paul. The redemption of language, like the bolt of lightning that strikes down Paul and the illumination of Heidegger's clearing, is described by Espriu in poem XXII of *La pell de brau* as an elevating and prepotent light: "Per l'alta escala / de les paraules, / la llum pujàvem, / alliberada." Like Ramon Llull's mystical steps towards God and the upward thrust of Teresa de Ávila's *grados de oración*, the "we" identified in the poem literally climbs the light, itself conceptualized as a stepping stone. All of this is to say that the poet's solitary, unshielded venture into the risky hearth of Being, which painfully expunges part of his subjectivity, is sacrificial to the extent that it is meant to be a gift to the inhabitants of Sepharad. This gift, naturally, is a redeemed language capable of expressing Iberia's lost religiosity that transcends the obsolete rhetoric of the recent past, which only constructed a *mur* of pain in *El caminant i el mur*.

The birth of poetic subjectivity in *Final del laberint* comes as a result of Salom's sacrifice, which places the poet in contact with others who have spilled blood. The poetic voice that has reached into the abyss – the risky openness of Being – and returned triumphantly as King of the Night is simultaneously a servant to *els homes de dolor*. *Final del laberint*'s and *El caminant i el mur*'s fidelity to a blood-spilling event, Salom's sacrifice, give purity and honesty to the poem. This thought is similar to Alain Badiou's application of his evental philosophy to the life of St Paul. Badiou sees in Paul's fidelity to the resurrection of Christ a subject that becomes divided in order to escape death. For Paul, "it is not a question of denying death by preserving it but of engulfing it, abolishing it" (*Saint Paul* 73). Death remains a patent force, but it functions as a founding site for an affirmative operation that is "irreducible to death itself" (73). In Espriu's poetics, the salvation of Sepharad is ultimately an affirmation of life prepared by engulfing and abolishing death, which begins with the resurrection of language in *Final del laberint*. The predominance of Christian echoes in *Final del laberint* argues against the cycle of grandeur and decadence in the history of Sepharadian civilization. This recalls Spengler's post-Hegelian historiography, but is also supported by Espriu's own characterization of the poetic subject of *Final del laberint*, which is a voice "atret més enllà de la *cançó* morta pels sons o pels brills d'una més alta harmonia" (cited in *Obres completes* 12: 163). Christian overtones remain strong throughout the collection, as the poetic subject's new *cançó* is thought of as what which fulfils and renders old rhetoric obsolete, similar to the relationship between the Gospels and the Old Testament. The notion of a higher, more perfect harmony also resonates with the balancing of accounts that Christ's assumption of human form entails for the human-divine dialectic in the foundation of a new covenant. The "end of the labyrinth" or the end of a destitute time therefore entails a founding where the beginning is nothing but the word – a reformed *cant*.

One finds throughout *Final del laberint* repeated poeticizations of "una més alta harmonia" that demands forgetting the past to reduce the stranglehold of the dead. The speaker of poem XXI, for example, admits to once desiring a "cançó de marbre" constructed with blood-spattered walls, but "l'esborra la pluja, / paraula per paraula. / La llosa de l'oblit / a poc a poc va caure. / Ni el llarg plorar dels morts / mai més no podrà alçar-la." The *mur*, in other words, and the bloody words painted onto its facade by Salom's sacrificial hurtling of himself against the stone, is erased through the forgetfulness of time's passage and its cathartic effect on inscriptions grounded in pain. Beyond the "llosa de l'oblit," however, is nature's tendency to cast aside evidence of human conflict, which in Espriu's poetry is often linked to water – such as the sinking of the temple into the sea in "Pontos" – or to the rain, in this particular lyric.

The conclusion of poem XXVI gives an indication of the burgeoning hope that Espriu eventually attaches to *La pell de brau* in noting, "M'arriba de sobte la claror d'aquest nou dia / que esdevindrà plenitud del meu somni feliç." Espriu thus replaces motifs of darkness and the miserable, abyssal environment of the *oblidats* with the clarity of the new *cançó*'s plenitude of light. Poem XXV describes a nearing of the night's outer limits as a trial that is won: "guanyo la riba de la nit." And to conclude the collection, poem XXX steps definitively outside of the *laberint* with an alliterative stanza stressing freedom from a past populated by the deceased:

deslliurat del pes
del temps, d'esperances
dels morts,
dels records,
dic en silenci
el nom del no-res

The poetic subject in "Sentit a la manera de Salvador Espriu," a prisoner to his name, manages by the end of *Final del laberint* to shed subjection to the symbolic order. In other words, the poetic voice follows Salom's sacrifice with a disengagement from "Salvador Espriu" and his manner of feeling, revealing a "nom del no-res." The "nom del no-res" expresses itself in silence, implying that the acquisition of a *nova cançó* produces an agency that can annunciate a Being formerly lost from human language. One could say that Espriu frees his poetic voice from what Badiou calls a "subjective disposition" and the regime of discourse allotted to it (*Saint Paul* 41). Badiou argues that St Paul territorializes the two key dispositions of his time, "Jew and Greek," and in so doing creates a "schema of discourses. And this schema is designed to position a third discourse, his own, in such a way as to render its complete originality apparent" (41). With this observation we arrive where we started: the Spenglerian dialectic of constructing a metaphysics of Iberian Being through the intermingling of sacred discourses, many of which lie in ruins on the Sepharadian landscape. Badiou's attribution of a third discourse to Paul carries with it a universality in the sense that it not only erupts from the key dispositions of his time, but brings the two together in a commonality. For

Espriu, then, "Sepharad," as a poetic signifier, is a third discourse that introduces the Iberian Peninsula's various centres of cultural identification into a plural public sphere unregulated by an exclusive, essentialized determination of Spanish sacredness. This requires that he shed his own subjectivity in order to adopt a "nom del no-res" – an empty tabernacle to be filled with multiple voices and discourses.

In *Final del laberint*, Espriu's emptying out of subjectivity does not simply produce a clearing of the past that defines the "nom del no-res" as an absolute nothingness, or at least as a negativity without positive attributes. The past, and the deaths pertaining to it, produces a founding discourse that is wholly original and suited to a poetics of the present, or more specifically, Sepharad's present and the *diverses parles* that reside on the peninsula. Espriu's poetic subject emerges from the entangled passageways of inner consciousness – his own personal labyrinth – as a universal singularity. I say singularity in the subject's fidelity to a particular event, which I have theorized as a long sacrificial process that reaches an apex in key moments, such as the conclusion of *El caminant i el mur* and the final stepping outside of the labyrinth. Fidelity to one's deaths permitted the breadth of existence to be measured and a full cognizance of the limits of mortality. As a subject split into multiple parts – Salom, Salvador, and the nameless priest of the "no-res" – Espriu's poetic subject measures those parts of the self that are absolutely particular, in order to connect with what is immutable and is therefore a universal truth. This clarifies the identity of the "nom del no-res": a voice that, in Badiou's words, "addresses itself to all others, and it effectuates itself as a power through this address" (*Saint Paul* 109). Through its disconnectedness from any individual subjectivity, the "nom del no-res" unifies discrete particularities through a universal matrix, which I argue is a kind of a Sephardian second religiousness or restoration of the plurality of sacred kinship in Iberia.[14] Alongside a plural public sphere, however, Espriu also searches for a key commonality that links the tribes together. The deepest, most rooted commonality that all Sepharadians share is a common ancestry in Hispania's first settlers, who are metaphorized in *La pell de brau* through a comparison with the Jewish *golah* in the book of Exodus. At this juncture, the poet morphs into a priestly figure that mediates multiple national particularities.

Rethinking Iberia: A New Temple of Sacred Communion

In order to theorize Espriu's mediating position between Iberian particularisms, to borrow Almirall's designation, and Spain's universal first causes, one could profitably refer to Hegel's theory of the unhappy consciousness, particularly in reference to the joy identified in *Final del laberint* at the poetic subject's discovery of a language attached to the plenitude of light. Hegelian thought has key applications to Espriu's sacrificial process, which depends on an unessential consciousness moving to become one with the unchangeable: the transcendent beyond, or "first religiousness," of a cultural sacredness that is lost in the Francoist winter of Sepharadian civilization. Poem VI of *La pell de brau*, in a didactic address to Sepharad, stresses that an idol, the "imatge del teu mal," was raised during a "llunyà dia del nostre hivern." The poetic voice, which at once belongs to the collective ("nostre hivern") yet is set apart from profanation ("del teu mal"), assumes a priestly role that negotiates the contradiction of both belonging to and being set apart from a community through a connectedness with the sacred.

Espriu's multi-volume trip through a poetic labyrinth reaches the forgotten dead through a mystical descent into consciousness and locates universal truth within the individual self. Hegel believes human consciousness is unhappy when individuality and universality are out of touch, though he stresses that the two poles are normally not thought to be located within the same subject: "The Unhappy Consciousness *is* this contact; it is the unity of pure thinking and individuality; also it *knows* itself to be this thinking individuality or pure thinking, and knows the Unchangeable itself essentially as an individuality. But what it does *not* know is that this its object, the Unchangeable, which it knows essentially in the form of individuality, is *its own self*, is itself the individuality of consciousness" (*Phenomenology of Spirit* 130–1).

Espriu, if the descent into his own inner Hades in *El caminant i el mur* is any indication, is aware that the "unchangeable," immutable part of himself linked to the transcendent truth of a historical community is indeed accessible within the individual's capacity for recollection. Delving into himself in order to remain cognizant of his people's sacred precepts unearths the deific presence that Sepharad's idols, the "imatge" of Iberia's "mal," have masked. This awareness of the unchangeable part of himself attached to a collective Sepharadian cultural history permits the poetic voice of *La pell de brau* to assert the truths of Iberia's present decadence with a conviction wrought from faith. This is a faith in the connectedness of the present to a historical continuity – a sacred communion of national belief.

In *La pell de brau*, the sky poetically functions as a conduit between the firmament and the mundane present: "El nostres avis varen mirar, / fa molts anys, / aquest mateix cel / d'hivern, alt i trist / i llegien en ell un estrany / signe d'emparança i de repòs." This, from poem VII, signals that the Christian thematics of *Final del laberint* are substituted in *La pell de brau* by a dependence on Hebrew mythology and the Jewish *golah* founded on exile. The motifs of idol worship, the rebuilding of a temple, and animal sacrifice also reinforce a return to Old Testament thought. I reference Hegel while transitioning into *La pell de brau* to stress Espriu's intermediary position between the miserable, cowardly people of

Sepharad and their deeply rooted collective history. The poetic voice in *La pell de brau*, in other words, is not a prophet announcing the future; rather, Espriu is a mediating priest trying to re-establish a sacred communion in the present. The construction of the nation, or of any sacred community, requires surrendering one's will to that of the collective. It also requires surrendering an aspect of individual freedom at the point where the subject derives a component of his or her identity from the transcendent meaning of a political group. Hegel, accordingly, argues, "The surrender of one's own will is only from one aspect negative; in principle, however, or in itself, it is at the same time positive, viz. the positing of will as the will of an 'other,' and specifically of will, not as a particular, but as a universal will" (*Phenomenology of Spirit* 138).

For Sepharad to be a political project, and for *La pell de brau* to contribute an influential rhetoric to the organization of a post-dictatorial Iberia (taking into account both Portugal and Spain), a kind of sacrifice is also requested of Espriu's readers. Just as Espriu had to empty out and extinguish his own subjectivity in order to mediate the voices of the forgotten, he demands that the reader commit his or her own poetic life to memory, which implies a surrendering. To be sure, it is doubtful that a politics would even be possible in the event that the Hegelian subject became aware of its own inner completeness, where the unchangeable and the unessential form a complete picture within the single individual. Exporting what is immutable outside of consciousness and branding it as "sacred" forces individual subjectivities to go beyond the self in a belief that the essential is neared only through collective experiences mediated by priestly figures.

The first poem of *La pell de brau* begins with imagery of a bull attacking a hide stretched out over the sands of Sepharad, the Roman geographer Strabo's famous symbol of Hispania, and refashioning it as a flag. The end of the poem stresses a shift in grammatical voice, to the first-person plural, in the denotation of the poem as concomitantly an "oració nostra / i blasfèmia nostra." This contradictory couplet reinforces Sepharad's decadent state and its history of bloodshed. The violence that separated the bull from its hide, and its divisive influence on the community, is inscribed onto a new national symbol – the hoisted bull's skin – in remembrance of the fraternal conflict. This is a gesture to preclude its repetition, similar to the victimization to end all victimizations in Sales's *Incerta glòria*. The symbolism of a stained bull's hide, converted into a flag, refuses to disfigure or place history into a blind spot by placing responsibility for past sins on a banished and scapegoated class of individuals. The first poem thus concludes by asserting that Sepharad's citizens are, *alhora*, the *víctima* and *botxí*.

Following the Old Testament motif, the poetic subject of *La pell de brau* has a priestly function akin to Moses, who himself couples together the wandering, concupiscent people in the valley below to the divine, universal being atop Mt

Sinai. The poetic subject's intermediary placement is communicated in the collection's second poem: "Si m'endinso somni enllà, / sempre goso mirar / el meu cor i el seu esglai, / veig l'estesa pell de brau, / vella Sepharad." Though capable of reaching into the beyond and escaping the miserable state of an unhappy consciousness trapped in its meaningless existence, the poetic voice remains tied, seemingly against its volition, to the bull's hide that bears all the marks of Sepharad's violent history. This "unhappy" positioning of the poetic voice at an elevated state recalls the poeticization of being atop the *mur* in *Final del laberint* and reinforces the conversion of the speaker into a consecrating priest rather than a prophet. Hegel writes that unity with the Unchangeable, and release from the misery of an unhappy consciousness, requires a mediated relation, or middle term, that is given a sacral quality by the anointing philosopher: "Through the middle term the one extreme, the Unchangeable, is brought into relation with the unessential consciousness, which equally is brought into relation with the Unchangeable only through this middle term; thus this middle term is one which presents the two extremes to one another and ministers to each in its dealings with the other" (*Phenomenology of Spirit* 136).

Hegel's subject displaces the unchangeable – Aristotle's metaphysical first cause – from itself onto an outside source, which requires a third party to provide the illusion of connectedness. In the following paragraph, Hegel attaches a religious office to the mediator, as the unhappy consciousness is thought to cast its freedom of decision "upon the mediator or minister [priest]" (136). Hegel, therefore, is both theorizing the nature of sacrifice and providing a mythology of the birth of the sacred and how the delusional nature of consciousness requires religious practice. This discussion links to previous chapters, especially to the mythical dimension of Benet's Numa, Goytisolo's resurrection of Alvarito, and Martín-Santos's *gran buco*. In all cases, a *corpus naturale* fulfils the mediating role of a priest whose existence responds to the existential need for an unessential consciousness to be completed by connection to transcendental meaning.

In *La pell de brau*, the poetic voice adopts the sacred offices assigned to priestly duties in three key moments: the discussion of idol worship in poems V–VI, the sacrifice of *l'ocell solar* in XV–XVI, and the construction of a new temple in XLVI–XLVIII. In poem V, the name of Sepharad's "mal" is learned through an inscription on the face of the people's false idol. In a reference to Sepharad's winter, the poetic subject instructs the people that the receiver should contemplate the idol "en aquest glaç." The poem's focus is on Sepharad in the present tense, as the image of its evil – a very clear reference to Exodus 32 and the Israeli people's betrayal of Moses atop Mt Sinai. The biblical story posits that idol worship begins with the extended absence of a true and sincere leader – Moses – who is in touch with Yahweh, he who *is* Being. It is in the turning to a false leader, Aaron, that a golden calf is produced, which the brother of Moses identifies as the true source of the Jewish people's exit from Egypt. This, essentially, represents a false attribution of sacred power, which is nearly impossible to read apart from Franco and his own sacralization of Spain.[15] Naturally, Gassol i Bellet links the appearance of idolatry and disobedience of the law in Espriu's work to the rise of Fascism in Portugal and Spain: "Els feixismes són moviments pseudoespiritualistes que tendeixen a concentrar en la figura del cabdill trets propis de la divinitat. I això és el que s'ha tornat a repetir durant el franquisme" (71).

In poem VI, the poetic voice recalls a far-off day in Sepharad's wintertime in which "el gran crim de Sepharad" transpires in a "guerra sense victòria entre germans." The poem proposes a reconciliatory model for the fractured society through recollection of how peace returned in the wake of this conflict long in the past, which initiated the diasporic *golah.* The structure of the poem reflects this juxtaposition of the present with the past, as it begins with the proclamation of the people's false idol in the preterite tense: "Ídol que vares alçar, imatge del teu mal." The next stanza, which comprises the remaining eleven lines of the poem, switches to the first-person plural, indicating that the story recounted corresponds to a definite historical event and forms part of collective Sepharadian mythology. In a comparison of Iberia to the Jewish *golah* in the Old Testament, the poem situates Sepharad in the period between the destruction of the first temple and the construction of the second, which in historical terms corresponds to the Jewish captivity in Babylon and exile from Jerusalem between 586 and 538 BCE. Later in poem VI, Espriu reflects on Sepharad's period of slavery and the prohibition against the practice of sacred rites. In the absence of a temple, salvation was achieved "en el dolor del treball, / guiant-nos per la llum del temple recordat, / guanyàvem lentament una lliure pau." In Israel's case, seventy years of diligent work and fidelity to the first temple resulted in a return to Jerusalem and the edification of a new place of worship (or more specifically, a new place of sacrifice). As with all of Espriu's poetry, remembrance of a collective's sacred precepts, and the transcendent light they produce, achieves clarity and peace. This poem, moreover, introduces to *La pell de brau* the concept of work, which is needed to construct a new temple free of false idols.

Poem V, thinking back to the decision of the Israelites to betray Moses and follow Aaron, also sets the political parameters for the appropriate election of a leader. The poem stresses that "no pot escollir príncep / qui vessa sang, / qui ha traït o roba, / qui no va alçar / a poc a poc el temple / del seu treball." D. Gareth Walters interprets this passage as a critique of the people's proclivity to choose unsuitable leaders and "a reflection on the unworthiness of the tribe and its moral deficiency, reflected in its inability to elect a suitable leader" (131). It is unclear how Walters extrapolates the people's innate moral shortcomings from this particular passage, as the remembrance of the destroyed temple in poem VI and the reconstruction of the temple later in *La pell de brau* indicate not "unworthiness" or "moral deficiency" but something more along the lines of Aristotelian *hamartia*.[16] Worshipping a false idol is a misstep that sets a chosen people out of joint with their sacred roots in an unforgiving and barren land, a moral detour that is correctable.

What Walters overlooks in his otherwise excellent study is the conflation of work and temple construction in the final two lines of poem V. The coupling of work with sacred place is denoted in the very etymology of the verb *edify*, which combines *aedes* (temple) with *facere* (to make). To edify means to imbue a sacred place of worship with one's work, and the one who participates in the toil of building and commits time to the collective good earns the right to choose a leader. One can carry this secular idiom into a discourse of the sacred as it pertains to religious practice. One who participates in the construction of a common place of worship, a public space that symbolically represents the vital force of collective belief, gains access to the articulation of political truth. On a political level, critiquing a rapid sacralization inconsistent with the profundity of historical origins and not the fruit of a fidelity to work points to, in the words of Gassol i Bellet, Franco's "moviment pseudoespiritualista."

Though remembrance of the destroyed temple is key to salvation in a moment of bondage, poems VII and VIII lay down the law, so to speak, by proclaiming the end of mourning: "No ploreu més el temple / de temps enderrocat. / A ponent us esperen / lliures camins de mar." This statement should be read with respect to the "gran crim de Sepharad" in poem VI, where the arrival to "l'altra banda de la mar" corresponded to a remembrance of the temple and the slow winning of peace. Sepharad, as the poetic voice reminds his people, was not originally attached to violence and despair, but represented freedom within the collective imaginary of the people prior to their arrival. When notified that territories superior to Sepharad exist, "nosaltres, amb un lleu somriure / que ens apropa el record / dels pares i dels avis, / responem només: – En el nostre somni, sí." The dialectic between idealism and mundane reality – Sepharad's present state versus its image in the collective fantasy of the body politic – gives birth to the sacred and the mediating position of the priest. A sacred potential persists as long as the dream of Sepharad remains patent within the collective imaginary, which emphasizes a great advantage of envisioning national identity through the sacred. By idealizing an image of the polity, organized nations can be mobilized to transcend their shortcomings and inequalities.

At this juncture of *La pell de brau*, the poetic subject extrapolates his knowledge of the breadth of Sepharad's being in order to denounce false idols. First, this proclamation derives conviction from the poetic subject's awareness of an authentic sacrality linked to the remembrance of a destroyed temple (perhaps the same temple that sinks into the ocean in "Pontos"). Second, this priestly voice demands disengagement from a history of destruction in an attempt to interject hope into the people's mournful demeanour. This process first passes through a sacrificial phase where the people offer up a false idol – *l'ocell solar* – in a placating gesture. The poetic voice acquires fire capable of vanquishing Sepharad's winter and reinstituting a hopeful springtime through "la més clara paraula," yet the country's false idols still remain: "Però desperto / molt aviat del somni: / és amb nosaltres; / a la presó glaçada, / també l'ocell del sol." Espriu identifies the *l'ocell del sol* as "L'Àguila de Sant Joan, heràldica a l'escut d'Espanya" (cited in *Obres completes* 12: 303). Appropriating an emblematic component of the arms of the Catholic monarchs mirrors Goytisolo's use of the Spanish coat of arms in *Conde Julián*. In both cases, a literary treatment of a symbol projected by the regime, which functions for Espriu as a synecdoche, asserts power by reinterpreting the emblematic function of the image. In reference to Espriu's poem, Delor notes that the *ocell solar* symbolically represented "un enemic tradicional d'una determinada Espanya liberal i republicana, havia estat vexat per Franco. Monarquia i República … havien trobat a mans de Franco un mateix destí" (cited in 303). Delor and Gassol i Bellet attach other references to *l'ocell*, including the appearance of birds in Antigone. However, if *La pell de brau* is a counter-imagining of Iberian sacred symbolism, an emblematic sacrifice of both monarchical and Francoist Spain through *l'ocell* is a rebuttal to the centralizing, Castile-exclusive image of Hispania that Espriu objects to in Ortega y Gasset's thought. The "esglaiós sacrifici d'imperial captiu" – note the wordplay with "imperial," which refers to both the Spanish imperial eagle and the monarchy – liberates Sepharad, which had been captive to the animal "per segles." In a parting shot, the final line of poem XVI refers to the *l'ocell* as a "renegaire rat-penat" – a blasphemous creature whose sacred qualities are inauthentic.

Sacrificing *l'ocell solar* permits the construction of a new temple by accomplishing two functions. On one hand, as with all rites of sacrifice, the public spectacle of the bird's immolation draws a community back together and rekindles the collective force that drives the erection of new metaphysical identity symbols. The *ocell* does not merely disappear from the scene; it adopts new symbolic content fuelled by the collective thrust of Sepharad's rekindled force of belief. In other words, the *ocell* becomes a totemic image, which confers a communal identity onto those congregated for the sacrifice, signalling the end of a "poble de senyors" and re-sacralizing the political potential of the people: "Direm la veritat, sense repòs / per l'honor de servir, sota els peus de tots." The sacred communion of the nation is founded upon ritual and symbolic practices, and *l'ocell solar* fulfils both prerequisites. On a second level, the sacrificial scene creates a physical clearing that lays the foundation for the slow but steady work of constructing a new temple around a founding immolation. In the first stanza of poem XLVII, ritual and symbolic practice reappear in the edification of the temple:

En la llei i en el pacte
que sempre guardaràs
en la duresa del diàleg
amb els qui et són iguals
edifica el lent temple
del treu treball.

In order to legislate law and form social pacts, the poetic voice privileges dialogue and opposes it to the violent exclusion of enmity that characterizes the exercise of power throughout Sepharad's history. This is essentially Aristotle's *polis* and also resembles Habermas's democratic public sphere of negotiation, where the polity's collective dialogue becomes a common embrace. This public sphere permits all parties capable of practical reason to provide "justifications for the universalistic and egalitarian concepts of morality and law … in a normatively plausible way" (Habermas, "Awareness" 18). Espriu's temple is a place in which equals relate to one another without losing their national distinction, and an overlapping of consensus, through dialogue, defines normative law in an egalitarian manner. This poetically symbolizes the Iberian project identified in the prologue of *La pell de brau*, where the centre and the peripheries occupy equal footing in the dialogical organization of the state. Espriu's new temple encourages a consensus of opinion among centres of sacred belief, while maintaining consciousness of plurality and opposition to purifying violence.

In the stanza's second part, the sacrifice of the *ocell solar* is elevated to metaphysical status within the temple, and its ideational content is strictly tied to the notion of freedom. The raising of a new house mirrors the stringing up of *l'ocell solar* earlier in the collection:

alça la nova casa
en el solar
que designes amb el nom
de llibertat.

The *ocell solar*'s sacrifice leaves only a *solar*, which is a charged term and refers to the terrain where a house is to be edified. This process mirrors how Salom's sacrifice in *Les hores* translates into an ontological measuring in *El caminant i el mur*, which lays the foundation for a temple honouring Iberia's multiplicity of sacred communions in *La pell de brau*. The sun bird's sacrifice, as stated earlier, converts the ground of its immolation into a sacred space on which the temple is to be constructed, which appropriates the Old Testament once again, particularly the books of Ezra and Nehemiah. On a symbolic level, the bird's immolation signals the end of Franco's sacred envisioning of the Spanish state, to be replaced by a new political structure built upon the bonds of kinship. By banishing a symbol of cruelty and exception, a diverse group of beings who share a common history all congregate in the name of a single love of freedom.

This, in conclusion, is a summation of Espriu's sacred envisioning of Sepharad and of his political Iberianism: that all nations be treated as equals and welcomed into a communal dialogue on the slow, painful work of constructing Sepharad's temple. There could be no conclusion more fitting than Espriu's response to Joaquín Soler Serrano at the end of an "A Fondo" interview that first aired on Spanish television in December 1976. Serrano, in lieu of ending with a question, quotes *La pell de brau*: "Diversos són els homes i diverses les parles, i han convingut molts noms a un sol amor." Espriu, in a triumphant gesture of consecration, responds: "Amèn, amèn, amèn."[17]

8 Conclusion: The Aesthetic Disruption of Political Truth

Art is more moral than moralities.
For the latter either are, or tend to become,
consecrations of the status quo.

John Dewey

This book has filtered Francoist ideology through a theoretical framework that relates the sacred underpinnings of political imagination to several core tendencies. In a structural sense, I have postulated that the sacred is a concept that spills over into secular political imagination, to both positive and negative effect. On the negative side, the signature of the sacred within secular political thought tends to favour hierarchical governance and purifying, exclusionary violence. Resolving periods of discord and crisis often translates into a victimizing scapegoating mechanism in order to restore peace. Moreover, the sacred quality of political identification, which exists prior to rational contemplation, encourages irrational adherence to particular discourses, poses, and creeds, which is especially tied to the automatic turn to violence at the earliest sign of profanation. Despite these limitations, I have argued that the sacred, as a result of the very structure of human consciousness, cannot be decoupled from political imagination. A social collective, whether on a small scale or an entire body politic, affirms its identity and moral paradigms by consecrating certain images and attaching metaphysical belief structures to those symbols. These moral paradigms, as is evident in Espriu's poetry, can advance powerful ideals such as fraternal love and universal humanism. Metaphysical idealism wards off the contingency of change and gives any collective a sense of stasis, and the repetition that the sacred introduces into secular time also gives political imagination a historical consciousness. The final tenet of my study was thus the need to balance the valuable, indeed inextricable, contributions of the sacred to the political and nefarious consequences of taking to an extreme a program of purity and negation of the enemy that demands unflagging loyalty from the body politic.

Choosing to study a carefully selected group of authors within a definite time span unfortunately leaves outside of the book's purview important authors and traditions in which the sacred plays a crucial role. I do not, for example, include studies of cinema and the visual and plastic arts. With the exception of Salvador Espriu, the book focuses mainly on narrative. I attempted to integrate works from both the Castilian and Catalan literary canons, yet I have not included texts written in Basque, Galician, or even Portuguese. It would certainly be fascinating to compare the function of the sacred in the Estado Novo with what I have found in Francoist ideology. Beyond merely studying Juan Goytisolo and Mercè Rodoreda, my theory of the sacred would also be a useful theoretical lens through which to view other contestations of national identity in exile. Another future avenue of research would be to analyze the persistence of *la España sagrada*, in all of its iterations, in the post-Franco transition to democracy. As I mention in the introduction, understanding the regime's use of the sacred as a tool for secular political imagination might help pinpoint those areas of the Francoist ideology that insidiously persist into the democratic period. More than thirty years after the death of Franco, controversies regarding Spain's sacred national character continue, as the 2010 ban on bullfighting in Catalonia, for example, has shown. Despite appeals to the ethical treatment of animals, the Catalan disavowal of the practice caused many Spanish intellectuals and politicians, such as the philosopher Fernando Savater, to interpret the gesture as a nationalist statement against a sacred cultural patrimony of the state.

All in all, I do not wish to presume that other cultural objects not included in this study, whether literary or otherwise, produced during the Francoist dictatorship and beyond cannot contribute to an ongoing understanding of the sacred underpinnings of political imagination. It is my hope that the formal nature of this study, which places close readings within an overarching theoretical framework tied to the sacred, will not be a final say on the matter and act as a springboard for future research.

In the introduction, I argued, through a brief analysis of Jacques Rancière, that the aesthetic regime of art plays a particularly disruptive role in the perception of political truth. At the beginning of the book, this notion of the political value of aesthetic disruption was a speculative, untested theory. As a means of summary, I believe that one can use the aperçus derived from my close readings as a data set through which to test the merits of the theoretical framework proposed by Rancière. In the book's concluding pages, I suggested that the texts, beyond merely contributing to the understanding of a political problematic, actively participate in key aspects of the political by exposing the violence embedded within the Francoist policing of the field of cultural production, disrupting the framework of nationalist truth projected by the dictatorship, and proposing alternatives ideals through which to foreground political congregation.

The intended ripple effect of my methodological approach was to reveal how the aesthetic regime of art can destabilize the location of national truth, if not rewrite it entirely. This gambit required thinking through national identity not in empirical, self-evident terms but rather as a form of imagination. In contrast, the Francoist conceptualization of the political through the sacred posits the presence of a primordial national truth that is there in reality, inundated by the profaning layers of secular history and awaiting the arrival of a redeemer to be unearthed. Francoist propaganda exalted a restored ideal of Spanishness that, far from being arbitrary, supposedly corresponded to facts both external to discourse and, as a result of its metaphysical nature, beyond direct rational confirmation. However, the literature studied in this book reveals Franco's efforts to be one of many possible modalities one could adopt in order to mediate the space between collective consciousness and national reality. The metaphoric, imaginative nature of aesthetic discourse thus possesses a cognitive function and has a keen ability to profane the regime's central hypothesis that Spanish Being was an always-already concept beyond reproach. In a productive sense the literary discourses studied in this book also have shown the capacity to germinate new discursive models for the way in which the Spanish body politic might conceptualize the order of its sovereign space. As I proposed in the previous chapter, Espriu indeed conceived *La pell de brau* as a work that could induce a crystallization of his poetics into a new political reality through the solidarity of the reading public.

The sum effect of these aesthetic discourses is a disclosure of national truth for what is: not a first philosophy that throws the body politic along a prefigured historical vector but rather a discursive construct produced by the adoption of particular vocabularies. This idea, aided by Richard Rorty's interpretation of contingent truth and metaphor, proposes that Francoist claims to Spanish identity reflect a "disposition to use the language of [one's] ancestors, to worship the corpses of their metaphors" (21). One such worshipped metaphor would be the pretension of being *caudillo* of Spain by the grace of God, a self-fashioning that mimics the argot of past rulers, such as the Catholic kings, and a sacred document, such as the first book of Corinthians. Having gained a political foothold by emerging victorious from war, Franco also derived discourses from the corpses of atavistic forces in order to acquire the symbolic capital necessary for his variant of national imagination to wield a sacred character, a process worked out to great effect in the concluding metamorphosis of Alvarito in *Conde Julián*. The literary texts analyzed in this book reconfigure Spain's essential truths by profaning the sacrality of Francoist political reality, demonstrating that a concept like national truth gains visibility and intellectual legitimacy through the symbolic partitioning of reality that takes place within a culture's aesthetic field. Aesthetic cultural production, more than a merely reflective reaction to ideologies that precede the work of art, can function as an innately political act by challenging the truth-content embedded in the perceptible framework of the social.[1]

It is no coincidence, therefore, that authoritative regimes project ideal political identity images by policing the fields of visual and textual representation. This was true for Franco, just as it was for Fernando VII throughout the *década ominosa* in a similar attempt to quell liberalist advancement. This, in a general sense, may be the central preoccupation of all political work, as Rancière has postulated: "The essential work of politics is the configuration of its own space. It is to make the world of its subjects and its operations seen" (*Dissensus* 37). Rancière argues that aesthetics discloses the delimitations and hierarchies that a sovereign aims to impose onto a polity, meaning that political imagination is impossible without such things as literary discourse and the visual and plastic arts. The state, in a mode of policing, must maintain vigilance over the aesthetic mediums that proffer political visibility in order to ensure that the structure of social relations is not disrupted. In effect, the Francoist consecration of a particular national sacred communion at the expense of other Iberian nationalisms was an effort to construct a participatory framework that set the visible boundaries of Spanish political imagination. This systematic mediation of the perceptible environment, what Rancière refers to as *le partage du sensible*, sets the parameters of the common space within the polity; the distribution of the sensible is a "system of self-evident facts of sense perception that simultaneously discloses the existence of something in common and the delimitations that define the respective parts and positions within it" (*Politics of Aesthetics* 12).

Establishing a sovereign political space resembling an exceptionalist sacred cult through hierarchical partitioning and victimary exclusion was indeed a hallmark of the Francoist regime. In this study, I first proposed that one finds ample critique of this consolidation of power in the work of Joan Sales and in the fantastical reconquest of the Iberian Peninsula in the thought of Juan Goytisolo. Goytisolo's betrayal of Spain revolved around a complete inversion of the outwardly perceptible *señas* of Spanish identity, obliterating all hallmarks of a calcified, decadent *castiza* culture in favour of Moorish symbolism. Indeed, the implication of this inversion is a remapping of the nation's "system of self-evident facts of sense perception." Rancière's strict link between the political and the aesthetic explains the great pains that the Franco regime, as well as an untold number of similarly oppressive governments, took in order to censure the field of cultural production, though Rancière's thought would argue that all states, oppressive or not, fulfil a policing role. By patrolling the very borderline of what is sayable, and therefore believable, about external reality, the state disallows the aesthetic field from disrupting its desired self-image of the body politic.

In the introduction, I argued that aesthetics, including the literature studied in this book, is a political matter because of its subversive potential to reapportion space and time and offer visibility to those areas of cultural life previously silenced. Aesthetic visibility, in other words, correlates with what is politically thinkable. The aesthetic regime of art modulates truth-claims by establishing the filters through which the raw material of reality must traverse prior to acts of individual perception. Thus, it is profitable to understand aesthetics, as does Rancière, "in a Kantian sense – re-examined perhaps by Foucault – as the system of *a priori* forms determining what presents itself to sense experience" (*Politics of Aesthetics* 13). The Francoist promotion of Spanish identity as a system of self-evident and sacred facts offers to the field of cultural production the a priori forms that set the boundaries for what is politically thinkable. The kind of aesthetic works permitted within this well-policed space, if they were to bypass censorship, had to assimilate the a priori first causes of Spanish essentialism promoted by the regime, which were projected into all arenas of quotidian sense experience – the *nodos* prior to cinematic works, the propagandistic radio broadcasts, the ideological substitution of street names, the rearticulation of public architecture such as statues and public addresses, such as those I have cited in this text.

Aesthetics, both a potential ally and arch-nemesis in the modulation of sense experience, can at turns normalize and disrupt the forms of cultural life consistent with the state's political theology. In my study, I have attempted to analyze texts that perform the latter function. For Goytisolo, especially, the sacred dictates the shape of the field of cultural production, conferring a state of permanence and immutability that is antithetical to a primordial virgin material at the heart of a shape-shifting *nuevo lenguaje*. The *nuevo lenguaje* of Goytisolo's literature, by reconfiguring the field of cultural production, disrupted the Francoist *partage du sensible*.

Rancière divides the "political" into two parts – the police and politics – thinking of the latter as a means of disagreement and unsettling.[2] The state, in its partitioning of the sensible, occupies the role of policing watchman in charge of symbolic ordering, ensuring that the sensorial material delivered to the eyes of the body politic is consistent with the desired identity of the nation. Against the state's role of policing, aesthetics performs the function of "politics": to introduce disruption into the systematic order of signs determining the shape of cultural life. Aesthetics is particularly central to the role of subversion and the role of "politics," because of its ability to modulate the a priori forms that precondition the perception of reality. Politics – the disruption of the sensible through aesthetic representation – rather than reflecting the reality deduced from the normal gathering of communities, "is an exception in relation to the principles according to which this gathering occurs" (*Dissensus* 35). In a political, non-policing sense, aesthetic disagreement has the express aim of proffering visibility onto a formerly obfuscated recess of the cultural field, thereby subverting the political realities reflected by the state's collective gatherings. Simply expressing an exception to the normal relations of political gathering is highly productive and questions modes of organization that appear sacred and unchangeable.

At different points, the texts studied in *By the Grace of God* have either critiqued the Francoist state as a policing watchman of the sensible or embraced the role of "politics" – that is, of communicating disagreement or asserting an exception to the principles by which collective gathering took place throughout the dictatorship. On the first point, my analysis of *Tiempo de silencio* exhibited how Spain's reticulate of ideal cultural symbols comprises the system of a priori forms that preconditions collective political imagination. As Martín-Santos trenchantly observed, every political community responds to an unconscious set of *normas objetales*, which in Spain are embedded within cultural artefacts like the bullfighter, Goya's *El Aquelarre*, and the *supervedette*. These cultural symbols mediate the perceived truth of historical memory, the flow of time, and political identity. As I demonstrated in *Tiempo de silencio*, the *supervedette*, in particular, communicates monarchical greatness and the virile bull reminds the *buen pueblo acumulado* that they are descendants of "el águila de la guerra" (*Tiempo de silencio* 274). These symbols shield the public from awareness of Spain's decadence and propose as the highest point of political subjectivity models that are rooted in a distant past that maintain a connection to present reality only through a mythology. An aesthetic work like *Tiempo de silencio* thus reveals that the distribution of the sensible apportions space, regulates the experience of time, and sanctions the commonality of certain activities.

The policed borderlines of what is open to the senses is particularly evident in my analysis of Numa in *Volverás a región* and the reiterative, expulsive violence required for the production of sacred time. It is worth recalling that any intrusion into Región from the outside – by those without a defined part or position within the community's perception of space – is "extra-temporal." What is out there, beyond the boundaries of Región, is also beyond thinkability, on an intellective level, which mirrors the intruders' locus outside of time. Moreover, the disclosure of "something in common" within the church belfry – the political dimension of Región's life-world – comes through the collective perception, on a sensual register, of gunfire in the distance. In addition, in *La mort i la primavera*, the narrator's elision from the *partage du sensible* brought about by his suicide stresses further the disappearance of meaning when beyond the boundaries of the sayable. The policing of the sensible that Rancière locates at the crux of the state also appears in earnest in the critique of the scapegoating mechanism in *Incerta glòria.* Systematizing cultural life requires diffusing the chaotic violence of warfare by apportioning responsibility onto an innocent, scapegoated victim. The sovereign thereafter expels the scapegoat, which in Sales's thought can be equated with Catalonia, thereby demarcating the line at which political and cultural visibility gives way to absence.

Moving on to Rancière's second division of the political – politics instead of policing – the texts I have studied also perform a disruptive function by either communicating disagreement to the Francoist partition of the sensible or asserting an exception to the principles by which collective gatherings took place. A repeatedly contested notion concerns the postulate that national truth is a first philosophy external to consciousness and beyond rationalization. Richard Rorty, himself an avowed critic of the correspondence theory of truth, disabuses the notion of first philosophies, proposing that "truth cannot be out there – cannot exist independently of the human mind – because sentences cannot so exist, or be out there. The world is out there, but descriptions of the world are not. Only descriptions of the world can be true or false" (5).[3] Creating new forms of political truth requires a rupture within the aesthetic field, mobilizing new kinds of "sentences" and thereby invalidating the ancestral, atavistic metaphors that adhere one to past experience. What is taken to be truth – what Hegel calls the "true Idea" – possesses a reality only within language proper. Political truth, in other words, much like I have argued apropos Numa in *Volverás a Región*, is a mode of semiotic communication with a truth-value found not beyond language but in signification itself. One could say the same in regards to the hypostatic reflections of social identity embedded within consecrated cultural symbols in the work of Joan Sales and Juan Goytisolo. The authors studied in this book challenge the basic tenets of metaphysics and the epistemological conundrum posed by the existence of noumenal essences beyond the scope of rationality. Many of the writers – Sales, Goytisolo, Martín-Santos, and Espriu especially – take the nationalist paradigm presented by Francoist ideology only as a narrativistic and poetic starting point; like the troping of an ancestral discourse, a text like *Incerta glòria* presents an idiosyncratic counter-partition of the sensible that produces a variant of political truth at variance with the status quo. In the case of Sales, very much as in the work of Espriu, Iberian repartitioning dissolves the political hegemony of the centre in favour of a federalist empowerment of the periphery.

The authors in this book also demonstrate a keen ability to subvert the Francoist principles underlying collective gatherings in Spain, either through critique or an outright appraisal of counter-values. Against the horde congregated in and around Región's church belfry at every sign of an intruder and the ritualistic sacrifice of innocents every spring in *La mort i la primavera*, the seminarian demonstration in Barcelona at the conclusion of *Incerta glòria* is organized around an exception to the principles underlying the Francoist organization of political space. In place of the scapegoating principle at the root of post-war dictatorial "peace," in *Incerta glòria* Cruells counters with a gathering formed in relation to the ideals of love and embracing victimhood.

The final two chapters of this study especially focus on this innately political dimension of the aesthetic regime of art, in both novelistic and poetic form. In Martín-Santos's fiction, the aesthetic object transforms into a cipher-script that illuminates, through a *captación* of the partitioning of the sensible, the alienated freedom of quotidian Spanish existence. This desacralizing *concienciación* harnesses the possibility for change by awakening the latent political animal lurking within the Spanish polity. For Martín-Santos, the darkness of lived experience, which passes without self-reflection pushed along by the thrownness of history, garners visibility through the political act of writing.

The most explicit advancement of a new set of principles dictating political congregation, however, comes in Espriu's poetics. The poetic voice of *La pell de brau* is a mediating priest attempting to re-establish a sacred communion in the present. The gathering poeticized at the conclusion of the work has the express aim of reconstructing a common space of congregation, which possesses a political dimension by virtue of comprising *homes de diversos parles.* The aesthetic community, formed around a relation to the principle of love, corresponds to Espriu's political conception of the Iberian peninsula: "La meva concepció de la Península, el meu ideal d'organització social i política de l'Estat espanyol ... contempla una Espanya federal composta per quatre nacions" (cited in *Obres completes* 12: 243). The federalist principle of coexistence that Espriu espouses contrasts with his critique of Ortega y Gasset and the perception that the periphery could not comprehend essential Iberian problematics. The raison d'être of *La pell de brau*, a text one could never call an autonomous literary construct turned away from the world, is the disruption and reformulation of the partitions of the political sensible in Iberia, especially those theorized initially by Ortega and later put into practice through the Francoist idealization of *los campos de Castilla*, which I analyzed in the second chapter of the book.

In conclusion, Espriu also represents the limitations of aesthetic discourse vis-à-vis political galvanization. With each successive edition of *La pell de brau*, the tone of the poet took on a starker tone as it became clear that his poeticization of Sepharad was being left behind as a viable political project. Recently, the retired president of the Generalitat, Jordi Pujol, has in fact declared Sepharad to be a failure: "Hi ha hagut gent – aquí, entre nosaltres, i sobretot fora d'aquí, en altres indrets de Sepharad – que no ha cregut mai en tot això" ("El fracàs"). Disrupting the distribution of the sensible or creating a new metaphorical vocabulary with which to propose a distinct political truth must traverse from the mind of the author to the collective imaginary of the body politic in order to truly gain force. Rorty knew this all too well, arguing that aesthetic assertions of truth become literalized, thereby shedding their metaphorical state, through collective solidarity. "Solidarity is not discovered by reflection but created. It is created by increasing our sensitivity to the particular details of the pain and humiliation of the other, unfamiliar sorts of people" (xvi). In other words, the producer of an aesthetic work can lead readers or observers to water, but cannot force them to drink.

If this study has accomplished anything, I hope to have at least brought these writers' common preoccupations regarding the sacred foundations of political consciousness to light and contributed to the solidarity many yearned to find with their contemporaries. Espriu's Sepharad may have failed on a political level, but in terms of pedagogy the rhizomatic integration of these diverse Iberian *parles*, congregated together around the principle of loving inclusiveness, confers a keen understanding of the inviolable, set-apart space within secular political imagination in which the sacred thrives.

Notes

1. Introduction: *La España Sagrada* as a Political Category

1 Post-secularity is a diffuse movement but can be whittled down to two competing preoccupations. For writers such as Richard Dawkins, the threatening return of the sacred is posed as a challenge to the classical divide between church and state and an assault of irrationality on conceptual thought. Elsewhere, one finds a different kind of alarmism in writers such as Jürgen Habermas and Judith Butler, who argue that the secular political sphere in the West suffers from *too little* of the organizational and moral sensibilities of a religious mindset.

2 In the United States and in other parts of the Western world, martial law is one such circumstance that creates a state of exception. An infamous example, as a result of its use by the Nazis, was Article 48 of the Weimar constitution, which allowed for unbridled executive power upon declaring a crisis. Schmitt, a political theorist working during the Weimar Republic, is a product of this system. Despite a system of checks and balances, even the United States – a nation built around limiting the tyranny of absolutism – still allows for executive orders that Congress very infrequently overturns, not to mention allowing executive pardons, commutations of prison sentences, and so on. In terms of metaphysical morality, the ethical "intentions" of the American founding fathers – Washington, Jefferson, et al. – are in some circles appropriated to be used as justification for policymaking and spiritual inspirations, which highly resembles Franco's turning to the Catholic kings. For more on the relationship between Schmitt and the Weimar Republic, see Villacañas (148–61).

3 The Spanish historian Francisco Sevillano elucidates the theological nature of Franco's politics quite well, noting that "la invocación patriótica del Caudillo primó un sentido tradicional y católico con lo nacional" (63). As evidence of the easy slippage of the sacred into profane political imagination, Franco's use of Catholicism was not so much a turning to religion per se; importing a theological faith with great

social import opened access to a transcendental fount of national being: "La devoción patriótica de Franco conduce a lo trascendente, llevándose a cabo en su persona la unión del alma de un pueblo impío con la esencia patria" (63).

4 Beyond being a metaphysical anchor for Francoist ideology, the Roman Catholic Church also took on a very active role in creating a Spanish police state. As Julián Casanova notes, "In no other authoritarian regime in the twentieth century did the Church assume such political responsibility and play such a central role in policing the country's citizens as Spain … once the war was over, far from turning the other cheek, the Church used the memory of its martyrs to justify paybacks against the vanquished" (108). The church's central involvement in governmental affairs was heightened once Franco's interior ministries passed from falangist hands to the Opus Dei in the 1950s.

5 With reference to viewing Castile as the source of national identity, a posture that mirrors Generación del '98 regenerationist theories of the nation, Franco noted in 1948, "La verdadera España, la España honrada, la España unida, salió de estos pueblos viejos de Castilla" (cited in Vázquez Montalbán 180). As regards the Generación del '98, Vázquez Montalbán argues that "esa búsqueda del orteguiano 'proyecto histórico' subyace en la ideología de Franco" (50). In terms of Castile being the centre of Spanish identity, see, for example, Ortega y Gasset in *España invertebrada*: "España es una cosa hecha por Castilla, y hay razones para ir sospechando que, en general, sólo cabezas castellanas tienen órganos adecuados para percibir el gran problema de la España integral" (40).

6 Beyond opposing Hobsbawm, Smith is also refuting the horizontal structure of national imagining proposed by Benedict Anderson. For Anderson, the nation is an imagined fraternity: "a deep, horizontal comradeship" (7).

7 A common theme of the post-secularism movement is a call to reconsider the definition and historical development of secularity. Charles Taylor, for example, purports that democratic governments should buttress their secularity by not remaining "true to hallowed tradition," but rather by maximizing "the basic goals of liberty and equality between basic beliefs" (56). Talal Asad's influential 2003 study on the secular traces the uneven transition from pre-modern societies to the horizontal solidarity of Benedict Anderson's imagined communities. For Asad, the move from the vertical sovereignty of absolutism to the structure of Western liberalism is anything but a straight line. The "secular is neither singular in origin nor stable in its historical identity, although it works through a series of particular oppositions" (25).

8 The verse in the original Catalan: "Durs càstigs eren conservats en símbols vells."

9 "El brau, en l'arena de Sepharad / envestia l'estesa pell / i en fa, enlairant-la, bandera."

10 One can trace the omnipotence of the sovereign back to Hobbes's *Leviathan*, where "no man that hath Soveraigne power can justly be put to death, or otherwise in any manner by his Subjects punished" (141). This is also the root of Schmitt's thoughts

on exceptional, decisionistic power. Hobbes proposed that the "whole power of prescribing the Rules" is annexed to the institution of sovereignty, and it is difficult to disassociate Franco's frequent insistence on maintaining order by way of *la espada* with the original frontispiece of *Leviathan*, which precisely features a kingly figure towering over the landscape with a sword and a crosier, beneath a citation from the Book of Job that reads, "On earth it has no equal, a creature without fear."

11 Scholars typically have studied "La España sagrada" not as a modern political category or literary theme, but rather as an artistic or purely theological construct rooted in the distant past. First published in the eighteenth century, *España sagrada* is a running compendium of ecclesiastical history that documents churches throughout Spain. The edited volume *Sacred Spain: Art and Belief in the Spanish World* (2010) analyzes the relationship between the church and cultural practice in the seventeenth century, and *Inventing the Sacred: Imposture, Inquisition, and the Boundaries of the Supernatural in Golden Age Spain* (2005) by Andrew Kleitt researches the role of the sacred in the machinations of the Spanish Inquisition. There remains a sizeable gap in Iberian scholarship that might extend the historical development of the sacred in Spain into the twentieth century.

12 Mercè Rodoreda wrote the bulk of *La mort i la primavera* in the early 1960s, though she returned to the novel in the early 1980s shortly before her death, and the novel was not published until 1986.

13 The scope of my work focuses generally on the aesthetic shift away from the *novela social* and *objetivismo* that took place in Spain beginning in the 1960s. A group of novelists and poets, like Goytisolo and Benet, eschewed the mimetic reproduction of a destitute reality in favour of addressing the cultural realm indirectly through a thematic abstraction made possible by importing philosophical currents of thought from Europe and exploiting those realms of thought already present within Spanish intellectual circles. Vestiges of *objetivismo* certainly persisted, with *Tiempo de silencio* being one example, but the investigation of a metaphysical Spanish way of being, and the sacred structures that conditioned this modality, was made possible by assuming a critical attitude toward culture by way of the philosophical. Scholars have studied the formal aspects of Goytisolo, Benet, and Martín-Santos's fiction at great length, leaving aside the works' ideological aspects. For this reason, I focus less on aesthetic form and more on the novels' conceptual shape.

14 Christopher Soufas argues that it is difficult to tie the diffuse modernist movement, in all of its iterations across Europe, to one specific time period. Indeed, even within Spain what is considered Catalan modernism differs, both ideologically and temporally, from what Soufas terms early contemporary Spanish modernism. In general, Soufas argues that modernism differs from its predecessor, realism, in that "the realist believes in one, and only one, empirical, sensually communicated reality, while the modernist believes in a second reality invariably considered superior to ordinary, conventional reality" (12). In this sense, the modernist movement bears a marked

similarity to the texts that I am analyzing in the common desire to propose, through imaginative discourse, alternative proposals to empirical reality. In contrast, I propose a much more pliable separation between the imaginary realm and external reality, which is always shaped by the symbolic field. Imaginative assertions of political truth within aesthetic art thus inflect external perception and cannot be decoupled from "communicated reality."

2. "He aquí una plenitud española": Catholicism, Cultural Regeneration, and Spanish Essentialism

1 Balmes, with derision, argues that "es necesario contemplar la sociedad desde un punto de vista elevado para no dejarse deslumbrar por teorías pobres" (1943, 202).

2 In an effort to end successional conflict, Balmes famously pushed for a marriage between Isabella II and Carlos of Montemolín.

3 Schmitt saw in Cortés's thought an early cynicism about the possibility of reaching decisions through a Rawlsian overlapping of consensus. Cortés conceived bourgeois liberalism as *una clase discutidor* that allowed all decision-making to be "suspended forever in an everlasting discussion" (*Political Theology* 63). For Cortés, dictatorship was the opposite of discussion, and embodied what Schmitt saw as the core of the political idea: "the exacting moral decision" (65).

4 Valis sees this literary shift in the late-nineteenth-century emergence of the novelistic form, which is "an alternative secular site of community (or its absence)" and the "ideal imaginary space in which to reconstruct belief in something … the novel seems to take sustenance from a mental structure that is at once uniquely moral and unstable" (4–5).

5 It is worth noting that the notion of an infection or virus infecting the *raza*'s purity also played a substantial role in Franco's and the Falange's interpretation of the Civil War and in justifying repression throughout the post-war period. As Richards notes, "The Spanish Civil War was portrayed as a project to pathologically remake the physical stock of the *Patria* and its morality" (47).

6 Balmes levels the same charge against liberals in 1845, arguing that "el error fundamental de los liberales ha consistido en querer introducir en España doctrinas y sistemas que estaban en abierta oposición con todo lo dominante … comenzaron por zaherir a la religión, cuando la religión era lo más popular que había en España" (*Obras completas* 208).

7 Richards attaches Francoist ideology to Conservative theories of regeneration that encouraged a physical amputation from the Spanish tree of venomous foreign influences and the poisoning influence of liberalism. By advocating for sacrifice in the name of self-sufficiency, Franco projected what Richards argues is a clear preference

for autarky, "an expression of extreme nationalism, a rejection of liberalism, a desire for national industrialisation, a sympathy for fascist ideas" (92).

8 Hannah Arendt's theory of totalitarianism is more in line with Franco's style of governance, with some key distinctions. Like Habermas's vision of liberal democracy, Arendt argues that totalitarian governments, at their inception, also need to win over the masses: "Under conditions of constitutional government and freedom of opinion, totalitarian movements struggling for power can use terror to a limited extent only and share with other parties the necessity of winning adherents and of appearing plausible to a public which is not yet rigorously isolated from all other sources of information" (*Totalitarianism* 39). Arendt argues that totalitarian regimes, unlike autarkies like Franco's Spain, win over the masses both domestically, in order to consolidate power, and externally, in preparation for world conquest. In Franco's case, the beginnings of totalitarianism, where propaganda initially converts the social classes into masses loyal to the government, before giving way to terror and repression, certainly match the everyday life of Spaniards in the 1940s. Though Franco claimed to be funnelling God's grace into dreams of empire, Spain never truly achieved the full breadth of Arendt's vision of totalitarianism by going beyond its borders.

3. Politics by Other Means: The Sacred Core of Collective Imagining

1 Note the lexical similarity to both Stendhal's Julien Sorel and to Joan Sales.

2 In 1960 Sales, through Gallimard, requested a similar *nihil obstat* from the archbishop of Paris for *Gloire incertaine* but was denied. This, however, did not impede its publication.

3 The two latest Catalan editions, published in 2000 and 2007 by Club Editor, were edited by Sales's widow Núria Folch, and both feature the title *Incerta glòria seguida d'El vent de la nit.* For clarity's sake I will hereafter refer to *El vent* … either by its title or as the fourth section of the novel.

4 Macià's declaration came before Madrid's, and it called for a Catalan republic within a federation of Iberian republics. Madrid republicans could not accept the federation and proposed a flimsy statute of autonomy, which even then encouraged the Spanish right to launch a coup in order to roll it back.

5 In Sales's *Cartes de la guerra*, the author describes a similar bout of melancholic anxiety while fighting on the Aragonese trenches in 1937: "Després d'haver escrit una llarguíssima carta a la Mercè parlant-li dels combats de Belxit … m'entrà com un encantament que m'ha durat uns dies. No sé com dir-ne; és la primera vegada a la vida que em passa. Com si m'envoltés una solitud absoluta; i em venia com una ràbia contra tota l'espècie humana" (164). After a few days, these feelings subside, but in retrospect Sales, very much in the style of Trini, will refer to the period as "una buidor tan insuportable" (165).

6 Sales, in a 1980 letter, credits his friend Ferran de Pol for encouraging him to return to the Christian faith, clearly echoing Trini's similar feelings of emptiness and her recognition of Soleràs's contribution to her conversion: "Jo li estic agraïdíssim per un altre motiu: ell va contribuir molt al meu retorn al cristianisme, ja que amb el do d'escriure que tenia, ningú – com ell – no ha sabut expressar tan vivament tota la buidor i l'absurditat de l'ateisme" (qtd in Arnau, *Compromís i escriptura* 172).

7 Carl Schmitt in fact argues that any ideological formation will eventually devolve into a political manifestation at the point that an antithesis is reached wherein a friend/enemy distinction is possible: "Every religious, moral, economic, ethical, or other antithesis transforms into a political one if it is sufficiently strong to group human beings effectively according to friend and enemy" (*Concept of the Political* 37).

8 Sales's perception of glory as a mover and the distinction of glory and vainglory might be a reference to St Thomas Aquinas, who is identified as one of Lluís's objects of study while perusing the library of the Olivel monastery. Aquinas, in response to Aristotle's *De Anima*, argues that the soul is incorporeal and subsistent: "The soul, which is the first principle of life, is not a body, but the act of a body; just as heat, which is the principle of calefaction, is not a body, but an act of a body" (62). Glory, if compared to Aquinas's soul, is a similar mechanism that inspires movement but is independent from corporeal existence. Trini's existential aporia and religious conversion would indicate the belief in an eternal impulse where the unmoved moves.

9 Schmitt argues that the partisan possesses four criteria: irregularity of fighting, increased tactical mobility, intensity of political engagement, and a telluric character that demands resistance of a particular, autochthonous region (*Theory of the Partisan* 22). In this sense, "the modern partisan expects neither law nor mercy from the enemy. He has moved away from the conventional enmity of controlled and bracketed war, and into the realm of another, real enmity, which intensifies through terror and counter-terror until it ends in extermination" (11). Sales proves that the path between internecine war and a partisan conflict, in Schmitt's terms, is extremely short and narrow. Schmitt argues that the Spanish Civil War is not partisan, per se, as it lacks a guerrilla style of warfare where soldiers attack irregularly, without clearly identifiable uniforms, and employ a style of attack that occurs outside of trenches. This style of fighting, however, closely resembles the anarchist militias – they weren't a regular army, lacked uniforms and discipline, and fought in poorly articulated units. What is important is that the partisan and the soldier in Sales's novel each approach violence from a mindset of resistance at all costs.

10 Though not stated explicitly, the conception of love referred to by both Sales and Girard is certainly akin to *agape*, which is translated as *caritas* into Latin and is very frequently used throughout the New Testament in Christ's teachings and by later Christian theologians such as St Augustine. Plato would define *agape* as a deeper expression of esteem than what would correspond to physical attraction, known as *éros*. As interpreted by Christianity, *agape* would refer to a kind of unconditional and absolute

offering of love akin to the feeling expressed by Christ in his sacrifice for humankind. The act of offering is crucial, as *agape* implies both feeling and corresponding action, which places it above the third Greek term for love used in Plato, *philía*, which is a kind of brotherly camaraderie.

11 Frances Lannon writes that the Second Vatican Council "plotted a new, more liberal, and more tolerant course for the Church. This radical change left Catholic authoritarians in Spain, including Franco himself, disconcerted and suddenly displaced from the orthodox centre they were sure they had always occupied" (278). Pope John XXII was particularly influential in two encyclicals entitled *Mater et magistra* (1961) and *Pacem in terris* (1963), as they revealed a "vision of a just and Christian society, and it bore little resemblance to Franco's Spain. In this new model, human rights such as the right of association and freedom of worship were scrupulously respected, wealth was redistributed down the social scale by progressive taxation and social insurance, and citizens participated in the affairs of the state" (Lannon 278). Sales frequently lauds the saintly qualities of Pope John XXII, especially in this episode depicting Cruells and the seminarian's peaceful protest in Barcelona. Cruells questions, "I no obstant, Tu ens havies enviat aquell sant clarivident, aquell sant genial, de què el nostre segle tenia tanta necessitat; Tu ens l'havies enviat i l'havies fet arribar fins al soli suprem de la teva Eglésia. Nosaltres l'hem vist amb els nostres ulls i escoltat amb les nostres orelles, aquell bon papa Joan, i el glaç es fonia de pressa" (724).

12 The notion of a singular revolt spreading like a flame and igniting others who are oppressed calls to mind Camus's *The Rebel.* Published in 1956, near the time when Sales would have been writing *El vent de la nit*, Camus argues that the rebel's denunciative "no" to nothingness and intractable defence of a certain ideal leads to an identification with an awakened "natural community" (16). In terms of my own study, it is also important to note that Camus ties rebellion to a questioning of the sacred: "The rebel is a man who is on the point of accepting or rejecting the sacred and determined on laying claim to a human situation in which all the answers are human" (21). Cruells, in his redemption of the Catalonian political victim, questions – in rational terms – the sacred, irreproachable concept of Franco's cult of national belonging.

13 Joan Triadú writes that Sales's three commitments are literature, religion, and a "projecte nacional" (423–5). This point is obvious and even unquestionable from an empirical standpoint, but it is worth noting that there lacks an underlying connective thread. The difficulty clearly rests on negotiating a variety of seemingly incongruous planes, as the critic approaching Sales's work must consider a work of literature from a symbolic register and additionally intertwine a series of meditations on philosophy, religion, and nation.

14 Any discussion of the connection of love and friendship necessarily passes through Aristotle's *Nicomachean Ethics.* Aristotle defines three kinds of friendship, each predicated on love: friendship based on utility, on pleasure, and on mutual goodness. In a general sense, Aristotle appears as a forerunner to Schmitt's thought when he argues

that "friendship seems to hold states together, and lawgivers to care more for it than for justice; for concord seems to be something like friendship, and this they aim at most of all, and expel faction as their worst enemy" (142). It goes without saying that Aristotle's definition of the state is different from Schmitt's, but the basic premise of the political based on friendship remains valid. As for Sales, the point at which love becomes political friendship has roots in Aristotle's thought. Love is initially a feeling, but passes into a state of character when it is converted into friendship with another being. In a friendship of the good, where humankind loves the good in another, not for the sake of utility or pleasure but as a virtue, one expects not only what is good for oneself but also to return the same feeling to another. In other words, Aristotle is defining a benevolent reciprocity: "Mutual love involves choice and choice springs from a state of character" (148). Though Aristotle is using the term *philía*, the notion of a selfless decisive action is similar to *agape* as defined by Christianity. Producing the sacred through love, then, is dependent on making a transition into a state of character where a choice to congregate and establish friendship is made.

15 The *Diari Oficial*, published by the Generalitat, did in fact proclaim a Catalan Popular Army in December 1936. The army as such was both numerically small and temporally short lived. The resistance is eventually fought by a series of columns, each represented by a variety of ideological banners.

16 Sales, in his youth, was a member of the Catalan Communist Party and at one point considered joining Estat Català but felt deceived by the party's inability to do away with the Federación Anarquista Ibérica prior to the Civil War. He was also disheartened by the Partit Socialista Unificat, which eventually absorbed other entities such as the Unió Socialista de Catalunya, after it fell under Communist hegemony (*Cartes* 188).

17 One should note that Schmitt's argument is purely abstract and that in common practice the enemy is often dehumanized. The function of wartime propaganda is explicitly aimed at such a dehumanization.

18 This idea also appears in the *Cartes* in an analysis of the historical failure of Castile and Catalonia directing each other's affairs: "¿En què es coneixeria, doncs, que Catalunya és un país autònom si els dos governs, l'autònom i el de la República, haguéssim de ser sempre, obligatòriament, del mateix color? Hi hagué també molt d'aquella mania nostra tan idiota d'imposar als castellans allò que ens agrada per més que a ells els faci fàstic: en el segle XVII la casa d'Habsburg, en el XIX la rama carlina o la República federal, en el XX la d'esquerres. ¿Per què no deixem d'una vegada que es governin com vulguin a casa seva i ens dediquem a governar en pau la nostra?" (246).

19 Pi i Maragall echoes this idea in the nineteenth century: "Order supposes arrangement, harmony, convergence of all individual and social elements: order refuses all humiliations and sacrifices. Can you call order that fictitious peace with which you obtain by cutting with the sword all that you are too stupid to organize with your limited intelligence?" (qtd in Brenan 148; Brenan's translation).

4. Intimate Strife: Inside Juan Goytisolo's Sovereign Exception

1 See Bloom (1975).

2 In his first memoir, *Coto vedado*, Goytisolo recalls that when he emigrated to Paris in 1956 authors such as Artaud, Bataille, and Breton "significaban nada o muy poco para aquel joven español imbuido de marxismo y adepto a las tesis del compromiso de Sartre" but that eight years later, "libre ya de mis anteojeras ideológicas," he would discover their work (*Coto vedado* 209).

3 Goytisolo and Paz were both in Paris in the late 1950s and later crossed paths in Mallorca. Goytisolo mentions in a speech upon receiving the Premio Octavio Paz de Poesía y Ensayo in 2002 that Paz's name was first mentioned to him upon arriving in France in a conversation with Josep Palau i Fabre, though the two did not meet until 1959 at a literary conference in Formentor. In his acceptance speech, Goytisolo expresses his strong admiration for the Mexican poet and essayist's work, in particular *El laberinto de la soledad*, which has become "un texto capital de la literatura española del siglo XX" (*CLSF* 267–8). Another Spaniard in France at the time strongly influenced by Paz's notion of creative destruction was the poet José Ángel Valente.

4 Another Spanish intellectual who spent part of her exile in Paris, beginning in the late 1950s, was María Zambrano. Zambrano's theorization of masks in her essay "La destrucción de las formas," which begins with a reference to Nietzsche, certainly has ties to Goytisolo's linking of *máscaras* to the sacred, both in his essays and in reference to Álvaro Peranzules in *Conde Julián*. Zambrano writes that in the mask, "se levanta frente al hombre lo ambiguo, lo demoniaco, lo sagrado en suma, con esa ambivalencia característica de lo sagrado" (23). The mask is precisely what hides the Real in the depths of the *rostro* – "el rostro revela; el rostro humano es el lugar donde la naturaleza, el cosmos entero, sale de su hermetismo" (23).

5 See especially Levine (1976) and Epps (1996).

6 Throughout the first half of the twentieth century, Tangier was an international zone without any sovereign power of its own. This allowed the city to become a hotbed for "illicit" activities, especially sexual perversion and drug use, aimed primarily at Western tourists. This dynamic is also evident in the fiction of other authors, particularly André Gide, whom Goytisolo often cites as an influence. The city's legal status did not change until Moroccan independence was granted in 1956, only a handful of years before Goytisolo first travelled there in 1963. Linda Gould Levine writes that Goytisolo found the landscape of Almería and his trips to North Africa as "dos puntos de partida fundamentales en la génesis de su obra," and even considered Tangier to be a "prolongación de la « pasión » que sentía ante el paisaje y clima mental de Almería" ("Introduction" 16). Goytisolo's comparison of Tangier to Almería is a class perception as working-class immigrants from Almería were "discovered" by

Goytisolo as an "other" to his Barcelona upper-class society, which is quite clear, for example, in the work *Campos de Nijar*. Tangier's status as an international zone and as an extension of a Spanish no-man's land within Goytisolo's thought will be important when comparing his work to Giorgio Agamben's state of exception.

7 Giorgio Agamben writes that the two terms share an etymological root in Greek but "are semantically and morphologically distinct: *zoe*, which expressed the simple fact of living common to all living beings (animals, men, or gods), and *bios*, which indicated the form or way of living proper to an individual or a group" (*Homo Sacer* 1).

8 Goytisolo's brother Luis, in fact, became ill with a respiratory infection after being incarcerated in the Carabanchel prison in Madrid in 1960.

9 Or, as Goytisolo surmises, stolen outright by officials from the Spanish embassy.

10 Throughout the novel, the protagonist's identity merges with that of several other characters, including Julián and its alternative spellings, Ulbán/Bulian/Ulyan; an infantile alter ego of himself named Alvarito; Tariq ibn Ziyad; and others. As the novel progresses and its stockpile of archetypes and characters grows, this merging of identity becomes commonplace and more convoluted.

11 As Foucault writes, "For a long time, one of the characteristic privileges of sovereign power was the right to decide life and death" (*Foucault Reader* 258). Foucault posits that this privilege originated from the unconditional power given to the father of the Roman family, who had the right to do away with the subjects of his family and house. The exercise of the privilege, however, was eventually granted only at the extreme point where the existence of the sovereign himself was in danger (258).

12 On the opposite end of the spectrum, Goytisolo highly esteems Américo Castro for demystifying essentialist conceptions of identity at the foundation of nationalist or religious dogma: "La insistencia de Américo Castro en apuntar a los mecanismos de exclusión fundados en dogmas y mitologías … partía de un hecho incontestable: el de la manipulación y escamoteo de nuestra historia *incómoda* en aras, ayer, de un nacional-catolicismo obtuso y, hoy, de un europeísmo de fachada resuelto a normalizar el pasado conforme al patrón del euro" (*Contra las sagradas formas* 55–6).

13 I say "mythologized" because very little is written about Count Julián and there is speculation that the betrayal may not have occurred as described in Alfonso's chronicle, if at all. Levine notes that "mayor paria o traidor no ha existido jamás para la historiografía oficial española. Aunque son pocos los datos que actualmente se saben de él y aunque incluso se ponga en duda su nacionalidad … toda su vida se reduce a un solo hecho: él es la persona que abrió las puertas de España a las huestes de Tariq en 711" (1985: 20). What is most important is the history of the myth and the way it has infiltrated modern-day Spain's political and social consciousness.

14 Ganivet, however, basically claimed that Seneca was essentially Castilian and only circumstantially *bético*.

15 The name derives from Alonso Fernández de Avellaneda's "Romance del conde Peranzules," which is included in his sequel to Cervantes's magnum opus *Segundo tomo del ingenioso hidalgo don Quijote de la Mancha* (1614).

5. The Eternal Present of Sacred Time

1 Seventeen years later, at the inauguration of the Valle de los Caídos, Franco again emphasizes "las varias veces que, al correr de nuestra campaña, se repetían los hechos providenciales que nos favorecían" (Díaz-Plaja 305). The Valle de los Caídos functions as a temple that entombs access to an eternal past. It is a space located within a crushed time, therefore, where a single edification embodies the cosmology of the entire nation.

2 In *The Sacred Bough*, Frazier dedicates chapters to the worship of trees and to relics of tree worship in modern Europe (109–35).

3 Labanyi (1989) brilliantly interprets the naming of Numa's territory – Mantua – as a reference to Virgil's *Aeneid*, which recounts the story of the golden bough. Mantua is "the birthplace of Virgil, author of the *Aeneid* in which the golden bough is mentioned, and Dante's guide to the underworld in the *Inferno* where he is referred to as a 'son of Mantua'" (97).

4 Benet, in an author's note to Rabassa's English translation of the novel, concedes that *Volverás a Región* was influenced by a reading of *The Golden Bough* and was first written in 1951 (*El ángel* v).

5 While conversing with Marré Gamallo, Dr Sebastián channels Frazier's ghost: "Tenemos un solo árbol. – interrumpió el doctor – pero ¿ha visto usted cómo brilla?" (158).

6 The poet Antonio Martínez Sarrión, a friend of Juan Benet's, notes that another of Numa's mythological origins is "el ángel provisto de la espada flamígera que expulsa del Edén a Adán y Eva, tanto en el relato bíblico como en el gran poeta de Milton" (121). Numa, taking into consideration all of his possible connotations, is responsible for the purity of a refined, unadulterated space.

7 My study of the Mantuan forest as a sacred space that regulates the temporal reality of profane time in Región is greatly informed by John B. Margenot's analysis of "sacred cloisters" in parts of Benet's fiction, including *Volverás a región*. Margenot argues, "Mantua constitutes an inherently violent space, a modern *discordia concors* which efficiently imposes order throughout the rest of Región … the controlling order emanates from Mantua to various levels of human and geographical experience in this fictional world" (113).

8 Benet does, however, cite Nietzsche's *Thus Spoke Zarathustra* in the final pages of the novel, demonstrating at least a passing knowledge of the philosopher's work. I adopt Nietzsche's spelling of *ressentiment* in lieu of the English *resentment*.

9 The relationship between *rencor* and Spanish identity was also firmly established by Ortega y Gasset in his *Meditaciones del Quijote*: "Los españols ofrecemos a la vida un corazón blindado de rencor, y las cosas, rebotando en él, son despedidas cruelmente. Hay en derredor nuestro, desde hace siglos, un incesante y progresivo derrumbamiento de los valores" (49).

10 Benet frequently refers to an epidemic sickness endemic to Región that is more ontological than epidemiological. In the novel's second part, for example, Sebastián notes that "ciertamente todo el país padecía una enfermedad crónica y una epidemia porque … en la conciencia popular se había llegado a considerar punible, insensata e imprudente la más ligera advertencia acerca de los peligros que encerraban los atractivos del monte" (*Volverás* 145). Warning outsiders of Numa's homicidal prowess is punishable because his acts of violence invigorate the town's *ressentiment* morality. Warning an outsider of Numa's shots would implicitly endorse the continued presence of an external morality within Región's closed space.

11 Benet's stance on an inherently wicked God resonates with the idea that the sacred is merely a displacement of inner experience: "Dios puede transgredir e invadir el terreno del hombre, la recíproca no es cierta. Dios no será ubicuo pero si perfectamente externo y todo terreno que conquista el espíritu ha sido previamente desalojado por Dios" (*El ángel* 104).

12 Unlike Benet and the other writers considered in this book, Rodoreda wrote *La mort i la primavera* while exiled in Geneva. Rodoreda did, however, travel to Spain during the dictatorship, such as in 1956 to receive the Premi Joan Santamaria, and maintained ties with Catalan intellectuals, such as her editor Joan Sales. She also moved back to the Iberian Peninsula in the later years of her life, which were partly spent revising *La mort i la primavera*. In any event, Rodoreda was keenly aware of the ideological contextualization of Spanish Being promulgated by the regime.

13 For more information on the text's different iterations, see Carme Arnau's excellent critical edition (*La mort* 22–38). Rodoreda, after having submitted the novel to the *Sant Jordi*, added key protagonists such as the *pres* and the *ferrater*'s son. Thematically, the novel slowly became more imbued with meditations on human nature.

14 For an interpretation of *La mort i la primavera* as a textbook case of "late style," see Viestenz ("Death in the Spring").

15 Humankind inevitably denies the persistence of change by inflecting temporal parlance and practice with spatial concepts and vocabulary, which Henri Bergson remarks is most evident in the practice of measuring time according to mathematical principles, such as extension (*Creative Mind* 2).

16 In both *Quanta, quanta guerra …*, Rodoreda's last original work published in 1980, and *La mort i la primavera* a river plays a central role. In the latter, I argue that the river is linked to both repetition, as it is a site of annual sacred ritual, and the origin of mythic consciousness. In the former, however, the river occupies a linear function and

embodies temporal flow: "Sort que la guerra s'ha acabat. Jo vaig veure com s'acabava, va acabar aquí, en aquest riu, aquest riu se la va endur cap al mar" (*Quanta, quanta* 231).

17 The writer repeats her metaphoric use of the mirror in a self-portrait dictated to J.M. Castellet in 1973: "Si escriure és com passar un mirall al llarg de la vida, a mi m'agradava passar-lo, mantenir-me al darrera. Darrera el mirall hi ha els somnis, i jo tinc la impressió que tot el que he viscut ho he somiat" ("Mercè Rodoreda" 42).

6. "De-sacralization" and "Sacro-genesis," or How to Step Outside of Sacred Time

1 Without identifying a source, though it could be Martín-Santos, Goytisolo, or Rouquié, José Ortega also writes in 1969, "*Tiempo de silencio* era parte de una trilogía intitulada *La destrucción de la España sagrada*" (23).

2 "Oft-cited" because it is one of the very few instances where Martín-Santos offers a perspective singularly related to literature. Trained as a psychiatrist, Martín-Santos published much more frequently on his approaches to "existential analysis," which rebuffs the concrete mythologems, such as the Oedipal complex, that structure consciousness within psychoanalysis. Martín-Santos writes, in a criticism of Freud, that orthodox psychoanalysis "no valora el carácter esencial de *durée* propio de lo psíquico, no ve el « movimiento » propio de la vida humana, que varía continuamente" (*El análisis existencial* 60). As with Sartre, existential analysis sees the being-for-itself as a constant process of remaking through absolute freedom not dependent on a determinant subconscious.

3 In a review originally published in 1962, a few months after *Tiempo de silencio*'s publication, by *Destino*, Antonio Vilanova writes that "en el caso concreto de Luis Martín Santos, cuya adscripción a los módulos narrativos del *Ulises* de Joyce es patente y manifiesta, las ventajas e inconvenientes de esa técnica, que tiende a refractar la realidad a través del temperamento y las ideas del autor, cobran una importancia que no puede ser soslayada" (420–1).

4 Existential psychiatry – "la pretensión de dar cuenta y descripción de la totalidad del ser espiritual del hombre" (*El análisis existencial* 72) – is the result of a series of intellectual steps beginning at the turn of the twentieth century and culminating throughout the 1920s. Of these, Martín-Santos situates both the work of Dilthey and Jaspers in addition to Binswanger, Minkowski, and Bleuler (72–3).

5 Like Martín-Santos's conception of Spain's infirm national body, Machado frequently uses metaphors of illness to describe the country: "A España toda, / la malherida España, de Carnaval vestida / nos la pusieron, pobre y escuálida y beoda, para que no acertara la mano con la herida" (248).

6 Hegelian dialectics obviously influenced Engels and Marx's conception of dialectical materialism. I make the distinction as a reaction to the use and abuse of the term

in modern scholarship, where *dialectical* is thrown around to the point of becoming trivial, and at best, a synonym with *causing conflict.* Hegel's innovation, vis-à-vis Plato and others, is to situate a thesis's contradiction within itself and not as an external reality. For Hegel, a true synthesis is never truly reached in a classical sense, which implies a merging of opposites into one. Synthesis, in Hegelian terms, is a speculative totalizing that acknowledges the codependence, and mutual determination, of a thing and its opposite.

7 Compare Cartucho's entrance onto the dance floor like a flash of lightening in a fit of amorous vengeance with Mariano José de Larra's cuckolded Augusto in "El casarse pronto y mal" (1832). Arriving in Cádiz in order to confront his absconding wife and her lover, Augusto enters a hotel and "ya no es un hombre, es un rayo que cae en la habitación" (69).

8 The first line of an essay where Sartre himself defines his own unique take on psychoanalysis echoes Martín-Santos's take on symbols. Human reality is thought of as something that "identifies and defines itself by the ends which it pursues" (712). In *Tiempo de silencio*, objective symbols encapsulate the ideational content, what may be called a signified, onto which humankind projects its being. In short, Sartre's philosophy rejects the notion of a pre-ontological reality, such as a primal drive or "original given," that may be understood to determine human reality (*Being and Nothingness* 717).

9 Pedro, unlike the "muchedumbre femelle," shows no indifference toward other variants of the truth but the result is the same for both groups. In Pedro's case, his existential castration at the novel's conclusion is filtered through yet another of Spain's national symbols, that of San Lorenzo. On the train, which ironically passes by *El escorial de San Lorenzo*, Pedro concludes the narrative identifying himself as "ese sanlorenzón … dame la vuelta que por este lado ya estoy tostado" (295).

10 On this point, Roger Caillois writes that a taboo object sublimely inspires both an "awe of sanctity" and a "fear of defilement" (36). The ambivalence Caillois finds in the sacred, which is rebuffed by Giorgio Agamben in *Homo Sacer*, is important insofar as its principle aim is to stimulate feelings in the believer, whether these sensations be of anxiety, fear, power, or prestige (37). Durkheim maintains a similar thesis, arguing that in sacred rituals primitive peoples "shriek and become carried away, feeling the need to tear and destroy" (303). Durkheim precisely notes that the effervescent feelings provoked by the sacred are fed by a ritual's collective nature: "Just by being collective these ceremonies raise the vital tone of the group. Now, when people feel the life within them – whether in the form of painful irritation or joyous enthusiasm – they do not think of death" (303). Similar to what Martín-Santos perceives in the agglomerated group of people in the theatre's audience, Durkheim notes that the collective draw of sacred symbols somehow suspends a rational consideration of such things as death and encourages the release of a vital tone whose effectiveness relies on an appealing to the senses that ultimately clouds judgment.

11 This comment appears to contradict the very title of the novel, which is centred on destruction. It is important to remember that this was not Martín-Santos's chosen title for the work. José Carlos Mainer, who edited the manuscript Martín-Santos left behind, attempts to extrapolate Martín-Santos's authorial intentions from his interview with Janet Winecoff. Mainer interprets Martín-Santos's admission that his present work was of a "destructive character" as a "premonición de un título – *Tiempo de destrucción* – y un tono para la novela que globalmente tenía proyectada el escritor: un ataque frontal a los mitos mostrencos de la vida española y la construcción de una posible liberación de los mismos hacia otros nuevos" ("Prólogo" 22). I, of course, see this as the function of *Tiempo de silencio*, whereas I argue that the following novel, now universally known as *Tiempo de destrucción*, bears a strong "sacrogenetic" character and defines what those other possible myths might be. As a dialectic, elements of "de-sacralization" will always accompany "sacrogenesis." But in the same interview with Winecoff, Martín-Santos also references that transcending this sacred dialectic involves the creation of the "sacred scriptures of tomorrow," which is a movement that I believe begins to take shape in the career trajectory of Agustín as it is defined in the first two sections of the novel.

12 In a March 1995 issue of the *Journal of Philosophy*, Habermas published his remarks on *Political Liberalism* and on general theories first introduced in *A Theory of Justice*. In a very diplomatic fashion, Habermas writes that Rawls's construction is flawed not in its foundation but rather in its execution: "I fear that Rawls makes concessions to opposed philosophical positions which impair the cogency of his own project" (110). In a "Reply to Habermas," Rawls offers a rebuttal in the same issue of the *Journal of Philosophy*.

13 In an analysis of the relationship between the sacred and law, Martha Merrill Umphrey, Austin Sarat, and Lawrence Douglas argue that the legal system acquires a sacred character through its indeterminacy, which "provokes both desire and fear" (6). This indeterminacy owes to the law's excess of meaning and potential for an unlimited morphology of interpretations, which is due in part to its being a text. This points to the similarities between biblical exegesis and the infallibility of papal authority and, in the United States, the ongoing juridical project of discerning the intent of the authors of the Constitution. Umphrey et al. cleverly funnel the issue through an analysis of Kafka's *The Trial*, where K.'s interpellation in the Cathedral leads to the priest, as though he were a judge, remarking, "The right perception of any matter and a misunderstanding of the same matter do not wholly exclude each other" (qtd in Umphrey et al. 6). Martín-Santos, in the second part of *Tiempo de destrucción*, argues that, unlike the law, reality, though it too possesses an "exceso de detalles, un exceso de verdades," is not subject to subjective interpretation because the past "tuvo a su paso una realidad total" (343).

14 Martín-Santos was a member of the PSOE and was detained on several occasions by Franco's police, though he was not officially a party member when first arrested

in 1956 (Lázaro 151). In 1958, Martín-Santos was sent to prison for the first time and eventually placed in Madrid's Carabanchel prison, the same facility in which Juan Goytisolo's brother Luis would be detained two years later. These experiences surely influenced the novelization of Pedro's detainment in *Tiempo de silencio* and the consideration of law and justice in the following novel.

15 It is interesting to compare Agustín's notion of just punishment with Cartucho's "eye for an eye" murder of Dorita in *Tiempo de silencio*. In a sense, Cartucho's automatic response to being wronged sets in motion a projection that is never altered through the intervention of a representative of the judicial system. In this case, the lack of social complicity between the law and the public fails to awaken an awareness in Cartucho, and his sense of vindication never "climbs Jacob's ladder" toward a more evolved plane. I say "evolved" on the basis of René Girard's account of the justice system's origins. Girard notes that the modern justice system is a response to the possibility of unmitigated violence breaking out in earlier iterations of society. Girard writes, "There is no difference of principle between private and public vengeance; but on the social level, the difference is enormous. Under the pyblic [*sic*] system, an act of vengeance is no longer avenged; the process is terminated, the danger of escalation averted" (*Violence and the Sacred* 16).

7. Espriu's Sepharad and the Equitable Restoration of Sacred Sovereignty

1 Espriu had originally translated Llorenç Villalonga's Castilian version of *Phaedra* into Catalan and thereafter wrote his own text, which was published in 1937 in *Letizia i altres proses* during the Spanish Civil War. His version of *Antigone* would not appear until 1955.

2 Jordi Pujol, the former leader of the centre-right Convergència i Unió party and president of the Catalan Generalitat from 1980 to 2003, noted, "Espriu era el poeta que calia a la generació que havíem nascut sota el signe de la derrota, però que confiàvem que sempre hi ha una represa" (cited in Walters 127). Armed with the uncritical security of being outside the political limelight, the retired Pujol has recently declared Espriu's dream of Sepharad a failure, despite his own best efforts to translate *La pell de brau* into a political program. Pujol's tone has sharpened in the wake of the Spanish Tribunal Constitucional's curtailment of the most recent Catalan Statute of Autonomy in 2010, but even prior to this event Pujol noted in 2009 that "hi ha hagut gent – aquí, entre nosaltres, i sobretot fora d'aquí, en altres indrets de Sepharad – que no ha cregut mai en tot això" ("El fracàs").

3 Espriu also expressed interest in the character in the poem "Cançó de Tirèsias" published in *Mrs Death* (1952).

4 Christian mysticism in particular demands an emptying of the self so that Christ might enter. Compare to Santa Teresa de Jesús: "Vivo sin vivir en mí / y de tal alta vida espero / que muero porque no muero" (122). A close resonance between Espriu

and San Juan de la Cruz concerns the motif of darkness. Espriu's verse, however, perceives self-negation as a reinforcement of the gods' absence rather than an "alto estado de la perfección," as San Juan de la Cruz writes in "La noche oscura." Espriu, departing from a ransacked home in order to, in *El caminant i el mur*, become *el rei de la nit* contrasts with "La noche oscura": "en una noche oscura, / con ansias, en amores inflamada, / ¡oh dichosa ventura!, / salí sin ser notada, / estando ya mi casa sosegada" (151).

5 This is not to say that Espriu failed to consider his place within the Catalan post-war poetic tradition. The death of Carles Riba in July 1959 unquestionably left Espriu as the reigning poet laureate of Catalan letters. In a prologue that was added to *La pell de brau* in August 1959, Espriu dedicates the work to Riba, all the while suggesting that Riba "no coneixia aquesta obra, i em decanto a creure que no li hauria agradat, car la meva poesia, en l'arriscada suposició que existeixi, ha anat sempre per camins molt allunyats dels seus" (*Obres completes* 12: 236). Both Riba's and Espriu's post-war literary contributions investigated the notion of a decadent or lost patria. In Espriu's *Antígona* and *Fedra* and Riba's *Les elegies de Bierville*, Greece, as the original seat of a Mediterranean civilization now turned ruinous, is framed as a refracted displacement of Catalonia. In Espriu's prologue to *La pell de brau*, though the work was written prior to Riba's death, he identifies an openness to "l'esperança, a l'esperança de la gent honesta i de la joventut" (236–7) as a point of departure from his master Riba.

6 Hubert and Mauss investigate the profound complexity of sacrificial rites throughout a handful of cultures. One constant is that "every sacrifice takes place in certain given circumstances and with a view to certain determined ends" (95). Sacrifice is in many cases linked to ritual and occurs at a rhythmic pace. It is also often thought of as a tool by which to fend off discord, runaway violence, and an angering of the gods or loss of sacrality. These qualities all define Espriu's historical moment and it fails to be surprising that sacrifice figures so prominently in his thought.

7 Espriu's legacy reflects this phenomenon in the wild popularity of the singer Raimon's interpretations of his poetry. The poet is now absent, has sunken away, but his demand to be remembered is fulfilled in his absence by his readers.

8 For a more in-depth discussion of Ortega's Castilian-centrism, see the fifth note of the Introduction. Ortega roundly disavowed the possibility that Basque and Catalan nationalism was based on a deep, vertical structure of kinship rooted in a long shared history. In *España invertebrada*, Ortega explains that prior to the late-eighteenth and early-twentieth-century emergence of separatist movements, "Cataluña y Vasconia no eran antes … unidades sociales distintas de Castilla o Andalucía. Era España una masa homogénea, sin discontinuidades cualitativas, sin confines interiores de unas partes con otras" (39).

9 Gassol i Bellet notes that this is primarily a response to *España invertebrada* and the perception of Spain as "una unitat nacional, formada per tots aquells pobles que Castella integrà" (60). Espriu explicitly mentions Ortega, but he is clearly reacting to

a vision of Spain promoted by a number of the philosopher's contemporaries such as Ángel Ganivet and his heirs such as Julián Marías. Gassol i Bellet argues that *La pell de brau* in particular "neix com una proposta personal d'Espriu orientada a posar les bases ideològiques que fonamentin l'organització d'Espanya" (61).

10 Metaphorically using wintertime to justify a nationalist project of regeneration not only references Spengler but also Enric Prat de la Riba. Riba's *La nacionalitat catalana* begins, "Cada any la natura ens dona una imatge viva de lo que és el renaixement d'un poble. Cada any, l'hivern estronca la circulació de la vida, deixa nues de verdor les branques, cobreix la terra de neus y de gebrades" (9). In *La pell de brau*, the poetic voice repeatedly refers to the "Hivern de Sepharad," such as poem XXVII where the land is said to be given over to a "senyoria a la foscor i al glaç."

11 George Steiner, in a sweeping study of the history of the Antigone myth, notes, "1943–4, 1978 and 1979 were, in fact, years of 'Antigone-fever'. The Hölderlin version is translated into French and staged in Strasbourg. An *Antigone Through the Looking-Glass* surfaces in London. At least three major new productions, modulating on Sophocles, Hölderlin, and Brecht, are mounted in Germany … Over and over again, western moral and political consciousness has lived what Helmut Richter calls, in one of his political sonnets, *Antigone anno jetzt*, 'Antigone year-now'" (108). Espriu's initial version surfaced prior to the fever of 1943–4, which speaks to its being connected to Spanish history at that moment rather than responding to cultural taste. The 1940s, however, when Espriu wrote a prologue to the work, were as rife with Antigone, with a staging at the Théâtre de l'Atelier in 1947 and another at the Stadttheater von Clur in Switzerland in 1948. It is striking to note that in both instances, in the late 1930s in Spain and the late 1940s throughout Europe, "Antigone fever" appears in the wake of catastrophic conflict.

12 See Delor i Muns 485–513.

13 As with so many of the works discussed in this book, Nietzsche's *Thus Spoke Zarathustra* appears to be referenced by Espriu in his poeticization of a moment awash in light. Zarathustra himself is a wanderer – a *caminant* – and his noontide moment is a period of rest and relief from weary travels. While lying down on the grass, Zarathustra exclaims, "Soft! Soft! Has the world not just become perfect? What has happened to me?" (287).

14 In *La pell de brau*, for example, when "tornem pel record als vells passos," "no vèiem cap nova deu, cap senyal d'aigua / al pou de l'acontentament" in poem XLV. The God that is found at the bottom of the well is in no sense new; a second religiosity is precisely a new discovery of the old.

15 The myth of the sacred cow ends with Moses instructing those still loyal to God to kill their brothers, friends, and neighbours. Moses gives the resulting deaths a sacrificial dimension and ordains the tribe of Levi for future service to the Lord. The myth, in other words, is ineluctably tied to internecine strife and the expulsion, or outright

killing, of those whose belief structure places them outside of a cult's sacred sphere of belonging. Espriu importantly refuses to divide Sepharad in such a way, maintaining that the people are all in some way responsible – through their silence – for the ruinous state in which the Peninsula exists. The work of constructing the temple in Sepharad does not revolve around a consecration based on victimization, rather, as poem V of *La pell de brau* asserts, "no pot escollir príncep / qui vessa sang."

16 Smith in fact argues that, "unlike Joshua, Moses preserved the vision of the people as the ultimate repository of virtue. In this, he was followed by a whole line of prophets, sages, and saints, for whom 'the people', rather than their leaders, let alone the nobles and clergy, embodied the essence of the nation" (35). Compare this thought with poem XXV of *La pell de brau*: "Detestem els grans ventres, els grans mots, / la indecent parenceria de l'or, / les cartes mal donades de la sort, / el fum espès d'encens al poderós. És ara vil el poble de senyors." The reference to gold, clearly, might be read with the golden calf and the worship of false idols in mind. The lighting of incense to signal the sacrality of a false, tyrannical leader further stresses the raising of false gods by the people.

17 This parting gesture calls to mind the conclusion of *La pell de brau*'s poem XXXVIII: "Que sàpiga Sepharad que no podem mai ser / si no som lliures. / I cridi la veu de tot el poble: « Amén »."

8. Conclusion: The Aesthetic Disruption of Political Truth

1 It is for this reason that I will argue for a political dimension of the aesthetic regime of art through a reading of Jacques Rancière in lieu of paying heed to the tradition of ideology and literature promoted by several prominent thinkers in the second half of the twentieth century. A key example of this tradition is Irving Howe's *Politics and the Novel*, which argues for a particular genre of political novelization. This writer's task is simply to "show the relation between theory and experience, between the ideology that has been preconceived and the tangible feelings and relationships he is trying to present" (22).

2 "Politics stands in direct opposition to the police. The police is a distribution of the sensible (partage du sensible) whose principle is the absence of void and of supplement" (*Dissensus* 36).

3 Consider as well Nietzsche's notion that "time, space, and causality are only metaphors of knowledge by which we interpret things for ourselves" (*Writings* 149).

Works Cited

Adorno, Theodor. *Aesthetic Theory*. Trans. Robert Hullot-Kentor. London: Continuum, 2002.

Agamben, Giorgio. *Homo Sacer: Sovereign Power and Bare Life*. Trans. Daniel Heller-Roazen. Stanford: Stanford UP, 1998.

– *The Kingdom and the Glory*. Trans. Lorenzo Chiesa. Stanford: Stanford UP, 2012.

Almirall, Valentí. *Lo Catalanisme*. Barcelona: Edicions 62, 1979.

Anderson, Benedict. *Imagined Communities*. London: Verso, 2006.

Aquinas, St Thomas. *On Human Nature*. Indianapolis, IN: Hackett Publishing, 1999.

Arendt, Hannah. *On Violence*. Orlando: Harcourt, 1970.

– *Totalitarianism: Part Three of the Origins of Totalitarianism*. San Diego: Harcourt, 1976.

Aristotle. *The Metaphysics*. Trans. John McMahon. Amherst, NY: Prometheus, 1991.

– *The Nicomachean Ethics*. Trans. David Ross. Oxford: Oxford UP, 2009.

– *Poetics*. Trans. Kenneth McLeish. London: Nick Hern, 1998.

– *The Politics*. Trans. Carnes Lord. Chicago: U Chicago P, 1985.

Arkinstall, Christine R. *Gender, Class, and Nation: Mercè Rodoreda and the Subjects of Modernism*. Lewisburg: Bucknell UP, 2004.

Arnau, Carme. *Compromís i escriptura: Lectura d'Incerta glòria de Joan Sales*. Barcelona: Cruïlla, 2003.

– ed. *La mort i la primavera*. By Mercè Rodoreda. Barcelona: Institut d'Estudis Catalans, Fundació Mercè Rodoreda, 1997.

Asad, Talal. *Formations of the Secular*. Stanford: Stanford UP, 2003.

Badiou, Alain. *Obras completas*. Vol. 7. Madrid: Biblioteca de autores cristianos, 1950.

– *Saint Paul: The Foundation of Universalism*. Trans. Ray Brassier. Stanford: Stanford UP, 2003.

Balmes, Jaime. *Lógica y ética*. Santiago de Chile: Zig-zag, 1943.

– *Obras completas*. Madrid: La Editorial Católica, 1950.

Barthes, Roland. "The Discourse of History." Trans. Stephen Bann. *Contemporary Criticism* 3 (1981): 7–20.

– *Mythologies.* Trans. Annette Lavers. New York: Hill and Wang, 1972.

Bataille, Georges. "Sacrifice, Mutilation and the Severed Ear of Vincent Van Gogh." *Visions of Excess: Selected Writings, 1927–1939.* Trans. Allan Stoekl. Minneapolis: U Minnesota P, 1985. 61–72.

– "Sacrifice, the Festival and the Principles of the Sacred World." *The Bataille Reader.* Ed. Fred Botting and Scott Wilson. Oxford: Blackwell, 1997. 210–19

Benet, Juan. *El ángel del Señor abandona a Tobías.* Barcelona: La Gaya Ciencia, 1976.

– *Return to Region.* Trans. Gregory Rabassa. New York: Columbia UP, 1985.

– "Numa." *Una tumba: Numa (Una leyenda).* Madrid: Alfaguara, 1987. 57–114.

– *Volverás a región.* 1967. Barcelona: Destino, 1981.

Berger, Peter. *The Sacred Canopy: Elements of a Sociological Theory of Religion.* Garden City, NY: Doubleday-Anchor, 1967.

Bergson, Henri. *The Creative Mind: An Introduction to Metaphysics.* Trans. Mabelle L. Andison. Mineola, NY: Dover, 2007.

– *Matter and Memory.* Trans. N.M. Paul and W.S. Palmer. New York: Zone, 2005.

– *Time and Free Will.* Trans. F.L. Pogson. London: George Allen & Unwin, 1921.

Bloom, Harold. *A Map of Misreading.* New York: Oxford UP, 1975.

Bourdieu, Pierre. *The Field of Cultural Production.* New York: Columbia UP, 1993.

– *Language and Symbolic Power.* Trans. Gino Raymond and Matthew Adamson. Cambridge, MA: Harvard UP, 2003.

Brenan, Gerald. *The Spanish Labyrinth.* Cambridge: Cambridge UP, 1990.

Butler, Judith. *Antigone's Claim: Kinship between Life and Death.* New York: Columbia UP, 2000.

Caillois, Roger. *Man and the Sacred.* Trans. Meyer Barash. Urbana-Champaign: U Illinois P, 2001.

Campillo, Maria, and Jordi Castellanos. "La novel·la." *Història de la literatura catalana, 11.* Ed. Joaquim Molas, 45–117. Barcelona: Editorial Ariel, 1988.

Camus, Albert. *The Myth of Sisyphus.* Trans. Justin O'Brien. New York: Vintage, 1991.

– *The Rebel.* Trans. Anthony Bower. New York: Vintage, 1991.

– *The Stranger.* Trans. Stuart Gilbert. New York: Vintage Books, 1946.

Casacuberta, Margarida. "*Incerta glòria*, una novel·la desventurada?" *L'Avenç* 333 (Mar. 2008): 40–50.

Casanova, Julián. "The Faces of Terror: Violence during the Franco Dictatorship." *Unearthing Franco's Legacy: Mass Graves and the Recovery of Historical Memory.* Ed. Carlos Jerez-Farrán and Samuel Amago. Notre Dame: Notre Dame UP, 2010. 90–121.

Castellet, J.M. *Iniciación a la poesía de Salvador Espriu.* Madrid: Taurus, 1971.

– "Mercè Rodoreda." *Els escenaris de la memòria.* Barcelona: Edicions 62, 1988. 29–53.

Cortés, Juan Donoso. "Discurso sobre la dictatura." *Ensayo sobre el catolicismo, el liberalismo, y el socialismo: Otros escritos.* Barcelona: Planeta, 1985. 241–61.

– *Ensayo sobre el catolicismo, el liberalismo, y el socialismo.* Madrid: Biblioteca Nueva, 2007.

Cortés i Orts, Carles. "Godless Religions in *La mort i la primavera*." *Voices and Visions: The Words and Works of Mercè Rodoreda*. Ed. Kathleen McNerney. Selinsgrove: Susquehanna University Press, 1999. 195–207.

Delor i Muns, Rosa. "Fonts dantesques a l'obra de Salvador Espriu." *Annali Istituto Universitario Orientale, Napoli, Sezione Romanza* 34.1 (Jan. 1992): 485–513.

Derrida, Jacques. *The Gift of Death*. Trans. David Wills. Chicago: Chicago UP, 1995.

Díaz-Plaja, Fernando, ed. *La España política del siglo XX: Tomo cuarto*. Barcelona: Plaza & Janes, 1972.

Dilthey, Wilhelm. *Dilthey's Philosophy of Existence*. Trans. William Kluback and Martin Weinbaum. London: Vision, 1960.

– *Selected Writings*. Trans. H.P. Rickman. Cambridge: Cambridge UP, 1976.

Durán, Manuel. "Juan Benet y la nueva novela española." *Cuadernos Americanos* 195.4 (July–Aug. 1974): 193–205.

Durkheim, Émile. *The Elementary Forms of Religious Life*. Trans. Carol Cosman. Oxford: Oxford UP, 2001.

Eliade, Mircea. *The Sacred and the Profane: The Nature of Religion*. Orlando, FL: Harcourt, 1987.

Eliot, T.S. *The Sacred Wood: Essays on Poetry and Criticism*. London: Methuen, 1948.

Epps, Bradley. *Significant Violence: Oppression and Resistance in the Narratives of Juan Goytisolo, 1970–1990*. Oxford: Clarendon, 1996.

Espriu, Salvador. *Antígona, Fedra, Una altra Fedra, si us plau*. Barcelona: Edicions 62, 2008.

– *El caminant i el mur*. Ed. J.M. Castellet. Barcelona: Edicions 62, 1983.

– *Cementiri de Sinera / Les hores*. Barcelona: Edicions 62, 1978.

– *Narracions*. Barcelona: Edicions 62, 1967.

– *Obres completes*. Vol. 1, *Poesia*. Barcelona: Edicions 62, 1968.

– *Obres completes*. Vol 12, *Edició crítica*. Ed. Olívia Gassol i Bellet. Barcelona: Edicions 62, 2008.

Foucault, Michel. *Discipline and Punish: The Birth of the Prison*. New York: Random House, 1995.

– *Foucault Reader*. Ed. Paul Rabinow. New York: Pantheon, 1984.

Fraser, Benjamin. *Encounters with Bergson(ism) in Spain*. Chapel Hill: U North Carolina P, 2010.

Frazier, James. *The Golden Bough: A Study in Magic and Religion*. London: Wordsworth, 1993.

Freud, Sigmund. *Beyond the Pleasure Principle*. Trans. James Strachey. New York: Norton, 1989.

– *Totem and Taboo*. Trans. James Strachey. New York: Norton, 1950.

Fuster, Joan. *Literatura Catalana Contemporánea*. Madrid: Editora Nacional, 1975.

Gassol i Bellet, Olívia. *La pell de brau de Salvador Espriu o el mite de la salvació*. Barcelona: Publicacions de l'Abadia de Montserrat, 2003.

Gaughan, Judy E. "Killing and the King: Numa's Murder Law and the Nature of Monachic Authority." *Continuity and Change* 18.3 (2003): 329–43.

Girard, René. *The Scapegoat.* Trans. Yvonne Freccero. Baltimore: Johns Hopkins UP, 1989.

– *Things Hidden since the Foundation of the World.* Trans. Stephen Bann and Michael Metteer. Palo Alto, CA: Stanford UP, 1987.

– *Violence and the Sacred.* Trans. Patrick Gregory. Baltimore: Johns Hopkins UP, 1977.

Goelet, Ogden, ed. *The Egyptian Book of the Dead: The Book of Going Forth by Day.* Trans. Raymond Faulkner. San Francisco: Chronicle Books, 1998.

Goytisolo, Juan. *Contra las sagradas formas.* Barcelona: Círculo de Lectores, 2007.

– *Coto vedado.* Barcelona: Seix Barral, 1985.

– *En los reinos de taifa.* Barcelona: Seix Barral, 1986.

– *Obras completas.* Vol. 2, *Relatos y ensayos.* Madrid: Aquilar, 1978.

– *Reivindicación del Conde don Julián.* Barcelona: Seix Barral, 1988.

Habermas, Jürgen. "An Awareness of What Is Missing." *An Awareness of What Is Missing: Faith and Reason in a Post-Secular Age.* Trans. Ciaran Cronin. Cambridge: Polity, 2010. 15–24.

– "'The Political': The Rational Meaning of a Questionable Inheritance of Political Theology." *The Power of Religion in the Public Sphere.* Ed. Eduardo Mendieta and Jonathan Vanantwerpen. New York: Columbia UP, 2011. 15–33.

– "Reconciliation through the Public Use of Reason: Remarks on John Rawls's *Political Liberalism.*" *Journal of Philosophy* 92.3 (Mar. 1995): 109–31.

Hegel, G.W.F. *The Hegel Reader.* Ed. Stephen Houlgate. Oxford: Blackwell, 2002.

– *The Phenomenology of Spirit.* Trans. A.V. Miller. Oxford: Oxford UP, 1977.

Heidegger, Martin. *Being and Time.* Trans. John MacQuarrie and Edward Robinson. New York: Harper, 2008.

– *Elucidations of Hölderlin's Poetry.* Trans. Keith Hoeller. New York: Humanity Books, 2000.

– "Letter on Humanism." *Basic Writings.* New York: Harper & Row, 1977. 193–242.

– *Poetry, Language, Thought.* Trans. Albert Hofstadter. New York: Harper Collins, 2001.

Herder, Johann Gottfried. *Philosophical Writings.* Cambridge: Cambridge UP, 2002.

Herzberger, David K. "Enigma as Narrative Determinant in the Novels of Juan Benet." *Hispanic Review* 47.2 (Spring 1979): 149–57.

Hobbes, Thomas. *Leviathan.* Ed. Rogers and Schuhmann. Bristol, UK: Thoemmes Continuum, 2003.

Hobsbawm, E.J. *Nations and Nationalism since 1780: Programme, Myth, Reality.* Cambridge: Cambridge UP, 2010.

Howe, Irving. *Politics and the Novel.* New York: Horizon, 1957.

Hubert, Henri, and Marcel Mauss. *Sacrifice: Its Nature and Functions.* Trans. W.D. Halls. Chicago: U Chicago P, 1981.

Jaspers, Karl. *Basic Philosophical Writings.* Trans. Edith Ehrlich. Athens: Ohio UP, 1986.

Juan de la Cruz, St. "Noche oscura." *Paraíso cerrado: Poesía en lengua española de los siglos XVI y XVII*. Ed. José María Micó and Jaime Siles. Barcelona: Galaxia Gutenberg, 2003. 151.
Kantorowicz, Ernst. *The King's Two Bodies: A Study in Mediaeval Political Theology*. Princeton: Princeton UP, 1957. Paperback edition 1997.
Koselleck, Reinhart. *The Practice of Conceptual History*. Trans. Todd Samuel Presner. Stanford: Stanford UP, 2002.
Kronik, John. "Leopoldo Alas, Krausism, and the Plight of the Humanities in Spain." *Modern Language Studies* 11.3 (Autumn 1981): 3–15.
Labanyi, Jo. *Myth and History in the Contemporary Spanish Novel*. Cambridge: Cambridge UP, 1989.
Lacan, Jacques. *Écrits: A Selection*. Trans. Alan Sheridan. New York: Norton, 1977.
– *The Seminar of Jacques Lacan: Book I*. Trans. John Forrester. New York: Norton, 1988.
Lannon, Frances. "Catholicism and Social Change." *Spanish Cultural Studies*. Ed. Helen Graham and Jo Labanyi. Oxford: Oxford University Press, 1995. 276–82.
Larra, Mariano José de. *Artículos*. Barcelona: Planeta, 1981.
Lázaro, José. *Vidas y muertes de Luis Martín-Santos*. Barcelona: Tusquets, 2009.
Lefebvre, Henri. *The Production of Space*. Trans. Donald Nicholson-Smith. Oxford: Blackwell, 1991.
Lefort, Claude. *Democracy and Political Theory*. Trans. David Macey. Cambridge: Polity, 1988.
Levine, Linda Gould. "Introduction." *Reivindicación del Conde don Julián*. By Juan Goytisolo. Madrid: Catedra, 1985. 9–69.
– *Juan Goytisolo: La destrucción creadora*. Mexico City: Joaquín Mortiz, 1976.
Lukács, Georg. *The Theory of the Novel*. Trans. Anna Bostock. Cambridge, MA: MIT Press, 1996.
Machado, Antonio. *Campos de Castilla*. Madrid: Cátedra, 2003.
Mainer, José Carlos. "Prólogo a *Tiempo de Destrucción*." *Tiempo de destrucción*. By Luis Martín-Santos. Barcelona: Seix Barral, 1998. 9–44.
Marcuse, Herbert. *Eros and Civilization*. New York: Vintage Books, 1962.
Margenot, John. "Cloisters and Cloisterers in Juan Benet's *Volverás a Región*." *Hispanic Journal* 10.2 (1989): 113–26.
Marett, R.R. *The Threshold of Religion*. London: Methuen, 1914.
Martín-Santos, Luis. *Apólogos y otras prosas inéditas*. Barcelona: Seix Barral, 1970.
– *El análisis existencial: Ensayos*. Madrid: Triacastela, 2004.
– "Realismo y realidad en la literatura contemporánea" [1963]. *Guía de lectura: Tiempo de silencio*. Ed. Juan Luís Granda. Madrid: Alhambra, 1986. 141–2.
– *Tiempo de destrucción*. Barcelona: Seix Barral, 1998.
– *Tiempo de silencio*. Barcelona: Seix Barral, 1991.
Nietzsche, Friedrich. *On the Genealogy of Morals / Ecce Homo*. Trans. Walter Kaufmann and R.J. Hollingdale. New York: Vintage Books, 1989.
– *Thus Spoke Zarathustra*. Trans. R.J. Hollingdale. New York: Penguin, 2003.

– *Writings from the Early Notebooks*. Trans. Ladislau Löb. Cambridge: Cambridge UP, 2009.

Ortega, José. "Compromiso formal de Martín-Santos in *Tiempo de silencio*." *Hispanófila* 37 (1969): 23–30.

Ortega y Gasset, José. *España invertebrada*. Madrid: Revista de Occidente, 1962.

– *Meditaciones del Quijote*. 1914. Madrid: Cátedra, 2001.

Otto, Rudolf. *The Idea of the Holy*. Trans. John W. Harvey. Oxford: Oxford UP, 1925.

Paz, Octavio. *Configurations*. New York: New Directions, 1971.

Pérez, Janet. "Time and Symbol, Life and Death, Decay and Regeneration: Vital Cycles and the Round of Seasons in Mercè Rodoreda's *La mort i la primavera*." *Catalan Review* 5.1 (1991): 179–96.

Pla, Xavier. "Joan Sales and *Incerta glòria*: The Polyphonies of a Roman-Fleuve." *Transfer: Journal of Contemporary Culture* 3 (2008): 111–20.

Pope, Randolph. "Benet, Faulkner, and Bergson's Memory." *Critical Approaches to the Writing of Juan Benet*. Ed. David K. Herzberger and Roberto C. Manteiga. Hanover: UP New England, 1984. 111–20.

Prat de la Riba, Enric. *La nationalitat catalana*. Barcelona: Escola d'Administració Pública de Catalunya, 2007.

Pujol, Jordi. "El fracaso de Espriu." *Centre d'Estudis Jordi Pujol*. Centre d'Estudis Jordi Pujol, 24 November 2009. Web. 6 May 2011. http://www.jordipujol.cat/es/jp/articles/7170.

Rancière, Jacques. *Dissensus: On Politics and Aesthetics*. Trans. Steven Corcoran. London: Continuum, 2012.

– Interview by Peter Hollward. "Politics and Aesthetics." *Angelaki* 2 (Aug. 2003): 191–211.

– *The Politics of Aesthetics*. Trans. Gabriel Rockhill. London: Continuum, 2005.

Rawls, John. *Political Liberalism*. New York: Columbia UP, 1996.

– *A Theory of Justice*. Cambridge, MA: Harvard UP, 1971.

Resina, Joan Ramon. *Del hispanismo a los estudios ibéricos*. Madrid: Biblioteca Nueva, 2009.

Richards, Michael. *A Time of Silence: Civil War and the Culture of Repression in Franco's Spain, 1936–1945*. Cambridge: Cambridge UP, 1998.

Rodríguez García, José María. "Determinismo, Destino y Fatalidad en *Tiempo de silencio* (a propósito de dos nuevos subtextos ingleses)." *Anales de la literatura española contemporánea* 27.2 (2002): 261/547–278/564.

Rodoreda, Mercè. *Mirall trencat*. Barcelona: Club editor, 2008.

– *La mort i la primavera*. Barcelona: Club Editor, 2000.

– *Quanta, quanta guerra*. 1980. Barcelona: Club Editor, 2000.

Rorty, Richard. *Contingency, Irony, and Solidarity*. Cambridge: Cambridge UP, 1989.

Sales, Joan. *Cartes de la guerra*. Barcelona: Club Editor, 1986.

– "Contra alguns errors divulgats." *Els "Quaderns de l'Exili."* Ed. Josep Ametlla, Lluís Ferran de Pol, Raimon Galí, and Joan Sales. Barcelona: Quaderns d'Estudis i Treballs, 1994. 108–12.

– *Incerta glòria.* Barcelona: Club Editor, 2007.

– "Paraules prèvies." *Els "Quaderns de l'Exili."* Ed. Josep Ametlla, Lluís Ferran de Pol, Raimon Galí, and Joan Sales. Barcelona: Quaderns d'Estudis i Treballs, 1994. 11–28.

Sarrión, Antonio Martínez. "Juan Benet: El Numa, mito de Región." *Cuadernos Hispano-americanos* 684 (June 2007): 115–22.

Sartre, Jean-Paul. *Being and Nothingness.* Trans. Hazel E. Barnes. New York: Washington Square, 1984.

– *The Wall.* Trans. Andrew Brown. London: Hesperus, 2005.

Saussure, Ferdinand de. *Course in General Linguistics.* Trans. Wade Baskin. New York: Fontana/Collins, 1981.

Schmitt, Carl. *The Concept of the Political.* Trans. George Schwab. Chicago: U Chicago P, 2007.

– *Political Theology.* Trans. George Schwab. Chicago: U Chicago P, 2005.

– *Theory of the Partisan.* Trans. G.L. Ulmen. New York: Telos, 2007.

Schopenhauer, Arthur. *Essay on the Freedom of the Will.* Trans. Konstantin Kolenda. Mineola, NY: Dover, 2005.

Sevillano, Francisco. *Franco, Caudillo por la gracia de Dios, 1936–1947.* Madrid: Alianza, 2010.

Smith, Anthony. *Chosen Peoples: Sacred Sources of National Identity.* Oxford: Oxford UP, 2003.

Sophocles. *The Theban Plays.* Trans. Ruby Blondell. Newburyport, MA: Focus, 2002.

Sorel, Georges. *Reflections on Violence.* Trans. T.E. Hulme. London: Collier Books, 1969.

Soufas, Christopher. *The Subject in Question: Early Contemporary Spanish Literature and Modernism.* Washington, DC: Catholic UP of America, 2007.

Spengler, Oswald. *The Decline of the West.* Vol. 2. Trans. Charles Francis Atkinson. New York: Knopf, 1939.

Steiner, George. *Antigones.* New Haven, CT: Yale UP, 1984.

Summerhill, Stephen. "Prohibition and Transgression in 'Volverás a Región' and 'Una meditación.'" *Critical Approaches to the Writing of Juan Benet.* Ed. David K. Herzberger and Roberto C. Manteiga. Hanover: UP of New England, 1984. 51–64.

Taylor, Charles. "Why We Need a Radical Redefinition of Secularism." *The Power of Religion in the Public Sphere.* Ed. Eduardo Mendieta and Jonathan Vanantwerpen. New York: Columbia University Press. 34–60.

Teresa de Jesús, St. "Vivo sin vivir en mí." *Paraíso cerrado: Poesía en lengua española de los siglos XVI y XVII.* Ed. José María Micó and Jaime Siles. Barcelona: Galaxia Gutenberg, 2003. 122.

Triadú, Joan. "Joan Sales: compromís personal i creació literària." *Les Literatures Catalana i Francesa: Postguerra i Engagement.* Ed. Ferran Carbó, Dolores Jiménez, Elena Real, and Ramon Rosselló. Barcelona: L'Abadia de Montserrat, 2000. 415–29.

Umphrey, Martha Merrill, Austin Sarat, and Lawrence Douglas. "The Sacred in Law: An Introduction." *Law and the Sacred.* Ed. Austin Sarat, Lawrence Douglas, and Martha Merrill Umphrey. Stanford: Stanford UP, 2007. 1–29.

Unamuno, Miguel. *En torno al casticismo.* Madrid: Alianza Editorial, 2002.

Valis, Noël. *Sacred Realism: Religion and the Imagination in Modern Spanish Narrative.* New Haven, CT: Yale UP, 2010.

Vázquez Montalbán, Manuel. *La Aznaridad.* Barcelona: Mondadori, 2004.

– *Los demonios familiares de Franco.* Barcelona: Dopesa, 1978.

Vico, Giambattista. *The First New Science.* Trans. Leon Pompa. Cambridge: Cambridge UP, 2002.

Viestenz, William. "Death in the Spring: Mercè Rodoreda and the Unproductive Productiveness of Late Style." *Journal of Catalan Studies* 14 (2011): 86–106.

Vilanova, Antonio. "Luis Martín Santos: Entre el realismo dialéctico y el monólogo interior." *Novela y sociedad en la España de la posguerra.* Barcelona: Lumen, 1995. 418–22.

Villacañas, José Luis. *Poder y conflicto: Ensayos sobre Carl Schmitt.* Madrid: Biblioteca Nueva, 2008.

Walters, D. Gareth. *The Poetry of Salvador Espriu: To Save the Words.* Woodbridge: Tamesis, 2006.

Winecoff Diaz, Janet. "Luis Martín Santos and the Contemporary Spanish Novel." *Hispania* 51 (May 1968): 232–5.

Zambrano, María. *Algunos lugares de la pintura.* Madrid: Acanto, 1989.

Žižek, Slavoj. *The Parallax View.* Cambridge, MA: MIT UP, 2006.

Index

TORONTO IBERIC

1 Anthony J. Cascardi, *Cervantes, Literature, and the Discourse of Politics*
2 Jessica A. Boon, *The Mystical Science of the Soul: Medieval Cognition in Bernardino de Laredo's Recollection Method*
3 Susan Byrne, *Law and History in Cervantes' Don Quixote*
4 Mary E. Barnard and Frederick A. de Armas (eds), *Objects of Culture in the Literature of Imperial Spain*
5 Nil Santiáñez, *Topographies of Fascism: Habitus, Space, and Writing in Twentieth-Century Spain*
6 Nelson Orringer, *Lorca in Tune with Falla: Literary and Musical Interludes*
7 Ana M. Gómez-Bravo, *Textual Agency: Writing Culture and Social Networks in Fifteenth-Century Spain*
8 Javier Irigoyen-García, *The Spanish Arcadia: Sheep Herding, Pastoral Discourse, and Ethnicity in Early Modern Spain*
9 Stephanie Sieburth, *Survival Songs: Conchita Piquer's* Coplas *and Franco's Regime of Terror*
10 Christine Arkinstall, *Spanish Female Writers and the Freethinking Press, 1879-1926*
11 Margaret Boyle, *Unruly Women: Performance, Penitence, and Punishment in Early Modern Spain*
12 Evelina Gužauskytė, *Christopher Columbus's Naming in the* diarios *of the Four Voyages (1492–1504): A Discourse of Negotiation*
13 Mary E. Barnard, *Garcilaso de la Vega and the Material Culture of Renaissance Europe*
14 William Viestenz, *By the Grace of God: Francoist Spain and the Sacred Roots of Political Imagination*

www.ingramcontent.com/pod-product-compliance
Lightning Source LLC
LaVergne TN
LVHW090157080826
844660LV00013B/851/J

* 9 7 8 1 4 4 2 6 4 7 5 7 2 *